THE ONLY REAL ESTATE & RENTAL PROPERTY INVESTING FOR BEGINNERS BOOK YOU'LL EVER NEED

CLOSE YOUR FIRST DEAL, EASILY MANAGE PROPERTIES, & CREATE FINANCIAL FREEDOM

2 BOOKS IN 1

ANDREW & COURTNEY JAMES

PERMANENT
PTO
Spend Life Living

DOWNLOAD THE AUDIOBOOK VERSION FOR FREE

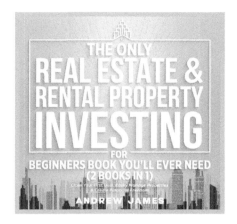

If you love listening to audiobooks on-the-go, you can download the audiobook version of this book for FREE (Regularly $14.95) just by signing up for a FREE 30-day audible trial!

Visit the link below to get started:
https://bit.ly/real-estate-rental-acx-us

CONTENTS

THE ONLY REAL ESTATE INVESTING FOR BEGINNERS BOOK YOU'LL EVER NEED

THE ONLY RENTAL PROPERTY INVESTING BOOK YOU'LL EVER NEED:

THE ONLY REAL ESTATE INVESTING FOR BEGINNERS BOOK YOU'LL EVER NEED

CLOSE YOUR FIRST DEAL IN 7 SIMPLE STEPS EVEN IF YOU'RE BROKE & HAVE ZERO EXPERIENCE

INTRODUCTION: WHY YOU ARE HERE

Do you crave freedom? Do you want the ability to do what you want, when you want, without worrying if you have enough money or if your boss will let you take time off work?

I know what you're going through because I've also been there, like many others. I used to dread clocking in not one minute later than 8 AM to my job, catching up on emails regarding problems I didn't actually care about, sitting in on what seemed like the same meeting over and over again, and waiting in agony for my coveted lunch hour. And even after this hour of freedom, I'd go back to my desk and watch the time tick by as slowly as possible as if it were mocking me and waiting for the most exciting part of my day, which was clocking out without any forced post-work gatherings to take up the rest of the evening. Then I'd peel out of the parking lot so I could complete a few necessary life tasks and, hopefully, still have time and energy at the end of the day to do something I enjoyed. But let's be honest. The day drained me so much that I usually ended up being too tired to do anything. Most of the time, I ended up cracking a few beers and watching Netflix before going to bed and doing it all over again.

If any of this resonates with you, you are reading the right book, and there is a way out. If you want to leave your 9-to-5 job and finally be free to pursue the life of your dreams, it IS possible!

Imagine being able to book a flight on a moment's notice in the middle of the week, take your spouse on a two-hour lunch date on a Tuesday, or spend the 40+ hours you usually work and commute with your kids without having to worry about making ends meet or upper management breathing down your neck. This lifestyle IS possible, even for the person who feels utterly stuck or far behind!

The best way to do this is by building passive income and generating wealth through real estate investing. I know this because I used to loathe my life as an employee. Now I am a full-time real estate and business investor living the life of my dreams, and I want to help you live yours.

So, if you want to dive into the world and endless possibilities of real estate investing, let's buckle up and get started!

PART I

THE POWER OF REAL ESTATE INVESTING

1

HOW REAL ESTATE INVESTING CAN MAKE ORDINARY PEOPLE EXTRAORDINARILY WEALTHY

The major fortunes in America have been made in land.

— JOHN D. ROCKEFELLER

Did you know that real estate investing has created 90% of the world's millionaires, and most started as beginners like you?

The secret is that regular people are getting richer than ever using real estate investing, and you can, too.

You might wonder, "If this is true, why don't more people invest in real estate?"

Well, there are many answers to that question. Some common reasons are that they don't think they can invest in real estate or know how to. However, the biggest reason seems to be that they believe they need tons of money, connections, or skills to get started.

The good news is this couldn't be further from the truth! Anyone can build a wealth-generating real estate portfolio with the correct knowledge and the drive to do so.

What is real estate investing anyway? Simply put, it's the purchase, management, or sale of real estate (homes, buildings, land, etc.) for a profit. There are many different types of real estate investments and just as many, if not more, ways to make money. This makes it a very flexible asset class to invest in that is also relatively easy to get started in. The average person can start with just one small investment and scale an extensive portfolio. They can do this relatively quickly or build it slowly over time, depending on their goals. The sky really is the limit!

So, how does real estate investing work? There are many ways that real estate investing can be done to generate wealth, but let's introduce the most common ways first.

To start, there's rental property investing. This is where someone buys a property, commonly with a down payment and a bank loan, and manages it while tenants rent it out and pay down the mortgage for them. Not only is the mortgage being paid down by other people, but hopefully, there is extra money left over from the rent payment after paying expenses to put in the investor's pocket every month. Most likely, the property is also increasing in value over time, making the investor even more of a return down the line. Imagine having 10s or 100s of these properties all operating at the same time! Probably the other most common way to build wealth through real estate is buying a property at or below its value, drastically renovating it to increase its value, and then selling it at a much higher price than what you bought it for and what you put into fixing it up.

These are just two high-level examples of hundreds of ways to build wealth through real estate investing. While real estate can significantly increase your wealth, this is not some "get rich quick" scheme; it can take several years. You have to come into the real estate business with the mindset that it's a long-term strategy. This often involves commitment, patience, and being hungry to learn anything you can about real estate to become a better investor.

Real estate investing has many other benefits beyond just wealth creation. Let's dive in to learn more!

The Secret Sauce of Real Estate Investing

While there are many benefits to real estate investing, there are four key elements to amassing significant wealth. All four of them, working together, are what make real estate a unique and powerful investment.

These four elements are: tax benefits, appreciation, cash flow, and leverage. I like to refer to them as the secret sauce of real estate investing. Let's take a closer look at each.

Understanding Tax Benefits

Let's begin with property tax deductions. I'm starting with these because these tend to be some of the most expensive taxes a real estate investor will have. However, they are often tax deductible, which means you can reduce them on your tax bill. Plus, if you already own your primary residence (the house you live in), you can deduct a part of your property taxes, too.

Another tax benefit is mortgage interest deduction, where you can deduct your mortgage interest payments. So, all the interest you pay on your mortgage can be taken out of your tax bill. This is great because, most of the time, you will be taking out mortgages to purchase your properties. It might not seem like much, but this is considerable savings, especially when you start your career as a real estate investor and when your interest payments are higher.

But perhaps one of the best tax benefits of real estate investing is depreciation. You can deduct the cost of acquiring a rental property over a certain period, which is usually 27.5 years or 39 years for residential and commercial property, respectively. This means that the depreciation expense can counterbalance your rental income, which reduces your tax bill.

Then there's the 1031 exchange, also called the tax-deferred exchange. This is more of a strategy where you can defer capital gains on a property when you sell if you use that money to invest in a similar property. The capital gains tax is a tax on the profit from the sale of real estate. For instance, if you sell a one-bedroom property and buy another one, any capital gains you've made with the sale can be deferred. This is a great way to continue to expand your real estate portfolio without a large tax bill. But more importantly, over a long period of time, the 1031 exchange can save you a lot of money.

Besides the 1031 exchange, there's another way you can save on your tax bill with capital gains. When you sell a property, any profit you make is taxable under capital gains, but the tax rate for long-term capital gains, which is usually more than one year, tends to be lower than the regular income tax rate.

It's important you understand and take advantage of these tax benefits once you start investing because they can really enhance your profitability. However, even if you know all of this, nothing replaces a qualified tax professional to oversee your business and point out any issues or more tax benefits that you can leverage. This professional can also ensure that you stay within the law—not that you'd ever be breaking it on purpose, but because it can accidentally happen if you don't fully understand what you're doing.

Appreciation

Let's now have a closer look at what property appreciation entails. This is one of the best ways for you to generate wealth with property investments. Because of that, it's vital that you understand exactly how it works and how you can take advantage of it, especially if you want to build long-term financial stability.

So, what exactly is appreciation? There are two types of appreciation – natural and forced. Natural appreciation is simply that—the natural tendency for prices to rise over time. While the price of everything goes up over time, you can also do your best to lean into natural appreciation by purchasing real estate in ideal locations. By choosing a property in a location that is or will soon be in an amazing neighborhood where there are good schools, a low crime rate, and great public transportation, the value of the property will tend to increase faster than others. But the market conditions, which are completely irrelevant to the property itself, are also an important factor. If the area of the property is prospering—that is, if the population, the economy, and job opportunities are growing—this will also influence the appreciation of the property.

Forced appreciation, on the other hand, is the concept of improving a property to increase its value. For example, taking a three-bedroom, one-and-a-half-bath and turning it into a four-bedroom, two-bath will immediately increase its value. This is incredibly powerful for the average investor because they can directly improve their investment and make more money rather than banking on external factors they can't control (like they would in, say, the stock market).

But why else does property appreciation matter so much for your real estate investments? Well, for one, it builds equity. This is because, as your properties appreciate, the discrepancy between the current market value and the amount you owe on your mortgage forms equity. You can use this equity by selling the property or remortgaging it. Either way, it provides you with the funds necessary for future investments. In other words, this appreciation can create leverage from your existing assets to acquire more properties. You can then use this higher equity in your properties as a down payment for new properties.

As time passes, property appreciation can significantly increase your net worth. This is huge! Do the work once, and watch your wealth grow over time.

Cash Flow & Generating Passive Income

In simple terms, cash flow is the amount of income left in your business after all the expenses like your mortgage, insurance, repairs, etc. have been paid. It is the lifeblood of any rental property business and vital for success.

Having a positive cash flow can also allow you to scale your business, meaning that for every property that you buy and rent out, this income increases—and due to inflation, it continues to increase while you pay the same mortgage (if you still have one). In turn, this means that your profit margins increase, as does your purchasing power. For example, if you have placed your money in a savings account, your purchasing power tends to decrease because, even though there's interest associated with the account, this interest is usually lower than the rate of inflation.

The amount of cash flow you can create largely depends on the property you have and the rental strategy you use. There are many different types of these strategies you can use, and you have to find the one that works best for you.

Short- and long-term are the most popular ones. Long-term leases happen when you rent out your property for more than six months, while short-term leases are usually for less time. While long-term rentals often involve renting the property to tenants, short-term rentals usually involve Airbnbing your property, especially if your property is in a location where there are plenty of tourist attractions. However, keep in mind that if you're going to rent out your property for short-term stays, doing so usually involves a lot more maintenance and upkeep than long-term leases. Even so, you can charge more, meaning your rental income is often higher.

Predicting the cash flow of a property can be difficult, but by using historical and industry data, you can get a realistic estimate of what it would be. We will get into the details of cash flow later in the book. However, if you can generate enough positive cash flow, you can reap the holy grail for most real estate investors: passive income.

Passive income is one of the most sought-after benefits of being a real estate investor and the central strategy of many. It refers to the income of money earned with almost no effort on your behalf, though it can provide you with financial security and freedom. I am telling you, there is almost nothing as satisfying as getting a check month after month while doing very little to no work.

As alluded to above, rental income is the main source of passive income in the real estate world. When you rent out a property, the rent paid by tenants comes every month. This is one of the most reliable sources of income in real estate because tenants have to pay rent if they want to live on the property. I cannot overstate how life changing it is the first time you get paid rent rather than paying it or a mortgage.

Leverage

Leveraging debt to build wealth is a very attractive part of real estate investing and is a great tool that will allow you to increase your potential returns by using the money you borrow to acquire properties that produce more income. Let's have a closer look at it.

Leverage in the context of real estate investing is when you combine the capital you have and the funds that you borrow, usually in the form of a loan or a mortgage, to buy investment properties. The main goal here is to increase your returns. Leverage also means that you can utilize the power of other people's money (OPM) – most commonly, the bank's or that of private investors. This is done by securing financing from lenders where you use a small amount of your own money to do it, which in turn frees up more of your available capital to put into improving the property or for anything else that you want to invest in.

For example, let's say a property is priced at $300,000 and the bank is willing to lend me up to 80% off the asking price. In this case, the bank will lend me $240,000 in the form of a mortgage. This means that I only have to put $60,000 of my own money for a down payment. Basically, I am paying $60,000 to get a $300,000 asset that will appreciate and be worth more in the future!

If you're thinking you could never come up with $60,000 for a down payment, don't worry. This is just an example, and we'll be talking about ways to find and create little-to-no-money-down deals later in the book.

But the real benefit here is that you can significantly amplify your returns on your own investments. For easy math, let's say you have $100,000 in cash to invest (again, please don't worry if you don't – this is an example). You could simply use that money to purchase a property that would cost $100,000 right away. If in a year, that property appreciated by 5% , you would have $5,000 more. But if you leverage, instead of buying the property with all the money you have right away, you leverage that $100,000 and use it for a down payment on a property that costs $500,000. If within a year, that property appreciates the same 5% , you would have $25,000 more! That's $20,000 more by using the power of leverage!

There are some considerations you have to take into account when you're leveraging debt. While it's a great strategy to increase your wealth, it's not without risks. For instance, it's vital that you can cover the mortgage payments and other expenses related to the rental. You also can't forget about the interest on your borrowed money. Moreover, think about market volatility, as real estate markets can fluctuate, and in some cases, properties might not appreciate for some time. Leverage use can increase your returns, but they can also increase your risk. So, make sure that you have a diversified portfolio to help you mitigate some of that risk.

Leveraging debt is a wonderful long-term strategy to build wealth. As time passes, your properties appreciate, and with that, your rental income grows, so you can pay down the debt and accumulate significant wealth while your portfolio continues to produce income and stays diversified.

Key Takeaways

- Real estate investing has created 90% of the world's millionaires—and you could be one of them.
- There are major tax benefits to real estate investing. Many successful investors pay less in taxes than most Americans, even though they typically make more income.
- Real estate has been a proven and reliable investment class, in large part due to appreciation: the natural or forced increase in value of the asset over time.
- Cash flow is king and the lifeblood of any business, including real estate.
- Leveraging debt is a powerful tool that allows you to buy expensive assets for a fraction of the cost.
- Tax benefits + appreciation + cash flow + leverage = the secret sauce to wealth building with real estate.

2

THE TOP 5 REAL ESTATE INVESTMENTS THAT CAN CHANGE YOUR LIFE

Ninety percent of all millionaires become so through owning real estate.

— ANDREW CARNEGIE

There are seemingly endless types of real estate investments, but five stand above the rest and have proven to be an approachable vehicle for ordinary people to become rich. Each category has its own pros and cons, so it will be your job, in line with your business plan, to choose the best option for your real estate investing journey.

One of the best parts of real estate investing is its flexibility. You can change your strategy along the way or employ many at once. It is, however, best to choose one strategy to get started with and stick to for a while before switching or adding more.

Let's dig deeper into each of these top five investment types to help you understand which may be more aligned with your goals as you begin your path in real estate.

Residential Real Estate

Residential real estate is a simple entry point for any new investor. It's popular because it has a lower barrier to entry regarding both cost and knowledge. Even seasoned investors who go into other real estate industries sometimes include residential properties in their portfolios because they understand the value of diversification.

As you might expect, residential real estate refers to properties meant for people to live in. It has distinct advantages that we will discuss, along with the various types of properties within this category. These properties are everywhere, as everyone needs a place to live. They consist of single-family homes, townhouses, mobile homes, condominiums, apartment buildings, and multifamily properties, such as duplexes, triplexes, and quadplexes.

Advantages of Residential Property

So, what are the benefits of owning residential property?

To start, these real estate assets have a continuous market demand level, making this category less volatile than others. However, it is essential to realize that variations are still possible. Residential properties are appealing because they have this particular characteristic of diversifying your real estate portfolio. You can buy any of them, including multifamily units, condominiums, and single-family houses.

Also, residential buildings have the benefit of providing consistent long-term rental revenue. Furthermore, they have higher appreciation rates than other real estate categories, allowing for the progressive expansion of your wealth over time.

As a real estate investor and an investor in general, you must often give up on different investments for various reasons. Residential properties are one of the simplest, most reliable, safest, and steadiest ways to build wealth. You can profit from these properties by renting, holding, fixing, and selling them. This type of property is also much easier to finance than the ones I'll discuss later in this section. This is because residential properties have significantly more financing choices than other types of assets.

Disadvantages of Residential Property

While residential properties might be more resistant to the changes in the market, they are also vulnerable to more significant economic cycles. Because of this, thorough research is required before making this sort of purchase.

On top of this, managing these properties can take a significant amount of time. If you don't have a property manager, you have to interact with and manage tenants yourself. You will face tenant-related concerns, such as background checks, resolving maintenance requests, rent payment issues, random appliances and equipment breaking, etc. There's also the property's upkeep, which must be done regularly to keep it in excellent condition and attract higher-quality renters.

There's also the dreaded vacancy issue. If someone isn't paying you rent to live in the property, you still have to pay the mortgage on time and out of pocket, and your cash flow decreases. So, it's essential to account for an appropriate vacancy rate in your financial analysis for when these things happen before you even buy the deal.

Finally, the landlord-tenant laws, which may be complicated at times, apply to residential premises. Regulations can differ by location, so it's crucial to know the rules you must follow, especially regarding evictions, squatters' rights, etc.

While these disadvantages may seem scary, don't let them stop you. There are many ways to mitigate the risk of these situations, plan for them, and strategize ways to handle them, which we will go through later in this book.

Commercial Real Estate

Commercial real estate is considered a step above regarding the complexity and cost of investment. Commercial properties cater to businesses. When it comes to tenants, while leases might take a little longer to be drawn, you can expect tenants to stay there longer, which allows you better cash flow.

When it comes to commercial real estate, there's a lot more diversity. You have office buildings, industrial facilities, or warehouses, for example. Nonetheless, the cost to invest in these properties is higher than the amounts you might be used to seeing in residential properties. Let's look at the various types of commercial real estate.

Office buildings are among the most common and are self-explanatory. They can serve as workspaces for single or many tenants and range in size from small offices to towering skyscrapers. These spaces can be filled by anyone, from a lawyer's office to a mortgage company, marketing firm, etc.

Retail properties include malls, shopping centers, freestanding stores, and restaurants, another common commercial real estate category. They are all structured to cater to businesses that directly service consumers, including clothing stores, grocery stores, daycares, and so on.

Warehouses or industrial buildings, such as manufacturing facilities, distribution centers, and others, are other commercial options. These are typically integrated into logistic hubs to facilitate the movement or creation of products.

Hotels and other hospitality properties are also classified as commercial real estate. They include, as previously mentioned, hotels, motels, bed & breakfasts, resorts, or any other sort of lodging facility.

Then we have multifamily apartment complexes, which, while residential, can also be considered commercial real estate if they have five or more units.

Lastly, there are commercial buildings known as special-purpose properties, which are created for highly unique uses. They vary from educational institutions to healthcare facilities and even religious institutions.

Advantages of Commercial Real Estate

There are plenty of benefits when it comes to investing in commercial real estate, but here are the six major ones:

1. There's a much higher income potential because commercial properties often charge higher rents than residential properties.
2. Commercial properties with an excellent location might also appreciate more than residential properties.

3. There is potential for much higher-quality tenants with solid finances, which reduces the risk of tenants not paying rent or damaging the property.
4. Commercial tenants tend to have much longer leases, which allows you to have a much more stable rental income.
5. These properties can have triple net leases where tenants take care of bills like maintenance, insurance, and property taxes. However, for this to happen, you typically charge tenants a lower rent.
6. Suppose you have specialized assets or the ability to build to suit. In that case, you can attract tenants that, in turn, sign leases with higher rents and stay far longer than traditional commercial tenants. For example, let's say the USDA is looking for office space. They want to rent out your property, but need the space renovated to meet specific requirements from the government. If you can meet their specifications, the USDA will likely pay you a high-rent, sign-a-10+-year lease, and renew this long lease.

Disadvantages of Commercial Real Estate

Despite all these advantages, commercial properties have certain downsides that must be carefully considered. One such disadvantage is the significantly higher initial expenditure necessary to invest in these properties. Purchasing a commercial property is frequently more expensive than buying a residential home, so a thorough understanding of deal analysis, financing, market trends, and a pulse on the local business ecosystem is essential to making effective investment decisions.

Also, keep in mind that the agreements for commercial leases tend to be more complex than those for residential properties. It's always best to bring in an attorney specializing in commercial leases. The same goes for the upkeep of your commercial property, which often requires more specialized professionals to work on it.

Raw Land Investments

Depending on what you do with it, raw land investments can range from very simple to being the most complex type of real estate investment out there. The two simple ways of making money with land investments are to buy and hold the property or rent it out as is. The buy-and-hold strategy is when an investor purchases a plot of land, keeps it for years, and sells it for a much higher price years or decades later. The other simple way to capitalize on raw land is to rent it out. This can be as simple as renting your land to farmers to grow their crops or as complex as renting to large companies like McDonald's, for instance, that want to build a location on your land. In situations like this, the company usually rents the land, but pays to erect a building themselves.

So, when do raw land investments get complicated? One word: developments. Many investors love this strategy, which is when investors take raw land and turn it into residential or commercial property by building on it. This commitment, however, adds a layer of intricacy and understanding that demands prior experience, and I'll emphasize that raw land may only be profitable if you have the necessary expertise. If you turn this land into a residential or commercial property, you will face a lengthy building period, significant upfront financial obligations, and the need to wait for eventual sales or tenant occupancy. In addition, a large amount of bureaucratic red tape and effort is required.

Still, investors love this strategy because they have almost total control over it—they can build anything they want the way they want it. However, there are things you have to consider, such as location, that will help you choose what you should build. Also, depending on the area, you can build any property, from residential to commercial or even more specialized properties, if you get it appropriately zoned.

Although there's more risk in this strategy of developing raw land, investors love to seize on these opportunities because when done correctly, they can make a killing off these deals.

Advantages of Raw Land Investments

An obvious advantage of these investments is your creative control over what you do with them—the possibilities are almost endless! You can build the property you have envisioned. If it's well located, it can have great potential for appreciation, just like residential or commercial properties.

A lesser-known benefit to land investments is that you will pay little to no property taxes on your undeveloped land until a property is built, so your holding costs are much cheaper than purchasing an existing property.

And finally, when executed correctly, investors can make significant money from developing residential or commercial properties on land they purchase.

Disadvantages of Raw Land Investments

Like anything else, these investments also come with disadvantages and risks, as you might imagine. For instance, local zoning laws and regulations can significantly impact what you can do with the land. They can stop you from building a commercial or residential property altogether, for instance. Before buying raw land, you should inform yourself and do thorough research on what you can and can't build.

Also, when it's time to build a property, the costs can be steep. This process is called developing the land, and you don't only have to buy materials and personnel to build it; you also need to pay for a myriad of things before you can build anything there. For instance, you may need to purchase utility installation, grading, environmental assessments, permitting fees, or road construction.

You also have to consider the current market conditions when you expect to buy raw land because this timing can affect its value. Another thing that you need to consider is access to infrastructure such as electricity, water, or sewers, which might increase the price even more if you have to install all of that.

REIT Investing

REIT investing, which stands for real estate investment trust investing, is a great way to enter the real estate industry. A REIT is a company solely aiming to manage, own, or finance real estate properties to generate income. In other words, you can look at REIT as a stock investment because stock is traded there, similar to a mutual fund dedicated to real estate. This way, you can buy shares of properties without purchasing, managing, financing, or paying a down payment on them.

Because they are like stocks, REITs are far more liquid than actually investing in a property. You can simply sell the shares and get money in your account, which doesn't happen as fast when you sell a property (this usually demands a lengthy process). REIT investments can apply to any property, from residential to commercial and anything in between.

While most REITs specialize in real estate investment, there are a few specialized REITs that hold specific types of properties if you want to diversify your portfolio. That being said, let's quickly go over the main types of REITs you can find.

There's a market for REITs: companies that lend money to real estate owners through mortgages or loans, whose earnings mainly come from net interest margins. Equity REITs, on the other hand, are more common. These companies often own and manage income-producing properties, so their income comes from rent, which often comes in monthly dividends as if you were receiving rent when you own a property. Then, there are hybrid REITs, a mix of the two above.

While these are the main types of REITs, they can also be divided into subgroups, such as publicly traded REITs, which you often find in the stock market; public non-traded REITs, which don't trade in exchanges but are still registered with the SEC; and private REITs, which only institutional investors have access to.

If you're starting out, publicly traded REITs are the easiest to start investing in. You can simply do this by having a brokerage account and purchasing shares of the REIT. Unlike individual company stocks, REITs tend not to grow in value as much, but pay dividends instead.

Advantages of REITs

I've mentioned some advantages of REITs, such as being highly liquid, but there's more. Investing in REITs can expand your portfolio's diversification, even if you're just a real estate investor. You can invest in different properties you wouldn't otherwise invest in.

Furthermore, cash flow is stable because you receive dividends, and you don't have to worry about screening tenants, so you know you will receive money from the REIT regardless. Lastly, REITs are flexible when it comes to adjusting your risk.

Disadvantages of REITs

As I've pointed out, don't expect a lot of growth from REITs, mainly because that's not really their way of operating, as any surplus they get is distributed in the form of dividends.

Also, the dividends you receive are taxed as regular income and are often associated with high transaction fees, though this depends on the REIT you buy shares from.

Tax Liens

Tax lien investing is often overlooked by real estate investors. What is a tax lien anyway?

Essentially, a tax lien is a legal claim against a business or individual's assets when they fail to pay taxes to the government. If the obligation to pay is not fulfilled, the creditor can repossess the assets. However, as a private investor, these claims can be traded and exchanged, and you can generate profit from those transactions. Of course, as with any investment, there are risks, and you must understand the rules.

In simpler terms, if a homeowner fails to pay their property taxes, the local government can place a lien on the property, which, as we've seen, is a legal claim. The home can only be refinanced or sold once the debt is paid. When there's a lien, a tax lien certificate is issued, which shows the amount of debt plus any interest added. These certificates can then be auctioned off to investors. When investors acquire the certificate, they must pay back the total amount immediately. Then, the homeowner must pay the investor all the money they invested plus interest, often between 10% and 25%.

Keep in mind that there's usually a repayment schedule between six months and three years. The legal claim comes in if the homeowner fails to repay their lien. If this happens, the owner of the tax lien—in this case, the real estate investor—has a legal claim to the property, and it is now theirs to do with what they wish. The investor can then get paid with either a 10% -25% interest payment or an entirely new property to keep, sell, or rent out. This can be a huge investment opportunity!

Advantages of Tax Lien Investing

Tax liens can see a higher rate of return than the stock market, anywhere between 10% -25% . They are secure investments, as they are in first position—meaning, they get first priority to be paid out. They are also more affordable to get started in, and they don't require as much of a learning curve as other types of investing.

Once you lock in a certain interest rate for your lien, that is what you get. Another big advantage to these investments is they are paid out by the government rather than by individuals or companies, so they're enforced by law and not as subject to fraud.

Disadvantages of Tax Lien Investing

You have no control when the taxes are paid, which means you may have to wait a long time to get paid yourself. Another risk is that the rules and regulations vary county by county, so some might sell liens for properties with little to no value. As a result, you really have to do your due diligence with the county you are buying from.

Lastly, there's not a ton of information available on tax lien investing or resources to learn about this topic. Most people don't know much about it because tax lien investors prefer to stick to themselves to keep the competition out.

Key Takeaways

- Residential real estate is the most common and often easiest way to get started in real estate investing.
- Commercial real estate costs more to invest in than residential real estate, but often has higher rents, longer leases, and higher-quality tenants.
- Raw land investments that are development deals are complicated, high-risk, and high-reward deals that can pay

off exponentially with the right approach. These investments are not beginner friendly.

- REITs are the easiest way to invest in real estate, as no property management is involved.
- Tax liens are one of the best-kept secrets in real estate investing. They allow you to pay someone's unpaid taxes for them and get paid back before even the banks and the government—or you—get to keep the property.

Regardless of which of these five types of investments you choose, due diligence is absolutely essential. It's the only way you can mitigate any financial losses, and the only way you can make the right decisions.

In the following chapter, we will go through various investing strategies in depth. I will focus on the most common ones and give you advice on how you can choose the one that suits you best.

3

THE SWISS ARMY KNIFE OF REAL ESTATE INVESTING & THE BEST INVESTMENT STRATEGIES

Real estate is an imperishable asset, ever increasing in value. It is the most solid security that human ingenuity has devised. It is the basis of all security and about the only indestructible security.

— RUSSELL SAGE

A Swiss Army knife is the world's gold standard of pocketknives, known for its reliability, versatility, and durability. This iconic tool is essentially the right tool for any job. It can help solve just about any problem, and can even save those in an emergency.

So, what is the Swiss Army knife of real estate investing? Your brain. It's all the knowledge you have about real estate investing.

You may be thinking that you don't know much yet about this topic, so you don't have much of a Swiss Army knife. However, the best part is that anyone can develop and learn about the ins and outs of real estate investing for little to no money invested. You don't have to have an expensive degree, a fancy job, or a network of exclusive people. The education needed for real estate investing is accessible through the Internet, books, conferences, networking, organizations, etc. You can learn about the different investing strategies to employ, the intricacies of a specific property type, the multitude of ways to finance a deal, the details of the local laws and ordinances in your area, the little-known ways to use the tax code to your advantage—you name it, you can learn it! The sky is the limit, and the more you learn, the more tools you will have at your disposal to solve just about any problem that comes your way. At the end of the day, that's what real estate investors are—problem solvers.

One of the best tools you can have as an investor is a thorough knowledge of the varied investment strategies. Knowing about all of them will allow you to be as flexible as possible when issues arise or when you need to pivot. They can help you see big money-making opportunities that other people can't.

So, let's get into the most popular investment strategies.

The Fix-and-Flip

The Fix-and-Flip is perhaps the most popular strategy investors start with outside of rental property investing. With this strategy, investors purchase a property below market value, renovate it to increase its value, and sell it at market value.

These properties are typically distressed or need much fixing to make them attractive. So, an investor needs to have a vision of what the end project will look like, how much it will cost to complete the project, and how much they can sell the property for to cover their purchase and renovation costs and to make a profit. Many people are afraid to invest in ugly-looking properties or ones with more significant issues beyond cosmetic ones. However, when executed correctly, this strategy can be highly profitable.

So why doesn't the owner do it themselves to make money off their property? Typically, the owners of these properties are not investors, so they don't know how, or even that they can. Even if they did, they may not have the money, time, or desire to renovate it themselves. This is good for investors because, most of the time, these owners want to get rid of their property as fast as possible, so they are willing to sell quicker and at a much lower price.

However, fix-and-flip is easier said than done. Significant research is needed when dealing with distressed properties. Doing an in-depth financial analysis and careful due diligence is required before purchasing these properties to ensure you accurately budget your finances and time to avoid losing money on the deal. It's vital to account for all that could go wrong or not according to plan because, by nature of the business, it will. On the flip side, if these properties do not require considerable changes and you can't increase their value enough, you'll get little or no profit from the sale.

Foreclosures are the most common type of distressed property. These occur when property owners default on their mortgages, causing the bank or another financial organization that granted the loan to repossess the property. Because of this, such properties are often more affordable. In other cases, foreclosure homes might not require renovations. This is great for investors because they can sell them at a higher price without incurring remodeling costs. Imagine how great that would be!

There are also short sales, which happen when the owner sells the property at a lower price than that of the comparable properties in a given market. This can happen because of numerous circumstances, but the most common is simply because the seller wants to complete the sale as soon as possible. Nonetheless, it presents an excellent opportunity for those looking to buy. Another instance of when this might occur is through auctions, where you can find properties to buy at a lower price.

With the fix-and-flip strategy (and the real estate business in general), networking is essential. This is because having connections with developers or real estate agents allows the opportunity to get off-market deals, meaning these properties have yet to be put on the market for everyone to see. As a result, you can negotiate a lower price for them.

Improvements and Renovations

While sometimes you don't need to renovate the property that much to increase its value, most of the time, you do. And there are many different things you might need or want to do to accomplish that.

The best improvements that can increase a property's value are simple cosmetic upgrades such as a fresh coat of paint on the outside wall, interior renovations such as flooring, or exterior changes such as landscaping. These are great because they often make a big difference at a small cost to the investor. Then, there are structural repairs that are usually more expensive and essential. For instance, there may be roof and foundation repairs or any other structural issues vital to the property.

Some improvements fall in between cosmetic upgrades and structural repairs. Remodeling the kitchen or bathroom or adding a room or useable square footage is a substantial improvement that could significantly boost a property's value. This increases the property's worth and makes it more attractive, so more people may be interested in buying it, thus increasing its demand as well.

Other things that can increase property value include improving energy efficiency or updating essential systems such as HVAC and electrical installations. Keep in mind that it is critical to ensure that any upgrade or renovation complies with local building rules and that the necessary licenses are secured.

What to Consider Financially

To execute a fix-and-flip properly and successfully, you must take into account a few financial considerations. Keep in mind the following things while creating your financial plan.

First, you must factor in the property's purchasing cost. You should buy the property for a price lower than its current market value. The lower the buying price, the greater the potential upside, and the more wiggle room you have for mistakes. You also have to think about the renovation budget. The goal here is to guarantee that you can still make a significant profit when the home sells after deducting both the purchase and remodeling costs. Minimizing delays or cost overruns during renovation will be critical to your success.

If you can get enough financing for the purchase and renovation, it can help you immensely in the event unexpected costs and delays arise. These things happen all the time. Again, the purchasing cost and renovations have to be lower than what you sell the property for to profit from the investment.

To know the price you should sell the renovated property for, you must research the local market and check comps (comparable properties in the area). For example, if you buy a one-bedroom and plan to make it a two-bedroom, research how much two-bedrooms in the same area are going for.

Challenges and Risks of the Fix-and-Flip Strategy

Of course, there are challenges and risks to every investment strategy. Market fluctuations always happen, so they are a risk, regardless of your plan. This is mainly due to the normal movements of the economy, which can be up or down at any given moment. Even specific local market conditions can affect the price of properties.

However, there are three main challenges when undertaking a fix-and-flip. Let's take a closer look at them.

Estimating the Scope of the Project

Properly assessing what is needed to improve a property is imperative to a successful fix-and-flip. This information forms the baseline for everything else. If you can figure out precisely what needs to be done and who will be doing it, you can plan much more accurately for your budget and timeline while lowering the risk of not making your target profit.

Besides knowing what needs to be done to the actual property, you also need to learn about any external factors like zoning requirements, permits, ordinances, or tax laws. You also need to determine if you want to put some sweat equity in the deal and personally paint rooms and tear down walls, or if you want to hire contractors or companies to do a partial or complete renovation. If you have the skills and time to do a lot of the renovation yourself, your profit margin will be much higher. Some investors love doing renovations themselves, while others don't. Not everyone has the skills or time to do it themselves, so they have to hire everything out.

Estimating Costs

Estimating costs for a renovation can be tricky. If you set a budget to use for your renovations, but in reality it costs more than what you budgeted, this could mean that your profit margins will shrink.

Trying to guess how much money you need without making sound calculations can be quite expensive in the real estate industry. This is why accurately estimating the project's scope and planning it ahead of time is so important. First, having an accurate understanding of what needs to be done to the property lowers the chances of an expensive surprise that will eat up all your profits or, worse, put you in debt. Second, you'll have a much more accurate picture of the total renovation cost. So, it is vital to decide beforehand if and what you will do yourself and what parts you are hiring out.

There are a lot of questions that need to be answered before you get into a deal like this. Do you need a plumber, roofer, electrician, or carpenter? How much do they typically charge for what you need to be done, and how long will it take? How do these things impact your bottom line and overall strategy?

To reiterate, if you have the skills and time to do a lot of the renovation yourself, your profit margin will be much higher. However, don't think you have to do this to make a lot of money. Many investors hire everything out and still make a lot of money at the end of a fix-and-flip. It's all about accurately planning and executing the project.

When planning the finances for your project, you'll have to consider more than just the renovation. Acquiring the property is the first cost, and usually the most expensive. And while you might come across low or no-money-down financing claims, these can often be false. So, when you do come across such claims, there are a few things that you should consider. For instance, while the interest on borrowed money can be deducted from your tax return, it's not 100% deductible. This means that every penny you spend on interest adds to the amount you will have to earn on the sale. Also, if you get a mortgage or even a HELOC (home equity line of credit) to finance your investment, remember that only the interest is deductible. Everything else – like taxes, insurance, or principal – is not.

When beginning with a fix-and-flip strategy, there are ways to limit your financial risk and maximize your potential return. In other words, avoid overpaying for the property and ensure you know how much the necessary renovations will be before investing in that property. Here, you can use the 70% rule, which dictates that you shouldn't pay more than 70% of the property's after-repair value

(ARV) minus any necessary repairs. The ARV is what the property is worth after the renovations are done. Here's an example:

Let's say the property's ARV is $200,000 and the repairs are $30,000. You shouldn't pay more than $110,000, as $200,000 x 0.70 = $140,000 minus $30,000 = $110,000.

Of course, sometimes you have to pay a little more for renovations because of unforeseen circumstances, but calculating the AVR is a good way to narrow down how much you should pay for a property. While correctly estimating a fix-and-flip budget can be difficult, it's not impossible.

Estimating Time

Nailing down an accurate timeline for fix-and-flips is just as challenging. Not having enough time budgeted is one of the biggest mistakes new real estate investors make with this strategy. While this method is relatively faster than buy-and-hold to make profits, it's still time-consuming and often takes more time to see it through. Once you are the property owner, you have to either do or oversee the renovations, which can take a lot of time.

Going through the average processes means demolition (which is common) and construction. Once the renovations are done, you still need to inspect the property and ensure everything is in order; otherwise, you will have to spend more time and money fixing it. Also, unexpected delays happen during renovations all the time. Whether a particular contractor is behind deadline, the delivery of parts is delayed, or there's a required specific local permit that you were unaware of, issues tend to pop up when you least expect them. Lastly, there's the selling of the property, which can also take more time than investors think.

While many of these challenges seem frustrating and scary to a new investor, they are par for the course. The important thing is allocating enough cushion time for the project without losing money. While these issues of estimating the scope of the project, costs, and time are common, if you do proper due diligence, thoroughly assess the conditions of the property and what it will take to complete the project, add in enough cushion for costs and time, you can mitigate a lot of the risks. Fix-and-flips can be highly profitable and, dare I say, fun if you're willing to put in the effort necessary.

The element that makes this strategy different from most of the others is this aspect of project management. You not only need to understand the real estate market, but you also have to be an expert when it comes to juggling deadlines, contracts, schedules, people, and many other moving parts. There may be a learning curve, but you'll get better and better over time and be able to manage many renovations at once, making you a large amount of wealth.

Buy-and-Hold Strategy

The buy-and-hold strategy is the most popular for real estate investors. As the name indicates, it involves buying and holding on to a property for a certain period (usually at least a year or more) before selling it. However, while you hold it, you get rental income by renting the property to tenants. This is perhaps one of the most profitable investment strategies because while you're getting rental income for years, the property is appreciating, so when you sell it, you are likely to sell it for more than you've paid. In theory, the longer you hold the property, the more you earn.

You can do this with almost any property type, from a duplex to a warehouse to a commercial property. Regardless of the property type you invest in, securing financing is typically key to maximizing your profits. The idea here is to invest a smaller amount upfront for a down payment to get a loan paid for by the rent your tenants pay you.

So, for example, let's say you put 20% down ($60,000) for a $300,000 property. You will have a loan of $240,000—with interest, of course— that other people are paying down for you! So, essentially, you're paying $60,000 for a property that will likely appreciate being much higher than a $300,000 value, making you hundreds of thousands of dollars in the future. On top of this, if you play your cards right, money will go into your pocket every month until then from the cash flow of your property.

Another important aspect here is that, as you pay your mortgage from the rent your tenants pay you, you are acquiring equity, which is to say that every time you pay your mortgage, you are acquiring a little bit more of the property, thereby increasing your wealth. Plus, the equity you build can be used for any future investments you want to make; this is called leverage. There are also the tax benefits I've previously mentioned, such as tax credits, depreciation deductions, or capital gains tax benefits from buy-and-hold rental properties.

Do you see the magic of real estate investing yet?!

The very first step when considering a buy-and-hold strategy is to look for and compare properties. Of all the steps, this one might be the most tedious, but it's important. Having a realtor by your side can make this process a lot faster because they can narrow down properties of potential interest and even help you through online auctions or through their multiple listing service (MLS), which is a database that realtors have access to. Then, you either purchase the property right away or finance it, which is similar to the process of buying a home.

Once all of that is done, you will have to rent out the property and manage it, which can be time-consuming in the beginning. But once you've rented it out, depending on the quality of your property, it doesn't have to be this way going forward. To find tenants, you need to market the property well to attract the best ones, screen the potential tenants by running background checks to ensure they can afford the rent, create a lease agreement, understand all the local and state laws, and get your landlord insurance.

Another popular strategy for buy-and-hold investors is short-term or mid-term rentals. This is when an investor buys a property, furnishes it, pays all utilities, and rents it out typically anywhere between one night to one month for a short-term vacation rental or anywhere from 3-9 months for a mid-term rental. Vacation rentals are typically high-maintenance properties because they need to be constantly flipped, cleaned, supplied, and guests can be demanding. However, in the right area, these properties can make investors high returns, oftentimes high enough to pay property managers to take care of all of the guest headaches that inevitably pop up.

Mid-term or medium-term rentals are usually for traveling professionals who work on a multi-month contract and need a place to stay. They are often a sweet spot for investors because these tenants are typically high-quality, with good records and reliable income to pay the rent. The best part is sometimes their company gives out high stipends or pays rent for them. Overall, these professionals are much more similar to having tenants than having guests in a short-term rental. They tend to be lower-maintenance and treat the property more like their own apartment than a vacation rental.

Buy-and-hold properties usually come with a lot of maintenance. Some items are best to take care of right away when you buy a property, while others you may be able to wait on fixing if you need to save up for them. This is why it's so important to pay attention to the ages of things like HVAC, roofing, appliances, etc., when doing due diligence of the property and financial analysis. When it comes to maintenance of the property, you have to consider updating carbon monoxide and smoke alarms, keeping up with the maintenance of the HVAC system and any other system, as well as managing structural issues that come up during an inspection, such as foundation issues. It's particularly important that you check for any structural issues before renting the property out so you can fix them right away and avoid a more expensive problem down the line.

Other tasks entailed in managing rental properties include rent collection and security deposits, keeping track of taxes, handling maintenance requests, getting proper insurance, dealing with utilities, and paying mortgages.

Risks and Challenges of the Buy-and-Hold Strategy

The biggest challenge in managing rental properties is tenant management, which largely involves dealing with tenant issues as well as vacancies. The maintenance of the property is another challenge, requiring you to regularly maintain the property, do repairs, and pay for unexpected costs.

With a buy-and-hold, you also need to think about an exit strategy, but unlike the fix-and-flip, this exit strategy is long-term. The most common exit strategies with the buy-and-hold are selling the property, using it as a retirement home, or simply passing it on to your children.

While you are renting the property, you should keep an eye on the housing market trends so you can understand the current and potential future of the housing market and know what your next step should be. Having a good grasp on the market will allow you to make the best decision when it comes to continuing to rent the property and know when it is a good time to sell for maximum profit.

This brings us to the next step: knowing when to sell your property. One way to find out if it's a good time to sell is if comparable properties begin to depreciate (and you already want to sell the property, of course). Another big reason to sell is if your current investment no longer serves your needs and financial goals. You should be regularly evaluating if your investments still align with your strategy and ultimate goals. Other reasons investors sell is that the property is costing them more money, time, or effort than anticipated. If the property is going downhill, it's better for them to cut their losses than hire a property manager to do their work for them.

If you do decide to sell, it's important that you consider taxes beforehand. When you sell a property, you have to pay capital gain taxes, and the time you sell your property will dictate how much tax you pay. For instance, if you've owned the property for less than a year, you will pay short-term capital gains, but if you've held on to the property for longer than that, you'll get preferential tax rates because of long-term capital gains.

Wholesaling

Wholesaling is a real estate strategy that is quite different from the others we've seen here so far. With wholesaling, you are essentially the middle point between sellers and buyers when it comes to making a transaction. So, you don't have to purchase the property yourself (well, kind of). Instead, you earn money by getting a commission when the sale is done.

While wholesale carries a much lower risk and you can make money faster, the profits are substantially lower than with other strategies. However, it's a great way to get into the real estate market if you don't have a lot of money to invest in properties.

The very first step with wholesaling is to find a distressed property, but unlike the fix-and-flip strategy, you're not purchasing the property. Instead, you negotiate with the seller to secure a purchase contract at a price that is much lower than the market value (it has to be much lower for this strategy to work). This is so that when you sell the property without any renovations done, you can sell for a profit that is likely still below market, but higher than the price you've paid.

After you've conducted your research and found a distressed property, you need to do your due diligence and your math. Here, finding out the property's fair market value will give you a little more information about how much profit you can make. You also have to look at comparable properties, cash-on-cash returns, and occupancy rates, as well as determine the cost of repairs. With this information, you can calculate the ARV. Then, you can calculate the maximum offer, which tells you how much higher you can go pricewise while still making a profit on the investment.

If all your math and due diligence check out, you need to contact the seller and tell them about your role as a wholesaler and how your services might be a great way to help them sell the property. You have to clearly explain how the role of a wholesaler can help them because many people might not be familiar with this strategy. Then, you have to obtain a property contract, but before that, you need to present your offer. Keep in mind that the property contract should have included the right to assign the contract to a different person (that's the main role of a wholesaler) and include some contingencies, especially one that states that you can back off from a deal if you can't find a buyer before the expiration of the contract.

Once that is done, you have to find a cash buyer, and here, your networking will really come in handy, as you can contact investors who might be interested in a fix-and-flip strategy. Alternatively, you can also contact real estate agencies and ask for a list of cash purchases made recently in the area.

When you do find a buyer, you have to reassign the contract to the buyer and make sure you get paid for the work you've done.

The most important aspect of being able to pull off this strategy is having the right connections. As a wholesaler, your most important job is to create a network of buyers and sellers, such as flippers (those who do fix-and-flip strategies), landlords (who want to sell), real estate agents, and other professionals in the industry. So, when you sign the purchase contract, you don't necessarily close the property, but when you sell it, the buyer assumes the rights and obligations of the contract. When you do this, you obtain what is called in the industry a "wholesale fee," which is usually around 5% of the property's value.

Some benefits of the wholesale strategy are, as I've mentioned, quick profits and low financial risk. Starting with wholesaling is also a great way to learn the ins and outs of real estate without investing too much money, as well as improve your negotiation skills. Also, you don't need to go through certain requirements that are needed with other strategies, such as checks on your credit score, and you don't need previous experience in how to renovate a property.

Risks and Considerations of the Wholesale Strategy

While the wholesale strategy is effectively lower on risk compared to other strategies, that doesn't necessarily mean it's risk free. Here, it's crucial that you have a great understanding of the local market to ensure that you get the purchase contract at a low price and manage to sell it for a profit. You also have to pay attention to legal and ethical compliance, such as local real estate laws and local regulations. If you fail to comply with them, your deal can fall through. Also, if you don't have a strong network of professionals and strong negotiation skills, your chances of being successful with this strategy are drastically reduced.

It's just as important to have a great marketing campaign and marketing team to look for potential buyers. This is because you need to be able to find a buyer fast, and the longer it takes to do this, the more money you lose. If it happens that you can't find a buyer, you need to have an exit strategy ready, which could potentially mean renegotiating the contract with the seller or simply walking away from the contract.

As you can see, the wholesale strategy is very different from other strategies we've seen so far. You need very different skills to make this strategy successful and find the best opportunities for you. However, if you are successful with it, you can make a great profit with much less upfront money.

If you want to make a profit with this strategy, you need to have great networking skills. This might be a little challenging if you haven't done so already, but it's something that you can work on. You will not make any money with wholesaling until you have found suitable properties and investors. This means that there will be times when you've worked quite a bit on a property, but were unable to find a suitable investor in time, and so you've not only lost time but also your earnest money. You also have to consider the fact that distressed properties can be unpredictable because of how dependent they are on the other properties available.

House Hacking

House hacking is a strategy that is quite time-consuming. It involves the benefits of income generation through ownership. With this strategy, you usually purchase a multifamily property with multiple units where you will live in one and rent out the other units to tenants. A very important benefit to point out here is that you can almost offset your property expenses with the rent you generate while you build equity with the multifamily property. If you're just starting out, house hacking is a great strategy because you might be able to get a great loan, buy your first property, and generate income while doing it.

As I've mentioned before, if you're looking to buy your first property, conventional or traditional loans are the easiest and cheapest way to secure financing. But to make your strategy even easier to execute, if you have friends who are looking for a place to rent, you can have them occupy the other units. This way, you don't have to screen people that you don't know, and it's a much easier process this way.

Either way, if you follow through with this strategy, you will become an owner-occupant, which simply means that you will be living with your tenants on the same property. You still need to do some management, especially if you have to screen tenants and market the property. Nonetheless, this strategy has great benefits, from lowering your housing expenses to high cash flows, equity accumulation, and tax benefits linked to your property ownership. Let's look at an example.

You've bought a duplex for $300,000 with a 20% downpayment (or $60,000) and the remaining balance of the loan ($240,000) will be paid in the form of a fixed mortgage over 30 years with a 4% interest rate. This means that you will be paying $1,145.80 a month. Now, if you live in one unit of the house and rent out the other unit for

$2,000 a month, the tenants will be paying more than you have to pay for your mortgage, plus you get $854.20 in profit that you can use to pay for repairs, taxes, or insurance. After only a few years, you would have built quite a bit of equity in the property while the property itself appreciated.

While you can use house hacking for many properties, some types work better than others. A multifamily home, for instance, is a great one, such as duplexes or triplexes. Alternatively, if you have an extra room that you won't be using, you can rent it out for the short term, such as using it as an Airbnb. This way, you don't have to always live with a tenant on your property, and you make more money on rent because short-term rentals usually yield a higher income.

Risks and Challenges of the House Hacking Strategy

The biggest challenge when it comes to house hacking is managing the property. As discussed, you might be able to mitigate this challenge if you already know the tenants you're bringing in. If you don't, managing the property can be quite a time-consuming activity.

Also, you have to keep in mind that the level of privacy you experience is not the same as if you were living in a single unit.

Furthermore, remember to think of an exit strategy. Usually, this means moving out and renting out all the units once you are done paying the mortgage.

As you can see, this type of strategy is very different from the fix-and-flip or the buy-and-hold, but it might be ideal for you if you're looking for a primary property to live in. Still, it requires some effort and can be quite time-consuming, so keep those things in mind.

Choosing the Right Strategy for Your Goals

As you can see, each investment method has its own distinct qualities and its own set of benefits and downsides. It is your responsibility to choose which technique best fits your present level as an investor. Recognize that extensive research is required when choosing a strategy at any given moment, as your selection will significantly influence your financial objectives, risk tolerance, and eventual success. Your strategy choice will also have a significant impact on your property acquisition method and, ultimately, the return on your investment.

How can one properly go through this assessment process? You've probably figured out what you want to do with your money at this time. If not, it is crucial to begin this process by outlining your financial goals. Ask yourself, "Am I aiming for short-term or long-term wealth or a combination of both?" Numerous key things must be examined to determine your answer. Consider cash flow, for instance, if you expect a consistent income stream from rental profits to fund costs. Also, ask yourself if you want to rely on property appreciation to increase your net worth, examine your risk tolerance, and determine your level of comfort with financial obligations.

The next stage is analyzing your resources, and here, you have to find out how much you have before picking a strategy. This is not only about your financial resources, but also your understanding of the strategies and the real estate industry as a whole. However, knowing the state of your finances will help you narrow down the types of strategies you can go for because some strategies need more upfront capital than others.

Time is another resource you need to take into account, as some of these strategies, such as buy-and-hold to then rent, will likely make you a landlord, which is significantly time-consuming. Of course, you can always hire a property management firm, but if you're starting out, that measure will take a lot of your profit. Lastly, having the necessary knowledge to pursue the strategy you want to perform is a must.

While choosing the investment strategy to use, you also have to take into account the current market conditions. Depending on how the market is going, different strategies might work better than others. But here, you should consider factors like the demand for rental properties or the current economic stability. Of course, location will also inform the strategy you might want to use, as well as the laws and regulations in that area.

There are factors that you have to dig into a little more in order to fully understand the right strategy for you to use. A risk-and-return analysis can really help you out by making a risk-reward profile for the different strategies you're considering, as well as helping you determine whether each strategy aligns with your goals. So, looking at financing risks, market volatility, and potential tenant problems might help you figure out the strategy for you. At the same time, you need to get an estimate of the returns you will have, which means you have to account for overall profitability and appreciation.

You must also take into consideration the diversification of your portfolio, and understand that adding different strategies will allow you to mitigate some of the risks and stabilize your portfolio. Keep in mind that some strategies complement one another so you can consolidate the diversification of your portfolio. However, being flexible and open to new strategies, as well as adjusting things as you see fit, will give you a leg up when mitigating risks. In other words, having a static strategy will not get you very far; you have to keep tweaking your strategies because the market is always evolving. The same is true for an exit strategy, which you have to set up for every single investment you make.

Once you figure out what strategies to use, you can start to narrow them down even further to land on one that is the most suitable for you at this point in your career. As I've said before, many young real estate investors prefer to start with the buy-and-hold strategy because it doesn't require much experience or initial capital. Here, you purchase a property, rent it out, and after a few years, you can sell it for more money than what you've spent on it while collecting rental income.

The fix-and-flip strategy is also quite common, but you need to gather a little more experience first. In addition, it often needs more initial capital, given you are purchasing a distressed property and have to renovate it. With this strategy, you don't necessarily have to have tenants in mind, but instead, other investors or homeowners. So, cater your renovations to that type of buyer because you will sell it as soon as you've completed renovations. Nonetheless, there are also other things you need to consider, such as your budget for renovation, the financing you want to take on, and so on. You have to fully understand the opportunity, and manage the property and renovations effectively, if you want to make a profit when you sell the property.

Wholesaling is a totally different story. Here, you are the intermediary between the buyer and the seller, and you don't have to purchase the property. However, you do have to look for distressed properties where the owner is very keen to sell the property quickly. Because you don't actually purchase the property yourself, the initial capital required is quite low. Also, the skills used in this strategy are very different from the ones applied in other strategies. For instance, your negotiation skills have to be on point, and your network has to be vast.

House hacking is another viable strategy, especially if you're starting out and don't have a primary property yet. By purchasing a multifamily property, you can rent out the other units while you live in one yourself, which can offset your housing expenses.

Key Takeaways

- Estimating an accurate project scope, timeline, and budget often makes or breaks fix-and-flip investments.
- Buy-and-hold properties are the tried-and-true investment strategy for most investors to start building wealth.
- Rental properties allow you to buy a mortgage at a small cost and have other people pay it off for you.
- There are massive tax benefits to real estate investing.
- Wholesaling is a networker's dream, and you don't need a real estate license or money to get started with it.
- House hacking is perfect for young investors or those wanting to drastically reduce or eliminate their personal mortgage. It is by far one of the easiest ways to get started in real estate investing.

FREE GIFT #1

The Only Apartment Investing Book You'll Ever Need: *The Exact Steps To Building Wealth Through Apartment Investing That Anyone Can Follow*

Get your comprehensive guide to apartment investing as a free e-book!

This definitive guide is designed for both beginners and seasoned investors alike. This book walks through the steps to build wealth through apartment investing from finding profitable properties, managing tenants, and maximizing returns, this book can help you gain the knowledge and confidence to succeed in growing your portfolio.

To get instant access this free e-book, scan the QR code below or visit this link: https://readstreetpress.com/iwantpermanentpto1

PART II

HOW TO CLOSE YOUR FIRST DEAL IN 7 SIMPLE STEPS

4

STEP ONE – BUILDING A SOLID
FINANCIAL FOUNDATION

I f your personal finances are in good shape, feel free to skip this chapter, as it may not apply to you. However, if you struggle with money, learning good money management skills to invest in real estate and build and maintain wealth is imperative. While this is not a personal finance book, and an in-depth dive into personal money management is outside the scope of this book, we will touch on the basics of what you need to know and do to get started investing in real estate and close your first deal.

Most people are too afraid or embarrassed to admit that their financial situation is not where they feel it should be or want it to be, or that they don't handle their money as well as they could. The good news is there are always ways to improve and change for the better. Everybody makes financial mistakes, and there's no shaming here!

The main reason to check that your finances are in order is to ensure you can be approved for traditional financing should you need it. Banks will only loan you money if they are confident you can repay them. Their team of underwriters assesses your personal finances and the property in question to determine if and how much they are willing to loan to you. The better your finances and track record are, the less risk it is for the bank, and the more likely you are to secure a loan—and secure one with good terms.

While conventional loans are the most common, there are other ways to finance a deal. In fact, you can finance a deal with very little or none of your own money (we'll get to this later in the book), but it is still essential to get your ducks in a row financially. First, you may need or want to use your personal finances at some point in your investing journey. Second, it's easier to find investors and partners who will trust you more when your own finances are in order. Third, good money management habits are extremely important to managing your business and investing finances well. If we don't manage our personal money well, how will we manage a business, where things tend to be much more complicated?

Depending on where you're starting from, it can take a year or more to improve your financial situation, so you must have patience. Trust me—it's worth the time and effort and the wait! So let's get into it.

Setting Goals and Realistic Expectations

The first step to getting your finances in shape for investing is knowing your goals and setting realistic expectations. If you're looking to invest your own money into your properties, you should have a number in mind of what that is. A good place to start is researching how much the type of property you're looking for is selling for, on average, in the area you want to invest in. Then, as a rule of thumb, you can take 25% of that selling price, which will give you how much money you would need (again, on average, depending on your financing situation) in cash for a down payment. This data will provide you with an estimated amount of money you should aim to have on hand before searching for deals when using traditional financing.

The next step is to take an inventory of your finances, if you don't already know. So many of us are too afraid to look at them to avoid the shame and guilt of our choices. Again, let's set that aside here. No shame or guilt allowed! We must forgive ourselves for our past mistakes and take an objective, almost surgical look at our money situation to fix it and move forward.

So, how much money do you need to get to that 25% cash, if that is your goal? How much can you save monthly to reach that number, and how many months will it take to get there? Can you do something to make extra income to make that goal go faster? Having a realistic plan and timeline will help you stay inspired as you meet your monthly savings goals and keep you motivated to stay the course, knowing there is an end in sight. You are getting closer to it every day.

Reducing Debt & Improving Your Credit Score

Reducing personal debt can improve your cash flow and save up cash reserves to invest. Imagine if you didn't have your monthly car, student loan, or mortgage payment (yes, there is a way to reduce this, which we will go into later in the book) and could put that money towards your savings goals. You would progress so much faster!

What if you have multiple forms of debt? How do you choose which to pay first? Make a debt paydown plan. There are two main strategies for how to do this. The standard way is to make all your minimum payments, but then pay extra on the debt with the highest interest rate that costs you the most money. Dave Ramsey's Snowball Method is the second most popular way to pay down debt. Here, you pay all the minimums on your debt. Still, you pay extra money to the debt with the lowest balance first, allowing you to pay off the total debt in full so you can move on, focusing on the next one. This method tends to encourage people as they go along because they feel like they have a win each time they eliminate a debt from their finances.

Let's move on to your credit score. What is it, and why does it matter? Your credit score, or FICO score, is a single number ranging from 300 to 850. It represents your credit risk to lenders. The higher the number, the better you look in the eyes of lenders, as it shows them you are a lower risk. Lenders take your credit score and other information, like your salary, age, assets, etc., to determine if they will lend you money and, if so, how much interest they will charge you. A good credit score is critical because it could save you hundreds of thousands of dollars in interest and be the difference between getting a loan for your investment.

How is a credit score calculated? It's broken down into percentages of specific categories, including 35% payment history (which shows how reliable you are at making payments on time), 30% amounts owed (also known as your credit utilization rate), 15% length of credit history (older accounts are best because they show how reliable you are at making payments), 10% new credit, and 10% types of credit (it's best to have a mix of debt history, including credit card, student loans, car loans, mortgages, etc.).

Don't know what your credit score is? It's extremely easy to check it. There are places like Credit Karma (creditkarma.com) or annualcreditreport.com, where you can get your credit score for free. Sometimes, your bank can provide your score. You can also find your official credit score for a small fee at myfico.com, which tends to be more accurate than the free versions.

What is a good credit score anyway? According to Experian, a major credit bureau whose data comes from the Fair Isaac Corporation (FICO), the quality of credit scores is rated this way:

800+: Exceptional – You'll get approved quickly and for the lowest rates.

740-799: Very Good – You're considered low-risk and will likely get better rates.

670-739: Good – This is where the average American lies. It is regarded as an "acceptable" risk.

580-669: Fair – You'll get mediocre loans with higher interest rates.

579 and below: Poor – If you can get a loan at all, you'll most likely have to put down collateral or a deposit and possibly even have to pay a fee.

So, what should you do if you need better credit? Here are six ways to improve your credit score:

1. **Make payments on time and never miss a payment.** Your payment history is one of the most essential elements of determining your credit score. One way to ensure this happens is by setting up automatic minimum payments where possible (however, if you're going to do this, make sure

you don't overdraft your bank account). Paying on time will also help prevent your account from being sent to collections, which would cause your score to dip lower.

2. **Get up to date with all your accounts.** Pay any bills you are behind on to make them current.
3. **Pay down revolving account balances.** Having a high balance on revolving debt like credit cards can hurt your score even if you pay them on time.
4. **Limit the number of new accounts you apply for.** You want to keep hard inquiries on your credit few and far between.
5. **Request higher credit limits.** If your credit limit increases and your balance stays the same, it will automatically decrease your overall credit utilization, improving your credit.
6. **Dispute credit report errors.** Mistakes happen! I personally woke up to my credit score dropping 100+ points one day. I knew I did not do anything for it to drop that drastically, so I immediately reached out to the credit bureau, found out there was an internal error, and they fixed it.

Save More Money

While saving money sounds boring to most people, it is vital to reach the goal of having cash to put into a real estate deal. This doesn't mean you have to stop doing everything you love, but you do need to prioritize your spending. There are multiple approaches to saving money, and we'll focus on the main two.

The first way to increase your savings is to reduce your personal expenses. Many online tools like Empower (empower.com) or Mint (mint.com) can help you keep track of your financial situation and show you precisely how much you are spending in a given category. If there are certain things you don't want to give up, that's fine; quality of life is important, too. However, I'm willing to bet there are things you only care a little about that you are spending much more money on than you'd like. For instance, one expense people are often surprised by is how many subscription services they have that they barely use. So, find out which expenses you care about the least and be ruthless about cutting them out of your budget.

The second way to save money for a down payment is to make more money. Maybe you don't want to reduce your quality of life, or you already have, but it's not moving the needle enough. Fortunately, there are endless ways to make extra money. Whether it be a side hustle, getting a raise, getting a higher-paying job, or selling items or assets you own, you can increase your income and acquire real estate faster.

That's all I'll say on this topic, as most people know how to save money but need to actually do it. Trust me—you can!

Key Takeaways

- You must have your finances in good standing to be approved for a conventional loan with a good interest rate. A bad interest rate could cause the deal to lose its cash flow potential, thus turning a good purchasing decision into a bad one.
- Even if you plan to use creative financing to invest in real estate, mastering your personal finances is still necessary, if for nothing else than to have good habits for managing the money involved in your real estate investments.
- Get rid of debt as fast as possible!
- Your credit score is essential, and there are many ways to improve it.
- Saving money doesn't have to hurt, but it needs to happen to reach your goals. Just do it!

5

STEP TWO – FINANCE YOUR FIRST DEAL WITH CONFIDENCE

Real estate cannot be lost or stolen, nor can it be carried away. Purchased with common sense, paid for in full, and managed with reasonable care, it is about the safest investment in the world.

— FRANKLIN D. ROOSEVELT

Financing your first deal is the second step in the journey of becoming a real estate investor. The first deal you make is always an important one, and one that you want to get right so you can build up confidence. For that to happen, you need to get great financing.

This is exactly what we will be talking about in this chapter: what your options are when it comes to financing your first deal. I'll go through the different loan types you might be able to acquire, how you can find other partners and investors, what other creative financing options are out there, and the different strategies for buying properties when you have no money or bad credit.

Different Loan Types

There is a large array of loan types, but this doesn't mean that you will have access to all of them just yet; some of them might not be ideal for you at the moment. But understanding all of them is valuable knowledge, so you know your options.

The most common loans are conventional loans, usually from a bank or other financial institution. These consist of the traditional mortgages many investors take out. They often require you to have quite a high credit score and make large down payments, but their interest rates are some of the best when it comes to financing options. Conventional loans are also a great option if you're following the common buy-and-hold strategy.

There are a few important things that you need to know about conventional loans, including the requirements for down payments, credit score, loan amounts, the terms of the loan, and interest rates. Let's quickly go through them.

The down payment is the initial deposit on the property you want to invest in. This means that you need to pay up front a percentage of the cost of the property, which, on average, is about 20% but can go as low as 3% . There's a lot that goes into the down payment, but typically, the higher the down payment you make, the lower the interest rate you get.

Another thing to take into consideration is credit score requirements. While it's possible for you to get approved for financing with an average credit score—say, around 620—the higher your credit score is, the higher the chances of getting accepted for financing, and the lower your interest rate. Just as a reference, lenders tend to accept a credit score of 660 or above.

The loan amount is how much the bank or financial institution is willing to lend you. Here, the higher the down payment you've advanced, the lower the amount—which is, in many cases, better because it means you don't have to pay as much back to the lender. The loan amount also depends on the property you want to invest in, as well as your credit score. The loan terms for traditional loans are, on average, 30 years; however, between 15 and 20 years is also quite common.

Lastly, interest rates can come in two forms: fixed rate or adjustable rate. As you may have guessed, a fixed-rate loan means you have the same interest rate throughout the term of the loan. On the other hand, adjustable rates can go up or down, depending on the market.

However, the most important factor in determining your interest rate is your credit score and your overall credit history.

Another common loan is the Federal Housing Administration (or FHA) loan, which are designed to help first-time buyers or those who have a lower credit score. This can be a suitable loan for your needs. If your credit score is at least 580, you can borrow up to 96.5% of the total cost of the property (Segal, 2019). Therefore, you only really need 3.5% of the down payment to pay upfront. If your score is below 580 and above 500, you can still get financing through FHA, but your minimum down payment has to be at least 10% . Now, FHA is not a lender like a bank is. In these cases, a bank or a mortgage company are still going to be the ones lending you money, but if you get your loan through FHA, they essentially work as guarantors, making it a lot easier for you to get your financing.

There are other types of FHA loans you can look into, such as the home equity conversion mortgage (HECM), which is suitable for those over the age of 62 who want to convert the equity of their property into cash while still remaining homeowners. There's also the FHA 203(k) improvement loan, dedicated to those who want to make renovations to the property, or the FHA energy-efficient mortgage for those who want to renovate the property, but in a way that directly impacts renewable energies or lowers their utility bills.

If you're just starting out in the real estate investing world, hard money loans might not be ideal, but they are an option nonetheless. These loans are commonly offered by private lenders or other investors, and they are more suited for short-term investments such as fix-and-flip strategies. Because they come with high interest rates, you want to pay them off as quickly as you can. These types of loans are often based on the value of the property you want to acquire because they often serve as collateral, and unlike a traditional loan, they are not based on your creditworthiness. Let's see an example.

It's much faster to get the money with a hard money loan because there's a lot less bureaucracy, and often, you can get the money after 10 days. The average amount lent is usually between 65% and 75% of the value of the property, and the terms vary between six and 18 months. So, say you want to get a hard money loan because you want to buy a fixer-upper for $200,000. The estimation of the renovation costs is $50,000, and you are planning to sell it for $250,000. Say that the lender is lending you 70% of the value of the property after the renovation is done, which is $175,000. There's 11% interest, which means that per month, the lender is making $2,062.50 on interest only each month.

There's also a variant of hard money loans called private money loans. These are often more flexible when it comes to interest rates and repayment terms, but they often depend on the type of relationship you have with the lenders. A popular choice is a seller-financed loan. Here, the seller of the property is the lender and provides you, the buyer, with financing. This means that you need to negotiate directly with the seller, and anything from down payment, repayment terms, or interest rates also has to be discussed with the seller. I will go through these types of loans in more detail later in the book.

There are other less common loans, such as veteran affairs, or VA loans, which are exclusively for veterans or active-duty service members; United States Department of Agriculture loans, or USDA loans, designed to promote rural home ownership; portfolio loans, which are offered by credit unions or banks, but are not sold to secondary mortgage markets; or commercial loans if you want to find financing for commercial real estate, like retail spaces or office buildings. Commercial loans can be quite different from the more conventional loans in terms of interest rates, for instance. They usually cover not only capital expenditure but also operational costs that the company may have. These loans are often designed for small businesses to be able to pay for their basic operational needs, like buying supplies or funding payroll. Often, you are required to have collateral, frequently property, in case you default on your payments. We can look at these types of loans as short-term funding for businesses that are struggling to get started, and the terms vary between 3-5 years. The interest rates also vary between 7% and 8% .

Choosing the perfect loan for you is critical, but it also depends on numerous aspects, like your financial status, your plan, the sort of property you want to invest in, and so on. You must also consider down payments, interest rates, repayment periods, and everything else I've discussed. As usual, speaking with a professional, such as a mortgage broker or a financial counselor, will help you understand your best options.

Finding Partners and Investors

Choosing suitable partners or investors is critical in the real estate world, as they have the capacity to drastically change your trajectory in the industry. These connections not only allow you to diversify your portfolio and boost your funds, but also enable you to take on larger projects to improve your professional background. Because of this, acquiring the information and abilities needed to choose the perfect partner is essential.

There isn't always a need to locate partners or investors, especially if you're just starting out and have the funds and knowledge to take that initial step, but you must be able to recognize when you do need these people. Typically, you would seek investors and partners in two situations: when you wish to grow your firm, and when you want resources or skills in an area where you lack experience. When it comes to growing your business, you will most likely discover that your financial resources alone will not be sufficient to progress to greater initiatives; therefore, partnering might be a fantastic solution. Here, partners and investors can also contribute experience, contacts, and additional resources. For instance, if you want to start exploring fix-and-flip strategies, knowing someone with a background or skill in remodeling can come in handy.

Different Types of Investors and Partners

Depending on your individual goals, you have a variety of possibilities for choosing investors and partners. One example of a widely desired partnership is an equity partner, who injects funds into your investment in exchange for an interest in its ownership. The extent to which they are involved in day-to-day activities may vary depending on your agreement. Private investors, sometimes known as silent partners, take a somewhat different strategy. They offer funds without actively participating in the project but expect a return on their investment, which might take the form of a percentage of earnings or interest payments.

Joint ventures are something you might want to consider, and they are quite common in the industry. Here, you'd partner up with one or more individuals or companies that have the same goals as you. One thing that you have to take into account is the bureaucratic side, which is quite a bit more than doing it alone. This is because when creating a joint venture, you have to specify the roles each individual or entity is responsible for, what their exact responsibilities are, and the financial arrangements between each partner.

In the past few years, a different type of investment has become popular: crowd-funding platforms. These platforms can be websites that connect investors within the real estate industry, and as an investor, you can make small contributions to join a large real estate project. Relatedly, there are real estate investment clubs, which are similar to crowd-funding platforms but have been going on for way longer. There are usually local or online real estate investment clubs where you can network with other real estate investors.

Building Relationships

Knowing how to build relationships is crucial in this business, as I've stated before. When it comes to networking, there are many ways you can do it. For instance, as I've mentioned above, crowd-funding platforms or real estate investment clubs are a great way to start.

However, you don't necessarily have to join a club to do this. All you have to do is pay attention to any real estate industry event, conferences, or simple meet-ups happening in your local area. Here, not only do investors attend, but you can network with a large array of different professionals in the industry, such as developers, lawyers, realtors, and so on. Again, online platforms such as real estate forums can be a great way to network with other professionals, have discussions, or share your experiences and expertise.

Creating a Partner's Proposal

When it's time to approach a potential partner or even an investor, your proposal has to be clear, and you have to have everything detailed properly so there's no confusion in the future. You should, for instance, add an outline of the investment opportunity, roles, risks, or expected returns. You also have to come up with a risk mitigation strategy and show that you are committed to the project. Lastly, make sure you add any financial projections to show the potential of the investment.

Now, all of this has to be bound by law, so you need to draft legal agreements. There are two main legal agreements you have to know about. If you are seeking to bring in a partner, then a partnership agreement is what you are looking to draft. This is a way to formalize the arrangement, and the document should have a clear description of the roles of each partner, their ownership shares, their responsibilities, and any other things you might find important.

The other legal agreement is a private placement memorandum, or PPM, and should be done when you're seeking funds from a private investor. This document should disclose important information about the potential investment and other relevant things. In both of these cases, you should have a real estate lawyer draft these documents, and they should be rectified by the other party's lawyer, too.

Whether you are seeking a partner or an investor, communication is important, especially in the case of a partner because they tend to be more involved in the operations of the investment. You should be looking for open and transparent communication to ensure that any agreement you and the other party sign complies with any laws or regulations in place. Bringing in a financial advisor might also be important because they have experience with any type of tax implications the new agreement might bring.

To make sure you're on the same page, ensure your goals align with your partner's or investor's. At this point, you should also mention the strategies you want to apply and your risk tolerance. Before signing any agreements, it's important to discuss an exit plan with your partner or investor. For instance, how will the partnership or investment be dissolved?

Finding the right partner can be a hurdle, but to set that up, you need to come up with a great strategy before you even think about taking an approach. Once that is out of the way and you've found your partner, you have to know that all parties are equally committed to the project. I'm highlighting this because it often happens that one of the parties is not as involved in the process, which usually doesn't end well.

Altogether, you have to keep in mind that this is something you are likely to seek in the future as your career progresses. So, while this might not cross your mind at this point in your career, networking from the beginning will allow you these opportunities in the future, so when the time comes, you don't have to rush into getting the right contacts.

Creative Financing Options

We've already talked about some of the most common finance approaches you can get, which I highly recommend before utilizing more creative financing options. This is because creative options are often not as favorable as traditional methods, but that doesn't mean they are always bad. Many of them depend on your unique circumstances, and sometimes the only way to get finance for certain projects is through these creative finances. Let's look at some of these options.

One of the most common creative financing options is leasing. This method involves leasing a property and adding the opportunity to purchase it at a later date at a specific price. This allows you to generate revenue while not being fully committed (monetarily) to the investment. It's a great way to understand if this investment can potentially work if you go all in. It also allows you to have more time for traditional financing.

Another option you might want to consider is something called "subject-to-financing," where you take over an existing mortgage on a property, but leave the property under the seller's name. The benefit is that you keep the current mortgage the seller has without making a new one, potentially not increasing the mortgage on the property. This also means that you may have a reduced down payment or no down payment at all.

Another option is the seller-carryback mortgage, which happens when the seller provides you with a part of the financing and acts as a secondary lender (besides the primary lender). Often, this primary mortgage comes from traditional financing, such as from a bank, but simultaneously, the seller carries the second mortgage. There are benefits here, such as reducing the down payment for the property and making it a lot easier for you to qualify for finance. The hardest part of this approach is finding a seller who is willing to do this.

A wraparound mortgage is similar to the one described above, but it involves preserving the existing mortgage and adding an extra layer of financing, with payments sent to the seller who is paying the original mortgage. This enables you to purchase a new investment without having to pay off your previous mortgage.

Cross-collateralization, which isn't as prevalent as others on this list, consists of using one of your own properties to acquire financing for numerous others. This maximizes your leverage, but also significantly raises your risk because your property is being used as collateral.

There's another way to find a creative financing solution if you have a self-directed IRA or a 401(k). Using this strategy offers a few tax advantages, but you'd be using your retirement account to invest in property, which may have some consequences, as you might imagine.

Then there's the seller leaseback, which encompasses a seller staying in the property as a tenant after you've purchased the property. This is a great strategy if you're looking to generate rental income from the get-go.

With all of this said, creative financing options are any type of financing you can arrange that is not within traditional financing. This means that many of these creative options are customized for your and the seller's needs. The best way to reach a customized deal is by sitting down with the seller and another investor and finding ways to structure the deal that benefit each party involved.

There are plenty of things and angles you can use to reach a deal that are not necessarily based on any of the options I've talked about in this section. Things like profit-sharing agreements, various purchase options, or deferred payments are all possible as long as every party is happy. Despite that, due diligence is the way to go when approaching such deals and gain leverage when negotiating, as well as hiring professionals to guide you through these negotiations.

Strategies for Buying Real Estate with Little Money or Bad Credit

There are numerous ways you can invest in real estate and start your career, even if you don't have enough money for a down payment, or if you have bad credit. Wholesaling is one of them since, as you know, these sorts of properties are typically priced below market value for a variety of reasons, including those mentioned earlier.

Another technique that might offer you more time to locate cash is to lease a home with the option to buy it later at a certain price. Also, when you don't have enough money to invest in real estate, you might use partnerships or the seller's financing. Alternatively, you can employ certain unconventional financing methods, such as subject-to-finance or wraparound mortgages.

There are other strategies we haven't talked about yet. For instance, you can rent out a spare room you have in your current property. This way, you can generate income and use it for potential investments down the road. Alternatively, looking at local government programs is a good idea since these might offer down payment assistance or low-interest loans.

I think that the best way for you to find the best possible financing strategy when you don't have enough money or your credit score is not ideal is to explore creative financing resources. Go to real estate investment clubs or simply network in any way because you might be able to find many other opportunities. Owner financing websites can help you find properties with owner financing options, or you can go to community banks, credit unions, or any other small financial institution because they tend to be more flexible when offering loans and mortgages.

Being able to finance your first deal requires substantial planning and thought before you act on it. It's how you can set up your career for great heights and become a successful real estate investor. Everything we've seen here, from the different types of loans, their advantages and disadvantages, and how they relate to your financial goals, is crucial, as is your understanding of the current market and its cycle. While you should always consider traditional loans, creative strategies might work better for you in certain unique circumstances.

One thing you have total control over is networking, creating partnerships, and leveraging those partnerships to lead you to better opportunities. Building relationships with other professionals is a big part of the job of a real estate investor, and you should get to know professionals from other backgrounds if you want to increase the chances of great opportunities coming your way.

It's especially important to build relationships with other investors so you can find more and better opportunities in your career. Networking is a big part of the job. Here, you can go to conferences and real estate events and meet other investors face to face. You can also join online groups to meet online.

If you're looking for partners and think you've found the right one, it's important that you craft a strong partner's proposal. This agreement includes legal requirements that should always be drafted by your attorney or at least verified by them. Such a proposal should outline the tasks each partner has, any risks associated with them, financial projections, risk mitigation, and so on.

If you find yourself with bad credit or limited funds and still want to invest, there are certain options you can go for. Wholesaling, for instance, is a great way to get into the real estate industry without investing too much initially. A lease with the option to buy is another great opportunity, allowing you to rent a property with the agreement that you will purchase it at a later date. In real estate investing, where there's a will, there's a way.

Now that we've talked about the different ways you can finance your first deal, in the next chapter, we'll discuss how to get preapproved if you're going the standard traditional financing route. Then, we'll find your first deal.

Key Takeaways

- Finding financing for your first deal is a crucial step to starting your career as a real estate investor.
- Conventional loans: The most common loan mortgages are usually from banks that require a down payment and a high credit score.
- FHA loans: These loans are great for first-time buyers or those with a low credit score.
- Seller-financed loans: The seller finances the loan, and you can essentially come up with your own terms between you and the lender.
- Hard money loans: These loans are best used for short-term strategies such as fix-and-flip, as they tend to have high interest rates.

- Private money loans: Loans offered by private investors instead of banks and other financial institutions. They offer you more flexibility when it comes to the terms of the agreement.
- Other loans, like USDA or VA loans, can be used in very specific circumstances.
- Finding other investors and partners to work with can change the trajectory of your portfolio.
- Equity partners, or investors that inject capital into the investment and take part in the ownership, or private investors, which simply provide funds, are the most common types of investment partners.
- Crowd-funding platforms can be a great way to find other investors or people to partner with for joint ventures.
- Creative financing can be the key to unlock tremendous opportunities that most investors miss.

FREE GIFT #2

Free Bonus Chapter About Creative Financing: Don't let your bank account stop you from your dreams!

Learn the basics of seller financing, lease options, and cash-out financing to help you find creative options to acquire more properties! What are some of the pitfalls to avoid? Find out in this exclusive chapter!

To get instant access this free e-book, scan the QR code below or visit this link: https://readstreetpress.com/iwantpermanentpto2

6

STEP THREE – FIND YOUR FIRST DEAL

Buy on the fringe and wait. Buy land near a growing city! Buy real estate when other people want to sell. Hold what you buy!

— JOHN JACOB ASTOR

Now that you know how real estate investing works, the different types of real estate, and the most common strategies you can use, you have to find your first deal. There are a few steps that you need to follow.

The first thing we'll be looking at in this chapter is how you can get preapproved for financing. You need to first obtain financing for your property purchase before you can move on to the next steps. Then, we'll explore how to get an investor-friendly realtor who is more than happy to work with you and help you find a deal.

Keep in mind, however, that finding a deal with an agent is not always a sure thing. If this is the case, you might have to look at properties yourself, which is something that we will also cover in this chapter. This should be the third step when looking for a property to invest in.

Getting Preapproved for Financing

Your very first step toward securing finance is getting preapproved. Preapproval has many benefits, especially for the seller, as they will see you as a serious investor. It will also help you determine your budget and, in turn, narrow down the strategies you will want to use.

There can be a little confusion between preapproval and prequalification. They might sometimes be used interchangeably, but they are different things. If you are prequalified, it means the lender has made an informal assessment of your finances. It's faster to do it, and it's definitely a great start, but it's not nearly as strong as a statement as preapproval. On that note, preapproval involves a more rigorous evaluation where the lender checks your employment, your credit history, your income, and many other things to fully understand your financial situation.

As I've said, once you get preapproved, it essentially means that your budget is clear – the letter you receive specifies how much money the lender will lend you, which, in turn, helps you figure out what properties will be in your price range. Leveraging preapproval during your negotiations is perhaps the best advantage it will give you, and while it doesn't 100% guarantee a loan, it's as close as it can get to an approval for a loan or mortgage.

Steps to Get Preapproved

When you are preparing to apply for a loan and get preapproved, you have to look for a lender. If this is all new to you, larger banks might be easier to deal with, as well as mortgage companies or credit unions. However, they are far from being the only lenders.

Once you've found a lender, you will need to provide all the necessary documentation for preapproval, which usually involves bank statements, any information about your liabilities and debts, employment history, and income verification documents (pay stubs, W-2 forms, or tax returns if you're self-employed). As you know, lenders will do a credit check on you to find out your creditworthiness, and here, your credit score will be important.

Once you've satisfied all of those requirements, you need to complete your loan application. This process once again requires you to give the lender other financial information as well as personal information. The lender will then review all of the documents and assess them. If everything's good, you will get a conditional approval, where you will see the maximum loan amount you can get, though this approval is still pending additional documentation and a property appraisal. This is because the lender will need an appraisal of the property you want to purchase to make sure that the property value checks out with the loan amount. Once that is done and everything's right, you will get your final approval for the loan, and you will also get your preapproval letter.

One important thing to take into account is that preapproval letters have an expiration date, so make sure you find a property during the allotted time. If you let the letter expire, you will have to go through the whole process again. Also, while getting preapproved is a great thing, you have to keep managing your finances properly throughout the property-buying process. This means not making big financial changes like changing jobs, buying something expensive, or even taking out a personal loan. Taking these actions might make the lender reconsider your preapproval.

Finding an Investor-Friendly Realtor

An experienced realtor who is on board with working with real estate investors can be a great asset, especially when you're just starting out in this industry. However, if you haven't previously met anyone with those characteristics, it might take a while before you do. This is not to say that you can't go out there and find one, of course. In this section, I will first highlight the benefits a real estate agent can bring to you.

An experienced real estate agent has vast knowledge of investment and therefore understands all the common strategies I've talked about here. Their expertise goes beyond the common residential property purchase, as they also understand market trends, rental income analysis, property types, and more. Most importantly, they can give you excellent advice that is tailored to your own goals. In addition, they can find better properties that align with your needs a lot faster, they have a much better understanding of the local market, their negotiation skills are sharp and can help you tremendously, and they have a great network of resources available to them.

Now, this is all great, but how can you find a good realtor? The first thing you should do is to ask for referrals. This essentially means asking your fellow real estate investors for recommendations, as they might know someone who works with investors. But you shouldn't always take their word for it, and you might want to conduct some interviews. After all, you're looking for a partnership where the realtor also benefits. In these interviews, you can ask them about the type of experience they have, their knowledge of the local market, and so on. You should also check their credentials to make sure they align with what they say, or even check their portfolio.

Once you've found your realtor, you need to know how to work with them. Here, you want to first define your investment goals for them so they can offer you the best properties they have that align with those goals. You should also discuss your expectations when it comes to choosing a property and doing market analysis. Remember that your real estate agent has been in the market for a long time, so perhaps they can link you with other professionals so you can create a team of experts. I'm talking about real estate attorneys, property inspectors, contractors, appraisers, and so on—anything that can make your investment process easier.

As with everything, clear communication is essential, so you should communicate with your realtor on a regular basis and discuss any investment opportunities that might have appeared.

Searching for Potential Properties

Before you get out there and start looking for properties, you have to make your goals clear, have a great knowledge of the market, understand your risk mitigation, and know the type of property you want to purchase. Only then should you start looking for a property.

The first place I like to look is at online real estate platforms. I'm talking about Realtor.com, Zillow, and Multiple Listing Service (MLS), not only because they host many different properties, but you can also filter those properties to find the one for you. Again, make sure you use your realtor during your search, especially if they have knowledge of the local market. They can give you many different resources and even give you access to off-market listings.

If you haven't established your network, do it as fast as you can. To make this easier, you can attend local real estate investment groups, for instance, where networking is the main thing they do, and where you will find a variety of professionals in the real estate business.

Alternatively, you can send marketing emails to property owners in the area you want to invest in to show them your interest in buying their property. There are also auctions you can attend, which offer great opportunities for below-market prices.

Lastly, remember the wholesaler strategy? Even if you're not following that particular strategy, you can contact wholesalers because they often have access to distressed properties you might consider buying.

Property Due Diligence and Evaluation

Before you even do your due diligence on a desired property, you should already have your budget more or less defined. That means, by this point, you already have a list of properties you can invest in. Doing your due diligence and evaluation will narrow this list down even further.

Inspecting the property is the first thing you have to do, followed by a close examination of the local market. During the inspection, you need to pay attention to the conditions of the property, so here, hiring an expert is a necessity. When it comes to analyzing the local market, consider recent sales, appreciation of local properties, or expected rental income, among other things. At the same time, performing the financial analysis is important so you can understand your return on investment (ROI), cash flow, and other important metrics.

Also, research any regulatory and legal subjects to make sure the property you're thinking of purchasing complies with all the local zoning and regulatory requirements. While doing that, it's always a good idea to research the property's history, like past sales, past ownership, or any legal issues past owners had. This is to make sure you are prepared if any of those issues arise at some point.

All of this information can be gathered through your due diligence, which proves vital when you reach the negotiation phase. At this point, you can leverage any findings you've unearthed, like repairs that need to be fixed, which raises the issue of whether you or the owner should pay for them. If you're the one paying for them, make sure you negotiate the price of the property to a lower number so you can factor in the expenses of those repairs.

Due diligence is almost always a long process, so it's important that you are patient and don't try to rush things. Not every property you see will be a good fit. Keep that in mind and be mindful of making the best possible decision every step of the way.

Let's go through an example of doing due diligence. Let's say you want to purchase a single-family property, and it's listed at $150,000. It's a great location, just outside a major city in a suburban area. At this point, you've found that the recent appreciation rate is 4% , and the local real estate market is relatively stable. That particular area has been built recently, so it's attracting quite a few professionals and has a growing job market. Upon inspecting the property, you notice there are some minor repairs to be made that total $6,000 (as an estimate). You've done your financial analysis and compared the property to similar properties in the neighborhood, and you expect to generate around $1,800 a month through rental income. You also find that the expected annual expenses, including maintenance, property insurance, and property taxes, go for around $3,500.

You get financing by putting down 20% , which is $30,000, and for the rest, you get a mortgage loan at 3.5% over 30 years.

So far, this is what you have:

- Annual rental income is $21,600 ($1,800 x 12)
- Annual expenses are expected to be $3,500
- Mortgage payment: $538.85 monthly

This is assuming the property complies with local zoning and regulations, the title comes back clear, there are no environmental issues, and all the legal procedures were done correctly.

Networking

As mentioned, networking is one of the most important things you can do in the real estate industry. Its focus is to connect with other people, and those connections will eventually help you become successful in the long term. Having a broad network of connections is almost invaluable, but not only do you need to connect with other professionals in your industry, but in other industries as well, because you don't know what challenges you might come across.

I've highlighted the value of networking in past chapters. From the network you build, you can get advice, increase your chances of getting a good deal, or even find another investor to form a partnership. But we haven't yet discussed how you can find and form these connections.

Here, it's important that you apply some networking strategies. For example, attending business events is a great way to start, but there are plenty of other things you can do. You should leverage today's digital age and try to find communities on online forums or social media platforms. Alternatively, you can join your local real estate association, which often holds monthly meetings that might be beneficial to you if you're just starting out. Any of these strategies will allow you to share your thoughts, ask questions, and, of course, connect with other like-minded professionals. You can also do a mentorship, where someone with experience in the field teaches you how the industry works.

Although the most important thing to focus on is trying to build long-term relationships with these professionals and eventually form partnerships with them, this is not as easy as it might seem. A true networking connection has to be a relationship where you give and take; that's the only way to form strong relationships. Constant communication is also vital, as is being reliable when your network needs you and asks for your help.

This doesn't necessarily mean you should only work with one contractor or realtor, for instance. But you should prioritize your relationships while trying not to burn bridges with anyone. Having a diverse network will allow you to reach your goals faster; after all, you can't expect that your preferred realtor or contractor will always be available. Furthermore, the more diverse your network, the more exposure you get to other professionals and other industries, as well as strategies and perspectives that might lead to unique opportunities.

As you can see, networking is a critical part of being a real estate investor. To continually increase your network, you have to engage with other professionals on a regular basis and make an effort to always try to get to know more people. You also need to provide them with value and nurture your relationship with them so they become long-term partnerships. The time you spend making these connections is an investment in your business; it's impossible to be successful in the industry if you don't meet other people and partner up with them. You need other professionals to help you, and in return, you need to help them.

What we've been discussing throughout the chapter is the very first step for you to take to establish yourself as a real estate investor. Finding your first deal might make you a little nervous at first, but it doesn't have to be that way. Before that, you need to find finance, which often means getting at least preapproved for a loan. When that is done, you will have a much clearer understanding of what your budget might be, which will allow you to strengthen your position as an investor in the eyes of a seller. You should also try to find an investor-friendly realtor who can point out many opportunities you wouldn't have come across on your own and find the perfect investment for you more easily.

This doesn't mean you shouldn't do your due diligence; in fact, this step is essential so you can narrow down the list of potential properties you might invest in. Lastly, networking and building relationships are as important as investing and doing due diligence because they will allow you to take advantage of more diverse opportunities.

Key Takeaways

- Getting preapproved for financing is the first step to finding your first deal if you are aiming to do traditional funding. It shows sellers you are serious about purchasing the property and helps you determine your budget.
- An investor-friendly realtor can give you an edge in your search due to their better understanding of the local market, market cycles, and trends. They also may have access to listings you don't.

- Having clear goals and criteria of what you're looking for in a property is key to closing on your first deal as fast as possible and being efficient with time.
- Online platforms, email marketing, direct mail, and local investment groups are all ways to find good deals.
- Inspections are critical to know if you have to do any major repairs that would impact your financial analysis or overall plan for the property.
- Networking is always a good idea for any investor to keep a pulse on their local market and find properties before they're even listed.

FREE GIFT #3

Investor Networking Guide: It's all about who you know so get networking!

Real estate investing can be difficult, that is why you should not do it alone! From investor friendly real estate agents to potential business partners, it is important to have a team of individuals you can count when you need an extra boost. In this guide you'll learn about the importance of networking and provides practical advice on how to build and maintain valuable relationships within the industry.

To get instant access this free e-book, scan the QR code below or visit this link: https://readstreetpress.com/iwantpermanentpto3

7

STEP FOUR – BECOME AN EXPERT AT DEAL ANALYSIS & DUE DILIGENCE

Buy land, they aren't making any more of it.

— MARK TWAIN

A nalyzing your deals is the fourth step to finding and closing on your first deal. The process used to analyze deals is called due diligence. I've mentioned it here several times, but in this chapter, we will delve deeper into what due diligence entails and how you can hone the necessary skills to perform it properly.

We will also be talking about other things related to due diligence, such as how you can evaluate the condition of a property, how to assess different market conditions, how to make better decisions based on the data you've gathered from your due diligence, and when you should leverage all this information into action when it comes to making a deal.

Conducting Due Diligence

As you now know, doing exhaustive due diligence is the most efficient way to assess your investment options. This approach entails a wide variety of steps and consists of a thorough review of potential investment assets. While there are various objectives for due diligence, the main focus should be risk reduction, followed by making well-informed decisions and ensuring your assets match your financial goals. However, due diligence also serves as a strategy for verifying the property's pricing. All the data acquired during due diligence offers you additional bargaining power and make certain that all legal duties are carried out.

Let's explore the main points of due diligence, starting with property inspection. While I'll go in-depth on this subject later in this chapter, you have to hire a qualified inspector to check the property. This professional will then assess the property's structural integrity and the functionality of all its systems, including electrical, plumbing, and HVAC, just to name a few. You will also want to verify the title of the property, which is also known as a title search. This is simply a way to determine who actually owns the property and if there are any legal disputes that could potentially affect your investment.

After that, you want to make a financial analysis of the property, but we will explore this particular aspect later in this chapter. In sum, you will have to crunch some numbers like NOI, ROI, or rental demand to ensure the financials align with your goals.

Then there's the market analysis, which entails doing research on your local area to figure out appreciation trends, rental demand, and other market conditions that might have an effect on your potential investment. You might also have to do an environmental assessment, especially if you're investing in commercial property. This is to know if there are any environmental hazards or any other type of contamination on the property that might affect the tenants, the public, or both. While doing this assessment and considering the regulatory and legal compliance, it's crucial to understand if safety regulations have been put in place or if there are any violations of permits.

Due diligence also involves researching the property's history. This doesn't only mean looking at past ownership, but also any structural issues that might have happened in the past. Also, when applying to get preapproved, you have to get a professional appraisal done because this might help you draw contingencies on the potential deal to protect your interests.

One thing that many new real estate investors are not aware of is the time constraint to conduct due diligence. This timeframe is often outlined in the purchase agreement you sign with the seller. Due diligence not an easy process to go through on your own, so it's vital that you bring in experts to help you out. For instance, hiring property inspectors, appraisers, real estate attorneys, and any other professionals might be useful because they can provide you with invaluable insights into your potential property. Also, don't forget to look at local construction trends, local rental trends, and local large businesses, as well as tax breaks on properties in the area.

Once you've finished these steps, you'll have a wealth of data to guide your decisions and finesse your negotiations. Know that acquiring this information does not bind you to a purchase; in fact, that's why due diligence is performed. If the information you've acquired recommends it, you can negotiate additional conditions. Always keep in mind that your investment selection should be in line with your investing goals and risk tolerance.

Due diligence is a non-negotiable stage in the property investment process. It protects your interests by ensuring you make sound choices and protecting you from any future troubles. By evaluating a property's physical condition, financial feasibility, market context, and legal compliance, you improve your decision-making and dramatically increase your chances of success in the real estate investment sector. Let me give you a few checklists on the due diligence you might want to conduct.

When looking at financial due diligence, make sure you go through:

- Vacancy tax deductions
- Tax and insurance liabilities
- Rent variability
- Gross rental income
- History of rent variations and tenant breakdown
- Operating expenses

When looking at property and land due diligence, ensure that you go through:

- Costs required to repurpose the building (if necessary)
- Engineer and architect inspection
- Land survey
- Environmental rating

Looking at legal due diligence, remember to go through:

- History of ownership
- Legal encumbrances related to the property
- Any outstanding legal obligations currently on the property
- Building control, environmental, zoning, and any other relevant regulations
- Access rights

Altogether, the main reasons for due diligence are illiquidity, cyclicality, and understanding if the property is fit for purpose. Let me explain.

As you know, real estate is one of the most illiquid assets you can invest in. This means that if you were in need of money (as in cash), selling your property would take quite some time for you to see that cash. Once you sign the contract on a property acquisition, this often means you are tying yourself up for quite a few years (unless it is a fix-and-flip strategy, but still). Due diligence is also a great tool to understanding the cycles of the industry, as this particular industry is highly cyclical. This means that when you're in a good cycle, properties seem like a great investment, but not so much when the economy goes through a bad cycle.

Lastly, fit for purpose simply means ensuring that the property you're acquiring is suitable for the strategy you want to pursue.

Evaluating Property Conditions

An important aspect when conducting due diligence is how to evaluate the property you're potentially investing in. This often means evaluating the physical conditions of the property, such as its structural integrity, to ensure everything is fine and aligned with your goals.

The benefits of doing this are to reduce your risks, help you draw up a financial plan, and make your investment more suitable and aligned with your financial goals. Due diligence also gives you leverage when it comes to negotiating prices, as you will know exactly what the upsides and downsides of the property are.

As I've mentioned, the structural integrity of the property is one of the most important factors to consider when conducting due diligence. You should hire an inspector to look at the property's foundation, including its walls, roofs, and floors. They look at any cracks, signs of water damage, or anything else that might become an issue later on. But structural integrity is not the only thing inspectors will be looking at; they also look at the property's systems, such as HVAC, electrical systems, and plumbing.

The problem with not finding these issues before purchasing the property is that fixing them takes a small fortune. You also will not be able to rent the property while there is work going on. Often, inspectors also look at the interior and exterior of the property to detect any signs of mold, pests, water intrusion, or anything else that might damage the property going forward. As I've said before, inspectors thoroughly conduct inspections of roofs and gutters and check the condition of the shingles for any signs of leaks.

Hiring a qualified and licensed property inspector is your best shot at identifying any of those issues before purchasing the property. They are professionals, and that's what they do. Years of experience have given them the insights to look closer at things we wouldn't even notice that might eventually become a problem. Furthermore, after their inspection, they give you a detailed report with recommendations on how you can act upon any of the issues they've identified.

With the professional inspection done, you are better informed to add any contingencies to the purchase agreement and protect yourself better. This simply means adding clauses that might allow you to renegotiate some of the terms of the contract or even walk away from the deal if you can't find a consensus with the seller. For example, after you've received the inspector's report, you'll estimate the costs of fixing everything. At this point, you can renegotiate with the seller on how things can be fixed, if they want to do it themselves, or if they would rather lower the price of the property and have you fix any issues yourself.

Without the keen eye of a professional inspector, you may not be able to notice all the issues happening with the property, which means potentially paying for repairs yourself down the line. If, for instance, you agree with the seller that they do the repairs before the purchase is done, and they haven't completed them, one of the contingencies you might have added is to walk away from the deal. This way, you won't have lost a lot of money.

Before the inspector comes in, you can also do your own evaluation. It won't be as thorough, but it might be important. As you start checking some of the most evident issues the property might have, add them to your list of things to repair. The first thing you have to do is to understand your priorities. For instance, you shouldn't think about installing new light fittings if the wiring is not properly done and it's dangerous. Or, if the property is not secure enough, you shouldn't even think about adding any expensive fixtures. It's always best to take it from the top, and I mean this literally – starting with the roof. However, don't put yourself in a dangerous situation by climbing a ladder to get to the roof (that's the inspector's job). Instead, you can get a pair of binoculars to examine the roof more closely and look for any evident damage. If you can't see it from the street, you can always ask a neighbor to let you onto their property for a better vantage point.

Also, get into the loft or attic so you can better inspect the roof from the inside. Here, you can look for water stains on the timbers. Ideally, wait for heavy rain and check it so you can be sure that there are no issues when it rains heavily. There should also be ventilators on the roof slope, along the eaves, or in the gable walls. If there are not, you have to make a note of it because poor ventilation will create mold. If there's a chimney in the property, make sure to inspect it for cracks or other damage, as these are the most exposed parts of the property.

Also, check the yard if the property has one. You should be assessing the condition of the fences, the roof of the shed (if there is one), lighting on any paths, or trees that might need trimming.

You should also check the downpipes or gutters for any blockages. If there are water stains on the inside or outside of the walls, this can tell you where there might have been some water damage from blockages. You can see this damage better when it rains. Moreover, if there's quite a bit of woodwork around the house, such as balconies, door frames, and so on, look for rotten wood (wood is especially exposed to weather conditions when facing west and north).

You should not only look for ventilation in the roof, but in the entire house. If the property is built on exposed bricks, you can look for air bricks, but most properties should have grilles built into the walls (usually above ground level). Sufficient air circulation is vital to fight mold and damp conditions, so make sure there is enough ventilation and none of the grilles is blocked. If the property has wood floors, just by walking on them, you might feel them sinking lightly. This often means the joints have rotted, so it's best to get them repaired, as their tendency is to get worse over time and more expensive.

After the property evaluation is done, you can make better-informed decisions on how to move ahead with the deal. You will have a much clearer idea of how the property might align with your financial goals and if any repairs are coming out of your pocket or that of the seller. This step in your due diligence is crucial to ensuring that you get a good deal. One of the jobs of a real estate investor is to be well informed about their potential deals and maximize their returns, as well as mitigate their investment risks.

Assessing Market Conditions

Assessing market conditions is also essential when doing due diligence. Essentially, this process is about analyzing the real estate market in a broad way, but in the area that you want to invest in. Understanding market conditions is another way for you to make an informed decision and to make sure this aligns with your financial goals.

There are many benefits to doing an assessment of the local market conditions. For instance, it allows you to assess the level of risk associated with your potential investment. Here, you will be looking at the fluctuations of supply and demand, market volatility, or any other economic factors that can have an effect on the value of the property now or in the future.

As you know, whatever affects the value of the property also affects your rental income. A market assessment also allows you to perfect your investment strategy. I mean that depending on the market conditions, you might opt for a different strategy than you first envisioned. Also, as you know, different market conditions might be more or less favorable to the different strategies.

Assessing the market conditions gives you a greater understanding of the real cost of your investment, protecting you from overpaying for an investment property. It also aids in the development of an exit strategy; for example, if the market is now better for selling than for purchasing, you may choose to postpone your purchase until more favorable buying conditions happen.

Multiple elements should be considered while assessing market conditions. A full assessment requires things such as an evaluation of local market dynamics, which includes a review of data such as vacancy rates, property valuation trends, and local rental demand. Also, the strength or weakness of the real estate market is highly linked to economic measures such as income growth, economic stability, and employment rates in the area.

One of the most important elements is the balance between property supply and demand in the area in question. This aspect too demands a thorough examination. For example, a scarcity of available rental properties usually results in a rise in rental revenue, whereas an oversupply usually results in a drop in rental prices. The relationship between property demand and availability is certainly an important aspect in the context of property acquisition or selling; however, it is critical not to neglect the impact of mortgage rates, given they are one of the key drivers influencing property purchase or sale options.

You have to consider seasonal trends as well as your property's location. Let me give you an example: if you have a property near a tourist location and you rent it out, you are likely to expect an increase in rental income during the holiday season, right? However, you have to factor in other things, such as zoning and regulatory changes, that might have an impact on the property's value. The best way to get a sense of the prices and values of surrounding properties is to look at recent comparable sales, also known as "comps." These can be really helpful when trying to figure out the value of your property. Not only that, you also have to understand real estate cycles and figure out if you're in a seller's or buyer's market, as this can have a significant impact on the value and price of properties. Let's break this down.

Starting with the local economics, there's quite a bit to look into. One of these is employment trends. Doing your research here will tell you how healthy the market is currently and in the future. In a simple way, if people have jobs, they will be able to afford rent. If there are no local jobs or there's quite a bit of unemployment, people will often move away from the area. The best way to get concrete numbers is through the Bureau of Labor Statistics as well as the local chamber of commerce. You should also look into the net migration in the local area. This includes various parameters, such as household income, population growth, and the age distribution of the population.

Essentially, you have to look at the demographics of the area to understand the demand for different types of properties. For instance, if, looking at population growth, you find out that people are moving away from the area, this would mean that it would be harder for you to rent the property. If there's a large university nearby, maybe looking at properties that students are more likely to rent might give you an advantage. Looking at net migration and demographics in general has a massive impact on the demand in that particular market and even on the appreciation of the property. On the other hand, if the population grows, demand for properties grows as well, which helps with renting the property and increases the value and appreciation of the property.

Still, within the local economy, you should look at industry diversification. If the local market has enough diversification (or a large range of industries), this means that the market tends to be less volatile when the economy goes through bad times. If the local market has only one or two industries (meaning, it is driven only by one or a couple of industries), this might have a bigger negative impact on the market, especially when it comes to its recovery. This means that employment might decrease quite a bit and take longer to pick up.

As I've mentioned, understanding the housing market is important when you're looking to invest in a certain area. Besides looking at local zoning laws to understand any regulations or restrictions that might have an impact on the market, you should also be looking at market trends. These trends include changes in the value of the properties as well as sales volumes. This information is important because it gives you a clearer picture of how the market might be changing and how healthy the market is, as well as the demand for certain types of properties.

Market conditions essentially determine if you're in a buyer's market or a seller's market. As I've mentioned before, a buyer's market is when there's more supply than demand or there are more people looking to sell than to buy, which makes the value of properties decrease. A seller's market is exactly the opposite and happens when there's more demand than supply, which means the value of the properties increases.

But you should also look at the median price trends, which are a middle point between high and low and a great indicator of current market activity. If the median price shifts, this often means there has been movement in the market. For instance, if the median price increases, this often means the local market is increasing, which favors the sellers (and so the value of properties increases). If the median price decreases, this means there are fewer sales on properties, and the market might be shifting against sellers. However, an increase in the median price could have other meanings. For instance, it could mean that the properties in the lower part of the market are selling, but it doesn't necessarily mean that the properties that cost more are selling. It's important that you have a clear understanding of the different divisions between the higher-priced and lower-priced homes in the local market.

You might also come across something called the market inventory, and it's crucial that you look at its trends. Essentially, inventory in this context means the number of properties for sale. In other words, it tells you how much supply is available in the market. Seasons can have a big effect on the rise and fall of market inventory. For instance, it is known that during spring, the real estate market picks up during that time of year. The opposite is true for winter and fall, as real estate tends to slow down. If you take the seasonality of it from the equation, you'll get a better idea of the inventory in that specific local market.

Another important metric to look at is the average days on the market (DOM), which tells you, on average, how long properties stay on the market before they sell or how long it takes to sell a property in that market. This will tell you how long it might take for you to sell your property, as well as the demand for properties in the area.

How Can You Gather Market Data?

To fully assess the market's conditions, it is essential to obtain data from a number of sources. Real estate websites, particularly online platforms such as Realtor.com and Zillow, should be the first resource to check. These platforms make publicly accessible data available and provide full access to local market statistics such as sales prices and rental rates. Additionally, contacting local real estate agents for a report is a good step because their information is frequently more accurate than what internet platforms have. Moreover, if you have a relationship with a local realtor, they may have access to much more relevant data than what is available online. In particular, they can provide useful information about current market circumstances.

There's also broader data that you can gather from the government or economic data that might give you a hint of what the overall market looks like. You can go directly to government sources or the chambers of commerce to get that data.

Based on all the data you've collected and the assessment you've made, you should be better prepared to adapt your strategy to the current market. For instance, if the market assessment tells you that properties are appreciating quickly, you might want to adopt a long-term buy-and-hold strategy. But a market assessment is not something that you do only before you are about to make an investment decision; this is something that should be ongoing. It's important not only because it can help you mitigate any risks, but also because it allows you to anticipate any opportunities in the future.

Making Decisions Based on the Data Gathered

Most of the decisions you will make in the real estate industry have to come from the data you collect. As we've seen, the real estate market is influenced by many different factors, and going through and understanding them requires great analysis, not just intuition. In this section, I will be talking about why data-driven decisions are important. Without them, it gets very hard to become successful in this business.

As I've stated before, decisions based on data gathered and analyzed allow you to mitigate the risks of every investment. When you properly analyze trends, economic indicators, and so on, you can make much better decisions, which automatically reduces some of the risks of the investments you make. Data is objective and unbiased, so it tells you what might work and what won't, regardless of your preferences. For instance, you might really like a property you've found, but if the data tells you that it's not a good investment, you should drop it and find something that better aligns with your financial goals. Data also allows you to understand if an investment is aligned with your goals and how much you can expect in returns when you invest in the property.

While you might have a good understanding of the market cycles, nothing is more accurate than data when it comes to really understanding what cycle the market is in or even what type of market is taking place. Data helps you choose the best possible investment strategy and mitigate risks. It can also lead to optimized returns on your investments because it allows you to identify investments that might give you better income potential or have a better appreciation over time.

When you're making data-driven decisions, you have to consider different aspects. Some of these we've already covered, such as market research, property analysis, economic indicators, or comps, but there are other things to consider as well. For example, market sentiment is relevant. Here, you need to understand if there's a positive sentiment toward the market or a negative one. This feeling has to do with the confidence of real estate investors in general. It can also be a driver of investment activity, which often leads to the appreciation of property.

The tools and overall technology used to gather this market data are important, too. For example, it is a good idea to search for data sources and systems that provide real-time information, as more recent and exact data is preferable. Also, though they develop financial estimations, these projections are founded on the gathered data. They provide a framework for making better-educated decisions about possible earnings, financing, and costs, among other things.

Let's have a look at the different tools and other resources you can use to gather important market data. I've mentioned some of these platforms and tools before, such as Zillow, that have great databases, market statistics, and historical data that you can peruse and that will help you gather essential information. When collecting all of this data, I find it useful to add it to a spreadsheet, such as Excel or Google Sheets. What's important is that you have all that data organized and can have a clear overview of the data gathered so you can examine it when needed. There is also dedicated professional real estate analytics software such as SmartZip, TopHap, or TopProducer, all of which feature more advanced tools to help you analyze data with predictive modeling.

Regardless of your choice, market research is continuous work that you have to do, and you have to remain committed to it throughout your career. As you perform these tasks, you will get more experienced with them and develop more skills, which will make this work easier. While data is important, when analyzing it, your knowledge and experience are as well, so don't only rely on data to make your decisions. Take into account your skills and knowledge so you can better mitigate potential risks.

However, it is true that most real estate investors heavily rely on data to make their decisions. This is because this approach has proven to be quite successful in the past, and as technology evolves, the insights we get from this data become more accurate, and so do your decisions. These two components, data and knowledge, are intrinsically connected, and they will help you make better choices during your career.

Knowing When to Act

Knowing when to act in real estate investing is part of having a successful business. It's an important moment when you decide to commit to an investment and take action after you've carefully analyzed all the points we've discussed above. Timing is a vital factor that can have a significant impact on the success of your investment as well as its profitability. But why is timing so important?

Let's begin with timing and market conditions. These are critical considerations, whether you are currently going through a seller's or a buyer's market. Timing has a large impact on your ability to negotiate the price of properties. Often, investors prefer to wait for more favorable conditions before acting on their investments. However, choosing the best time goes beyond the initial investment and often refers to withdrawing from an investment. As you know, before you get into any investment, you have to have an exit plan, and timing is very important. This is because selling at the right moment can significantly increase your profits. This, coupled with market cycles, can play an important role in understanding when exiting a deal might be more profitable.

Knowing when to act comes down to all the factors I've mentioned above, such as market and property analysis, financial preparedness, local economic factors, market sentiment, comps, and even property inspection.

Something else you need to account for is your risk tolerance regarding your investment goals. For instance, if you don't like to take many or high risks, you probably have a more risk-averse profile, which means that you prefer stable goals and long-term returns. In this case, a buy-and-hold strategy might be more appropriate for your style. But if you think that timing is important and the faster you get profits, the better, then perhaps a fix-and-flip would be more suited to your investment style, though at the same time, the risks would increase.

Once you take into account all of these factors, you have to make a decision and put it into action. Timing is relevant once again, but timing doesn't always mean looking for the perfect moment where all conditions align (I mean, ideally, sure, but if you're always waiting for all the right parameters to align, you will never get anything done). You can act once you have the necessary data to make a decision and understand when you should shift your strategies. This is when experience comes in, and it's not all about data and numbers (although these are important). Again, timing is important when you enter *or* exit a strategy, so keep that in mind when you're about to put your strategies into action.

Knowing the ways you can analyze deals and reach accurate numbers through due diligence is an important part of a real estate investor's life. Due diligence is a thorough process, and you shouldn't rush through it. You need to understand the risks and rewards and ensure your goals are aligned with the strategy. At the same time, mitigating risks will lower the chances of losing money and increase your profits. As we've seen in this chapter, due diligence encompasses many different things, such as evaluating market conditions or inspecting properties. Every decision you make should be based on the data collected from your due diligence and the experience you gain along the way. Sure, timing also plays an important role, but this aspect will become clearer as you understand how the industry works.

Property Valuation

Knowing how to value a property can help you with analyzing your deals and later on when negotiating. While you should always get a survey or appraisal and look into comparable properties in the market or those that have recently sold, there are other ways you can consider a property's value. In fact, looking at comps while doing your own valuation is the best way to get a more accurate valuation of the property.

There are five main methods that you can use: the comparable method, the investment method, the profit method, the residual method, and the depreciated replacement cost method.

Comparable Method

The comparable method is perhaps the easiest one. You can do it by looking at comparable properties that recently sold in the local area.

If we look at two identical properties in the same market, one sold for $130,000 and the other for $100,000, there are two things that we can conclude. First, the buyer of the $130,000 overpaid because they didn't gather enough information or pay for a building survey to analyze the extent of the work needed. On the other hand, the buyer of the $100,000 underpaid, probably because the seller didn't market the property correctly and didn't do their research. So, it's vital that, when buying or selling, you look at comps.

As a rule of thumb, when valuing a property, the last 20% of the value is often subjective. The thing is, there are no clear rules when it comes to valuing a property, and everything is based on speculation. For instance, if you were to ask five different surveyors about one property, they would probably give you five different prices for the property. It all comes down to how much the buyer is willing to pay, and that's why you should also look at intrinsic value.

You might have heard of intrinsic value, or perhaps not, but it essentially means the value the property has to the potential buyer. While comparable sales prices help narrow down the value of a property, it is the intrinsic value given by the buyer that ultimately matters. Sometimes, we come across a property that surprises us by selling for such a high price; that's probably because it meant something to the buyer.

Often, the reason to pay an extra $20,000 or $30,000 has nothing to do with money, but with the buyer's preference. For instance, if, by buying that particular property, the buyer doesn't have to commute to work or the kids can walk to school instead of taking the bus, it might make a massive difference to them. Therefore, they will be willing to pay the extra to outbid any other competition.

While comparing properties is merely a guide, it's still important to understand how you do it. Say that you're looking at a property where the house next to it was recently sold. If that house is 20% bigger than the one you're looking at and the bathroom has been refurbished, it's only natural that the property you're looking at costs less. If there are repairs to be made that will cost, say, $30,000, you can also reduce the offer.

When you're purchasing your first investment property, it's quite common that you go for the asking price, not knowing that this price is often already inflated (at least 10% to 15%) so buyers can negotiate. This means that if you make an offer for the asking price, you are probably offering a little too much (not counting intrinsic value). Here, the best way to know this is by looking at the local property market trends and seeing if the prices are going up or down.

Investment Method

This method is specially crafted for investors, and it determines the amount of money you would pay for a property based on certain metrics. When using this method, you are comparing the prices of properties to anticipate the rate of return. When you find the rate of return, then you can better measure the estimated price you want to pay.

When it comes to determining the investment value, you have to go through some steps. The first is to do comparable sales, as we did in the last method. Here, all you have to do is compare the value of comparable properties in the same area. Then, you have to look at the gross rent multiplier (GRM), where you measure the value of the investment by multiplying the gross rent you're projecting the property will make in a year by the GRM. You also need to know the cash-on-cash return, and you can calculate this number by dividing the first year's pro forma cash (which is a projected cash flow statement) by the total initial investment.

Then, you have to calculate the direct capitalization, where you convert an estimate of the first year's income into value to determine the market value of the property. Let's get into more detail.

As I've mentioned, analyzing some of the metrics will help you make better decisions, especially when calculating cash flow and rate of return to understand how profitable the investment might be. But what exactly is the capitalization rate (or cap rate)? Essentially, this is the needed rate of return on your investment, depreciation, or net value appreciation. In other words, the cap rate helps you estimate the resale value of the investment when it's time to sell. You can then apply this rate of the net operating income (NOI) to find the present value of your investment.

So, say that you expect to get a NOI of $500,000 over the next five years. If you discount the cap rate of 10% , the current market value of the property would be $5 million since market value = net operating income/cap rate. If you buy the property for $4 million, that would be a good deal, but if you bought it for more than $5 million, you would have overpaid for it. (Of course, you can use any numbers corresponding to the reality of your situation.)

Coming up with the cap rate can be a great metric to start with when valuing a property investment. While there are different ways to calculate the cap rate, one of the easiest ways to do it is through the market-extraction method. Here, you have to find already available NOI and sale price data on comps. For example, if you want to purchase a property where you expect to generate $300,000 in NOI and you have found three comps, Property 1 has a NOI of $150,000 and a sale price of $1.5 million, so the cap rate is 10% . The second property has a NOI of $200,000 and a sale price of $2.5 million, so the cap rate is 8% . Lastly, the third property has a NOI of $100,000 and a sale price of $2 million, so the cap rate is 5% . Then, you have to find the cap rate average by adding all the cap rates of the comps and dividing it by three (in this particular case), which is 7.6% , which is a good representation of the current market. Now that you have found the cap rate, you can better determine the market value of the property you want to invest in.

In this investment method, to find the valuation of a property, you can go a little further and look at two sub-categories of valuation methods: absolute and relative. The absolute valuation tells you the current value of potential incoming cash flows to find the intrinsic value of the property. Here, the most common methods are the discounted cash flow (DCF) and the dividend discount model (DDM), but I'm not going to dwell on them, as these are quite advanced techniques. But then there's the gross income multiplier (GIM), which belongs to the relative valuation, which is far easier to use.

With the GIM, you have to assume that properties in the same location are proportionally valued to the gross income they generate. For instance, let's say that you want to buy a 50,000-square-foot property, and by looking at comps, you find out that the average gross income per month per square foot in that area is $10. From here, you can assume that the gross annual income is $6 million since $10 x 12 x 50,000, but you need to account for vacant units during that time (assuming you rent out separate rooms or units). If you find out that the vacancy rate in that area is 6% , then the gross annual income will drop. Then, you would have to find the GIM and multiply it by the gross annual income, which you can look up online, such as in the area's chamber of commerce.

Profits Method

The profit method is more for commercial property, but you might use it in the future, so I'm just going to give you the basics. The main point here is the profitability of the tenants—in this case, the companies that occupy the property. Here, too, you can use the comparable method, but you would be looking at other businesses' profitability. For you to be able to use the profits method, there has to be a profitable business running on the property already, such as a cinema, a bar, or a hotel.

The first thing to do is to understand the key financials of the businesses for at least the last three or four years. Here, there are two main calculations you want to use: the gross profit and the net profit.

Gross profit = gross earnings - purchases

Net profit = gross profit - working expenses

Essentially, the gross earnings are the total revenue the business generates throughout the year, and the gross profit is the number after taking away the business purchase costs from the gross earnings.

In this context, working expenses are those that occur on a daily basis for the business, such as gas, water, business rates, and so on. The net profit is the gross earnings minus all the expenses. But how do you calculate rent?

Of course, you need to calculate the rent so you can properly evaluate the investment. Here, you could divide the net profit by half to determine a more accurate number. For example, say the gross earnings of the business currently on the property you are interested in purchasing are $500,000. The business purchases are $200,000, and the business expenses are $150,000. Your calculations would go like this:

Gross profit = $500,000 - $200,000 = $300,000

Net profit = $300,000 - $150,000 = $150,000

Annual rent = 50% of $150,000 (net profit) = $75,000

Residual Method

This method is often used by investors who want to invest in land to determine its value. As always, you can also use the comparable method, but by using the residual method, you would be taking the developed value out of the land and subtracting the cost of developing it. Essentially, this method allows you to determine the value remaining after all the costs of developing the land are subtracted.

This is also a great way to estimate the costs, returns, and profits of land that you want to develop, as well as determine the budget needed and mitigate the risk of the development project. In other words, it allows you to find out if the land is worth buying and developing.

The calculations would look something like this:

Residual value = gross development value (GDV) - total development costs (including profit)

Let's break this down. GDV is essentially the market value of the project when developed, where you have to factor in the likelihood of renting the property after it is built. The profit is the value you might be willing to accept. Then, you have to consider the total development costs, which are the cost of the land plus any taxes you need to pay. Then there are the actual construction costs, which are likely to be estimated. There are also fees because you have to add in professional fees outside the building costs, such as environmental impact assessment, legal fees, or planning consultant fees.

You must also consider sales costs, which are usually the agent's fees and any commission you've agreed on; the cost of financing, which includes interest on borrowed money; and contingency costs.

Depreciated Replacement Cost Method

This type of valuation method is often used in properties that are highly specialized (as in custom-built) and would be hard to replace if lost. The depreciated replacement cost (DRC) can help you value an asset and take into account its depreciation over time, as well as the cost of replacing the asset if it is lost. This means that it is more applicable to commercial properties, such as labs or custom-made warehouses.

You can calculate the DRC by estimating the cost to replace the property, which can be done by assessing any changes in the cost of materials, as well as specialized labor when this property was initially built or purchased, and by subtracting the depreciation that happened over time.

For example, if you have a commercial property and want to know its value, you first look at how much it cost when it was first built—say, $2 million 15 years ago. The building has an estimated useful life of 40 years, as well as an annual depreciation rate of 3% . So, you would have:

$2 million - ($2 million x 3% x 15) = $1.1 million

If we assume that the cost of building something similar would be $1.5 million, and we want to know the DRC of the building, then:

DRC = current value + replacement cost - depreciation

DRC = $1.1 million + $1.5 million - ($1.5 million x 3% x 15), or DRC = $1.1 million + $1.5 million - $675,000 = $1,925,000

Thus, the DRC of the building is $1.92 million.

Key Takeaways

The emphasis of this chapter was on how you can analyze your deals. We first looked at how important due diligence is when it comes to making informed decisions. This is especially true if you want to protect your interests, which you definitely should.

Then, I broke down the different components of due diligence:

- Property inspection, where you hire a professional inspector to check the property.
- Financial analysis, where you need to dig into the finances of the property, such as rental demand, ROI, NOI, and other metrics to try and find out if the property is a good investment.
- Title search, where you verify the ownership of the property and check if there are any outstanding legal disputes.

- Market analysis, where you research the local market conditions, trends, and so on.
- Assessment of any legal and regulatory compliance to which you must adhere.

Remember that there is a time constraint when performing your due diligence, which you can find in the purchase agreement.

When evaluating the property, the inspector will then give you a detailed report about the structural integrity of the property and any other issues you will have to solve, which you can then add as contingencies in the purchase agreement to protect yourself.

You also have to research the current market conditions, where you have to consider different economic factors, such as property supply and demand, among others. This is also when you try to figure out the real estate cycle you are currently in to determine if it's a buyer's or a seller's market.

Gathering market data is also an important thing to do when analyzing your potential deals. You can use different websites, talk to real estate agents, or look at economic data online. But this is not something that you do only once; this type of data changes over time, so you have to be aware of any changes and be able to adapt your strategy accordingly.

With this data, you can then make better decisions to mitigate some of the risks associated with these types of investments. However, knowing when to act is just as important. While you shouldn't be waiting for the perfect time when everything perfectly aligns (which might never happen), you can't jump into an investment at any time. You have to consider certain factors, such as your finances, your risk tolerance, or your goals. Keep in mind that at the beginning, the right time will never seem to come, but as you get more experienced, it will become clearer to you.

Remember to continue to learn so you can continue to adapt your strategy as the market changes and as you gain more knowledge and experience. You will never know everything, but it's crucial that you never stop learning.

FREE GIFT #4

The Ultimate Due Diligence Checklist: Don't let anything slip through the cracks!

This essential tool will guide you through every step of your property evaluation and help you make well-informed decisions in your investment choices.

To get instant access this free e-book, scan the QR code below or visit this link: https://readstreetpress.com/iwantpermanentpto4

8

STEP FIVE – MAKE AN OFFER THEY CAN'T REFUSE

Don't wait to buy real estate, buy real estate and wait.

– T. Harv Eker

The first offer might be a little intimidating for a real estate investor. It seems like such a complicated step and overly overwhelming at times, but it doesn't have to be that way.

In this chapter, we will be going through the whole purchasing process so you can have a better idea of the different steps you have to take to make your first offer. We will go through things like how you can create a compelling offer, how you can negotiate effectively, and even how you can handle inspections and contingencies. Making an offer is the sixth step to entering the real estate industry.

Overview of the Purchasing Process

When looking at the purchasing process, the first thing you have to do is define your investment goals. These goals will guide you through the whole purchase process and help you stay focused on what you want. After that, you have to come up with a budget that determines what you can and can't afford. This budget should factor in expenses such as renovations, closing costs, and a myriad of other ones.

As we've talked about, you have to get prequalified and preapproved. Doing so will allow you to increase your chances of getting the financing you need, as well as estimate the investment you can actually afford.

Once all of that is done, you have to find the property you want to invest in. Here, as you might know, you have to do your due diligence and evaluate the property, and only then can you think about making an offer. When making this offer, you have to add a few things, like the purchase price, any contingencies you might want to add, and a proposed timeline to perform all the contingencies.

This all seems a little overwhelming, right? But at this point, you should have an expert who will guide you through it and help you draft the proposal.

Once you've sent your proposal, chances are that negotiation is imminent, but I'll go through this particular step later on, where we will also talk about counteroffers, discussions of terms, and anything else related to the proposal. For now, you should only focus on doing your due diligence, as it will help you through the whole process.

If you have enough money to make such a purchase, then it's best to work closely with the lender to make sure everything goes according to plan. You are at the stage where you have to have an appraisal done, figure out the approximate value of the property, and ensure all the requirements are met by the lender. Then there's the contingency period, or a certain time period when you can ask the lender to repair some of the things; if not, you can withdraw from the deal if you don't reach an agreement. At the same time, you must have property insurance to ensure that you are protected against any damage or loss to the property.

Then, of course, there's the closing of the deal, which is the last step of the purchasing process. At this point, you will have to sign any remaining documents and transfer the funds.

Crafting a Compelling Offer

This might not seem like a crucial step, but it is. Many real estate investors overlook the crafting of a compelling offer, though it can place you in a much more advantageous position. Essentially, you have to really show the seller how interested you are in purchasing the property. And by crafting a compelling offer, you can stand out from the crowd.

Of course, you need to know a few things, such as understanding the current market. To do this, you need to do your market research. Specifically, you need to be aware of current market conditions, the value of local properties similar to the ones you want to invest in, and so on, so you can create a stronger offer. Working with a realtor at this stage is quite important, given they have a great knowledge of the local market. But time is of the essence at this point, and you have to move fast, as there may be others interested in the property.

After all of that comes the offer price. When calculating your price, keep in mind that your offer has to be competitive, and you can determine this amount by looking at the average local market value. Again, this value is established through comps and your research. While lowballing might be tempting, try to send a fair offer, even if it is a little lower, so you can negotiate. Sending a very low offer decreases the chances of not having your offer accepted and the seller picking someone else's. At this point, you have to be ready to negotiate and always leave some room in your budget so you can increase the price during the negotiations if needed.

At this point, you have to add the earnest money deposit when sending your offer so that you show the seller you are a committed buyer. If everything goes as planned, your offer will appeal to them.

Let's move on to contingencies now. These are important clauses that allow you to protect yourself and your interests. These can be anything, but there are a few that are more common than others, such as appraisal, financing, or property inspection. It's important that you are as specific as possible when writing about these contingencies, especially about the conditions of meeting them.

The finance preapproval, which is commonly represented by the preapproval letter I previously mentioned, comes next in the process.

This letter, which established your position as a well-qualified buyer, should be included with your offer. Consider including a personal letter to the seller, emphasizing your serious wish to purchase the property and explaining your vision for its use. When setting a closing date, it's best to provide some wiggle room to accommodate the seller's needs.

You also need to take into account escalation clauses. These clauses allow you to increase the bid price for the property if it is matched by another potential buyer. This not only proves your commitment to buying the property, but also ensures that you are always above the highest bidder (of course, there should be amount restrictions).

Also, make sure you send your offer in a timely manner and maintain your professionalism at all times throughout the negotiation process. Having a positive attitude can go a long way with the seller.

To be honest, crafting an offer to invest in a property is as much an art as it is experience and knowledge of the local market. This offer is you trying to convince the seller that you are the best buyer with the best offer, and you really have to focus on it if you want to increase your chances of success.

Negotiating Effectively

Negotiation is a big step in the offer process for your potential property. Even when you eventually sell the property, it's important to have strong negotiation skills so you can maximize your profits. Now, as I've said multiple times, understanding the market is key, as is setting clear goals as to how much you want to purchase or sell. Bringing in an experienced realtor is also vital, as they can provide great insights throughout the process.

Now that we have that out of the way, building rapport with the seller (or buyer) is also one of the most important aspects. You need to be able to foster trust, maintain professionalism, and have open communication with them. During this phase, the more prepared you are, the better. Gather all the information you might need, and most important of all, know your limits. You have to determine your budget beforehand, or the price you are willing to accept if you are a seller. Understanding the other party's motivation can give you insights into their goals and give you more chances to tailor your negotiation strategy better, or even come up with solutions that might suit both of you.

I can't emphasize enough how important effective communication is at this stage. You not only have to maintain professionalism, but you also have to actively listen to the seller because you can figure things out without them even telling you; you can find common ground just by listening.

Now, onto the negotiation tactics. Ideally, you would want to go for a win-win approach where the outcome of the negotiations is favorable to both parties. Finding common ground is key here. However, this can't always be the case, but nevertheless, it should be something you strive to reach. Again, counteroffers are pretty common during negotiations, so be prepared for them. Consider every counteroffer that comes your way, and don't let emotions make the decisions. One last thing: You should be able to leverage the information you've gathered to help you with your arguments.

Above all, negotiations are a game of patience, and you should avoid rushing at all times. I'm going to be honest with you: most negotiations take time, and this is especially true if there are more than two parties involved. But trying to rush the process is not going to help you. Also, one thing that I always like to consider is introducing nonmonetary terms. This could be contingencies, closing dates (where you should always be flexible), or items such as appliances or repairs, for instance.

One last thing I think is very important throughout any negotiation is to have what in the real estate business is called a "walk-away point." This is the point where you need to know when to walk away from the negotiations if terms don't align or if the negotiations become irrational. If you continue after this point, you will just be losing time and potentially money.

So, when negotiating, there's a mix of knowledge, great communication skills, preparation, and patience. Above all, stay calm and don't rush the negotiation process because the more level-headed you are, the better the outcome will be.

When negotiating, it is important that you are aware of the type of market you're in: buyer's or seller's market. In a seller's market, as you know, the seller has the advantage in the negotiations, which means that if you're a buyer, you simply don't have as many options, and the sellers can further increase the prices on their properties.

For example, say you're a seller in a seller's market, and you place one of your investment properties on the market. On the first day, you have 20 showings, and on the second day, you have 15. In a buyer's market, having 35 showings in a month or two would be lucky, but in a seller's market, it's not. You receive five offers from these showings, and in two of these, the buyers would pay the difference (up to a certain amount) if the property appraised for less than the asking price. For example, if the property was on the market for $250,000, but the appraisal came only at $230,000, these two buyers would be happy to pay the $20,000 difference to close the deal quickly. This is just to say that in a seller's market, buyers are a little more desperate to buy a property, so they typically won't mind overpaying for a property.

In a buyer's market, the negotiations tilt toward the buyer. As you know, there's quite a lot of supply in terms of properties in this type of market, which means buyers have options. Because of this, the value of properties decreases.

If you're buying, then you can negotiate a few things. For instance, if a property is listed at $200,000 and has been on the market for four months without any good offers, you can argue that the current price exceeds the market, and you can try to bring it down. Because sellers are desperate to sell, they are more likely to take the chance to sell instead of continuing to pay costs, such as holding costs for a property they are not making any money on. You can also ask the seller to cover the closing costs, especially if they are not willing to reduce the price of the property.

Even when it comes to inspections, buyers have the upper hand. This is because most contracts have an inspection clause, which means that if the inspection reveals a big issue, the buyer can leave the deal or ask the seller to repair those issues. If this were in a seller's market, the seller might simply move on to another proposal.

Tips for Buyers and Sellers

One of the best tips I can give you as a buyer is to try to understand the needs of the seller. Many of the sellers will want to maximize their profits, of course, but sometimes, their goals might not have anything to do with money. This is where you need to try to come up with a solution. And so, you need to uncover the main reason that is driving the seller and how you can solve that problem for them. In other words, you need to understand their needs so you can negotiate effectively.

A couple of years ago, I found an off-market seller. In trying to understand his needs, I found out that he was moving into an assisted living facility and didn't have the money to pay for it. However, the house required a number of repairs. I figured out the needs of the seller by talking to him: he had to sell to get money to pay to move into the assisted living facility, and he needed the money fast. In my mind, besides getting the money quickly, the deal had to be convenient, and this is what motivated the seller even more than trying to maximize his profits. What I did was buy the property as quickly as I could (while still doing my due diligence), but I didn't require them to do any repairs, which was exactly what he needed. On the other hand, I got the property for a cheaper price.

As a seller, you need to figure out who your ideal buyer is. You should do this even before you put the property on the market. When you know exactly who your ideal buyer is, things become a lot easier, especially when it comes to marketing the property. You can look at it from two main categories, especially when you're negotiating a single-family home: those who are looking for their primary home, and investors looking for a distressed property.

The primary home buyer wants to find a house they can start living in right away, which means the property should be ready to be occupied and shouldn't need a ton of repairs. If you're selling a property to first-time buyers, you should have a home that is ready for them. This often means you need to envision yourself living there, so every repair or refurbishment you do has to cater to first-time buyers. Another thing to keep in mind is that chances are that these buyers will use financing to purchase the property, usually through traditional financing (which is, let's say, a 30-year mortgage), so the property has to meet some quality conditions for the lender.

If you are catering to real estate investors, then it is likely that these types of buyers use alternative types of financing, such as hard-money loans, cash, or any other type of creative financing. For you, the seller, the conditions of the property are not as relevant, as these types of buyers put more emphasis on the cost of the property, contingencies, and the closing timeline, for example. It is also likely that such buyers will use a fix-and-flip strategy, so it's important that you understand this process because they might have a predetermined budget and, during negotiations, they will try to lower the price. What happens quite often is that these buyers will bring an inflated renovation budget to try to lower the cost of the property. In these cases, you might want to perform an inspection so you can counter-offer their initial proposal.

Let's look at tips regarding off-market properties, given these types of negotiations might be a little different. The main difference here is the needs of the seller. Usually, sellers with off-market properties have equity in the properties. For that reason, they have a certain motivation to sell the property, but cannot list their properties on the Multiple Listing Service (MLS) or on the market because the property is in need of major repairs.

I'll tell you a little secret: many sellers don't have enough skills to sell their properties. Meaning, they don't fully understand the buying and selling process of properties, which means that for you, this can be a great opportunity to negotiate. This is particularly true if the property they are selling is an inheritance (often because a parent or a family member passed away) and they were given the property but have not planned for such circumstances. Moreover, these sellers often have other things to care about. This doesn't mean you should take advantage of such a situation, but from a buyer's standpoint, you can still make a good deal without ripping them off. Instead, you can act as the expert and help solve their problems while making a good deal. Often, these sellers will not bring a lawyer because they think they will just sell the property quickly, in which case you can bring a real estate attorney to make their lives easier and make the process smoother (here, you will also be paying for the services of the attorney as part of the contract and to decrease the property's cost). This is a win-win situation because the sellers don't have to go through the estate process by themselves, and you make a good deal for yourself.

When you prioritize the seller's needs, building a relationship with them will make it easier to find common ground. For instance, if you first contact the seller, you will ask them what their needs are. The truth is, you might not get to their true need right away, but you've started working on the relationship. Then, it is likely that you will meet face to face and see the property, and here, your chances of building that relationship increase if you look for common ground. You should also try to connect on a personal level. For instance, if there's any reference to their hobbies, such as playing the guitar or a poster of a sports team, you can start breaking the ice with that. Essentially, you need to find a way to bond. Make sure that this bond is truthful; don't come up with lies or any other type of disingenuous behavior. Eventually, you will find common ground. Any common interests you might have are the foundation of the relationship you want to build, so they have to be sincere.

While going to a property for the first time, you should pay attention to the details as much as possible. You can ask a few questions, such as, "When was the boiler last replaced?" "When were the drywall repairs?" and many other things. The main goal here is to try to find out as much as you can so you can use this as leverage when negotiating to lower the property's cost. The seller might also ask you questions, and a prominent one is how much you want to pay for the property. You should always try to deflect the question.

When you're on the lookout for a property (especially when these are potential sellers who have yet to make up their minds about selling), you can ask to be either the first-in buyer or the last-in buyer. The first-in buyer means you are the first buyer to make an offer, and the last-in buyer means you are requesting to be the last one to make an offer. There are advantages and disadvantages to both of these options.

If you are the first buyer to make a proposal, you have the advantage of being the first, which increases the chances that a seller will accept your offer, especially if they are motivated to sell. However, while the seller might be motivated, this doesn't mean they will accept your proposal right away, and they might want to wait for other offers before they commit to one. If you are the last-in buyer, you will know all the previous offers, which is an advantage so you can alter your offer as needed. However, while you wait (as the last-in buyer), the seller might have already accepted another offer. For that reason, many investors prefer to be the first-in, especially if the seller is motivated to sell and will jump at the first opportunity to sell the property.

Let's now consider negotiating tips on MLS properties, which are dedicated more to sellers. When selling with MLS, using an agent is important, especially if you have renovated the property. Essentially, listing the property with the MLS exposes your property to more potential buyers, whether they are homeowners or investors. Also, if your property is listed in the MLS, it means that agents can access your listing from anywhere, which means that primary buyers and investors wanting to purchase a property in your area will also see it, giving you more leverage when it comes to potential buyers, as you don't have to rush into the first offer. Here, when you're listing on the MLS, the two more important parameters for buyers are: the condition of the property, and the price.

To give you an idea of an agent's importance when selling a property, they can bring knowledge of the market and jump into negotiations with buyers, which is more than justification for the commission they receive. In fact, if you're selling the property after you've flipped it, you should add these costs to your budget from the beginning. The only exception to this would be if you're going through a great seller's market and know you will sell the property for a great price. Either way, if you list your property on the MLS, you are almost guaranteed a few shows, which is why you should have your agent do a follow-up on the potential buyers. Here, the agent can ask them what their general thoughts are of the property, or what they thought about the property's conditions. If nothing comes of it, at least you will know what potential buyers think of the property and start to see a pattern, even if it's negative. When this happens, you can simply wait and not change the price of the property until there's an offer from a buyer, but keep in mind that this might cost you while the holding costs continue to pile up. Or you can listen to the buyer's feedback and make the change so they can make an offer on the property.

Alternatively, you can always offer seller financing, especially if you are in a buyer's market. The truth is, regardless of the market, there are many potential buyers who might have a hard time qualifying for traditional financing. This could be because they don't have the money for a down payment or because they don't have a high enough credit score. So, for these types of buyers, seller financing might be the solution, and it might be a good way for you to get an offer on your property. But as we've learned, there are disadvantages to this, such as the fact that you need to be the lender. Many investors don't want to do this; however, if you're okay with it, then it might be a great solution for you.

Remember one thing: you can negotiate almost anything when dealing with transactions in real estate, regardless of whether you're buying or selling a property, but you should always try to get a win-win situation out of it. You should understand the needs of the other party first and foremost so you can gain leverage and negotiate a great deal.

Dealing with Counteroffers

You know that counteroffers are quite common during negotiations, and because of that, I'm dedicating a section to them. Many new real estate investors don't know how to deal with them in the first place.

The first thing I want to say is that you should always be expecting a counteroffer. If you do that, you can anticipate your response. When you submit your initial offer, always think about what counteroffer the other party might ask for. Always analyze the counteroffer even if, at first glance, it might look like a bad one. Take the time to review it and pay special attention to any specific terms and conditions, such as timelines, contingencies, or changes in price.

However, your objectives should be prioritized here, so when you make an initial offer and review a counteroffer, always refer to your goals and decide which terms might and might not be negotiable, as well as those areas where you might have a little more flexibility. Also, don't let the other party wait for too long. Timely communication is important and shows respect, and delayed responses might lead to frustration from the other party. Regardless of how bad or even ridiculous the counteroffer might be, always keep your emotions in check because, in the worst-case scenario, you can simply leave the negotiations.

Also, every time you get a counteroffer, you should check with your realtor for any guidance they might be able to give you. They have ample experience in this regard and can offer some help. Now, when you get a counteroffer, most people think you can do two things: you either follow with another counteroffer, or you accept it. But there are always three options: you can submit another counteroffer with revised terms, you can accept the counteroffer as proposed, or you can simply reject it if the terms of the counteroffer are nowhere near what you want.

Remember that, regardless of negotiations back and forth and the flexibility you might have, you have to stay within your budget. So, you have to make sure that any adjustments to the price align with your financial capabilities. Counteroffers are also great ways to gain a little bit more insight into the other party's motivations. Understanding their goals might help you counter their offer more efficiently.

Apart from consulting your realtor, you should also bring in a financial advisor as well as a legal advisor when you receive a counteroffer. This is to ensure that the terms of the counteroffer are legal and beneficial to you. Remember to set a walk-away point. This is the point when you don't believe you can reach a fair negotiation with the seller, so you simply walk away from the deal. This is important because it will allow you to just move on instead of wasting time on an investment that will not pan out or bring you any advantage.

When dealing with counteroffers, there are a few skills at work here. First, you need to be adaptable to any changing circumstances. Make sure your focus is on your goals, but be flexible in that you want to find a good solution for both parties. Rely on your advisors because they can give you great insights on how to navigate these counteroffers and still benefit you.

Handling Contingencies and Inspections

Contingencies and inspections are key parts of the purchasing process. They both protect your interests and help with the implementation of the deal.

Contingencies describe any requirements that must be met before a negotiation can be formalized. Inspections, appraisals, or financial requirements are some of the most common contingencies added to the purchase agreement. As I've previously said, you should always bring an expert when amending the purchasing agreement to ensure that the phrasing of these contingencies is done properly and there are no loopholes that might lead to conflicts down the line.

For example, if you add a home inspection contingency, you are allowing yourself the chance to hire an inspector to make a report on the condition of the property. The main goal of hiring one is to find any issues with the property you are not aware of that might influence your investment. After their inspection, the expert will give you a detailed report of any issues they have found, such as necessary repairs or safety issues.

If there are any urgent repairs that need to be done, you can negotiate them with the seller. Usually, it goes one of two ways: the seller fixes them before you purchase the property, or you fix them, but the selling price of the property lowers so you can take on the cost of repairs. If you can't reach an agreement with the seller after a few counteroffers, you can abandon the deal.

Financing contingencies are often on the buyer's side. If you can't get financing within a certain period of time, the seller can withdraw from the negotiations without losing a single dollar. You might be asking, "But I have been preapproved; how can I not get financing?" A preapproval doesn't mean you have been approved yet; it's only a good indication that you will get approved and show the seller that you are a serious buyer.

Appraisal contingencies allow the buyer to order an appraisal to find a more accurate value of the property. For example, if the property you want to purchase comes out for less than the purchase price the seller established, you can ask the seller to decrease the price. If that request is denied, you can leave the negotiations. The appraisal, however, is usually ordered by the lender and done by a qualified appraiser, who does a detailed evaluation of the value of the property based on comps.

Most contingencies have deadlines, and it's key to adhere to them. Failure to do so may result in the sacrifice of some rights.

Navigating all of this can be a little overwhelming, but you have to really consider it, especially with a professional who can guide you through it. Remember that all of this is vital to protecting your interests and ensuring everything runs smoothly, from the negotiations to the transactions.

So, we've seen how to make an offer and go through the contingencies and counteroffers. Remember, creating a compelling offer needs careful consideration of the market conditions, as well as understanding your budget and your goals. You can really turn around negotiations with contingencies by protecting your finances.

Also, always expect counteroffers, and always try to be one step ahead of the other party. However, never forget your goals, and if negotiations are straying a little too far from your objectives, feel free to walk away.

Key Takeaways

- Define your investment goals and know your budget so you can stay focused on them during negotiations.
- Prequalifications and preapprovals will give you leverage in negotiating terms and help you know what you can afford.
- Make a compelling offer with a competitive price based on the local market value.
- If you can, build rapport with the seller and find out their needs to reach a win-win situation and be ready for a counteroffer.
- Knowing the seller's motives can help you anticipate what they are going to counter with so you can respond effectively and quickly.
- Set a walk-away point when you think you won't get anywhere so you don't waste time.
- Build in financial contingencies to protect yourself if the deal doesn't go through. Have contingencies in the offer based on inspections as well.

9

STEP SIX – CLOSE YOUR FIRST DEAL & COLLECT THE KEYS TO YOUR KINGDOM

Find out where the people are going and buy the land before they get there.

— WILLIAM PENN ADAIR

Now that you know how to make an offer and how negotiations can go, it's time to understand how you can close a deal. You might think that all you have to do after the lengthy negotiations is sign the papers and it's all done, but it's never like that. This is the last step when it comes to acquiring an investment property.

The Closing Process

The closing process is the final step in the purchasing process. If successful, you will become the owner of the property, but this is not simply signing some papers; there's a bit more that goes into it. Let's go through the parts and first focus on what happens just before the closing process.

At this point, you have to conduct a title search to ensure the property is indeed under the ownership of the seller and that there are no outstanding disputes. Essentially, this will tell you if the seller does have the right to sell you the property. Also, at this point, it's important that you get another look at the property, especially if there exist any contingencies, such as repairs, to ensure that these are resolved.

After that is completed, you have to go through the closing disclosure. This is a document that outlines the final details of the transaction, such as the closing costs or the purchasing price. Only then can you start signing the documents. There are a few of them that you have to sign and can include promissory or mortgage notes, deeds, and so on, but your legal representative can help you understand all of this as you sign.

After everything is signed, the next step is the transfer of funds. Usually, this process can be separated into two distinct parts: funds for purchases and funds for closing costs. The first often happens when the buyer gives a cashier's check or has a wire transfer done. This is to cover the purchase of the property and the down payment. Essentially, this is the big chunk of the money. The funds for closing are always the responsibility of the buyer. These can include costs such as appraisals, legal services, and so on. Let's have a look at the most common costs.

The lender's fee is customary, which can include application fees, origination fees, and any other costs and charges regarding the mortgage. Title and escrow charges cover title searches, insurance, and escrow accounts. Recording fees are also standard, and involve the recording of the transfer of the property paid to the local government. Of course, if you've used a real estate agent, they will also take a fee or a commission, but this often falls on the seller's side.

At this stage, you should have a closing agent, an expert who will guide you in the transfer of funds, as well as with the ownership papers. This is often an attorney who knows about this particular aspect, but it can also be a title company. This is just so you know that the funds are allocated properly. Then there's the deed of transfer, which happens when the seller signs the documents and ownership is officially transferred to you. While this is happening, the local government is simultaneously recording ownership as well.

When that's all done, there are a few other things you have to finish. For instance, you need to establish a date of possession of the property, setting a date for the seller to hand the keys to you so you can finally have access to the property. The possession date is usually stipulated in the agreement, and while the handing of the keys and possession date can occur on the same day, it doesn't necessarily have to be that way. If that's the case, then the handing of the keys is always after the possession date.

You and your legal expert have to make sure that the closing process complies with both legal and regulatory requirements. You don't necessarily have to know the ins and outs of this procedure, but that's why you should have an expert with you. This is important because there might be some tax implications depending on the type of transaction or the jurisdiction in which you reside. At this point, bringing in a tax professional might ease the process and give you peace of mind.

While this all might sound a little complicated, with the help of experts, you shouldn't have to worry about it, and it can actually go pretty fast. Don't do this on your own, even if you think you have some expertise in the subject. It's always better to have a second or even third pair of eyes on these occasions, as you might stumble into some legal issues down the road that you could have easily avoided.

Once this is all done, you can finally become a property owner.

Required Paperwork and Documentation

You need to know, more or less, what you are signing. You don't have to know every detail of it, but at least have a general idea, even if you're working with a professional. There are typically many documents to sign, but they're mostly there to protect the interests of both parties.

I've mentioned the purchase agreement before, which is basically a document that outlines the terms and conditions of the proposed sale. These terms can include, but are not exclusive to, the purchase price, contingencies, or possession date. There are other papers that you need to sign as well. For example, there are inspections, deeds, appraisals, closing disclosures, or title insurance policies. There also tends to be a property survey, so you know with certainty that the property is legal under the seller's name.

If you are the buyer, then when it comes to the affidavit of title, you may relax because the seller is in charge of handling that. This document proves the seller's clear title and the absence of any claims. However, as the buyer, you must verify that you have all of the appropriate documentation related to the escrow account, including instructions and an agreement, in order for the monies to be distributed properly.

Don't forget to keep all loan paperwork, including the deed of trust or mortgage, the note, and any lender-specific documentation. In some areas, when specific property disclosures are required by law, the seller must make a seller disclosure. Both the buyer and the seller must provide proof of insurance coverage in the form of their separate insurance policies. Additionally, depending on your area, there may be numerous federal or state-mandated documents to guarantee compliance with regulatory and legal norms.

You see, there's a lot that you need to have or hand over. Navigating through these can be overwhelming, but this can all be accomplished with a competent real estate lawyer. They can also guide you through the whole process; it's what they do, after all. Still, it's vital that you comply with everything if you don't want the process to take longer than it should, or even go awry.

Working with Title Companies and Attorneys

When going through these transactions in real estate, working with title companies and attorneys is quite common. They provide essential insights into making sure that the financial and legal aspects of the transaction are all properly handled. Let's go through their roles and how you can work with them.

Title companies can provide many services, such as title searches, where they verify the history of the property's ownership and make sure there are no claims or disputes. They also offer title insurance policies that serve to protect the lender and the buyer in case there are any issues down the road. They often also provide escrow services, or accounts where funds regarding the transaction are held, and make sure that all parties fulfill their obligations and get paid.

Now, you should always do your due diligence when working with these companies, as you would with any company that provides you with services. You might want to go for one that has vast experience in the field and a solid reputation. Communication in this phase with these companies is extremely important, especially during the closing process.

Real estate attorneys offer other things. They have extensive legal expertise in real estate and can offer you guidance throughout the whole process. They can also prepare documents for you and review them, such as deeds or purchase agreements. And if there are any disputes, they can chime in, provide guidance, and even negotiate on your behalf.

Choosing a real estate attorney is even more important than choosing a title company because the attorney's competence can differentiate a good deal from a bad one. Having experience is not the only thing you should be looking for; you should also have knowledge of the local market and be familiar with any regulations. These attorneys also offer legal consultation throughout the process and, as I've said, legal representation if you need it.

It's not uncommon for title companies and attorneys to work together to make the whole process smoother. They often share information and align their efforts to protect your interests. Because they have managed all the documents, they will collaboratively help you navigate all the paperwork that is necessary.

Working with these two entities is just part of the process, and when you first start, you will have to do your research to find good ones. But once you form a relationship with them and are happy with the results, you can continue to use them so you don't have to research every time you make a new investment.

Remember what I said about creating relationships? These are some that you want to establish as quickly as you can because they are always necessary.

Post-Closing Responsibilities and Considerations

After you've closed the deal, there are still things you need to do. If your plan is to rent out the property, then you have to get started with preparing the property for tenants. But before that, you have to record the deed with the county so the transfer is finally formalized.

One minor thing that many new real estate investors forget way too often is changing the locks once you become the owner of the property. You don't know who else, apart from the seller, has the keys to the property, so if you want to protect the property and future tenants, you must change the locks. You also have to update the insurance, despite becoming a landlord or just a homeowner. This is to ensure that you have the right insurance policy and don't run into any legal issues in the future. Remember to transfer the utilities or any other services that the previous owner might have on the property, such as water, gas, internet, and electricity. All of these now have to fall under your name, and you are responsible for them.

Be sure to do any repairs and maintenance needed before you bring in any tenants. You can have another look at the home inspection report to check for anything that the inspector might have flagged, and fix it. At this point, talking to a tax advisor might be important so you understand any taxes you might need to pay now that you are the owner.

If you're renting out the property, it's important that you address any concerns your tenants might have and that they are deemed reasonable. A happy tenant increases the chances of staying longer on the property, which might stabilize your cash flow and maximize your earnings. Keeping all the financial records is also important so you can understand how your investment is going and track the overall performance of the property, as well as when you start making a profit on it.

You still have responsibilities when you become the owner of the property. If anything, those responsibilities might increase, especially if you become a landlord.

Closing the deal is just as important as choosing the right investment for you or negotiating the deal. There are a few steps you have to go through and many documents to sign. You should ensure these are delivered in a timely manner and properly signed so the process goes smoothly and quickly. During this phase, preparation is everything, and when done properly, it can really pay off.

Get your team ready so they can help you navigate this process, which can take a little while. But with great professionals by your side, there's a higher chance that all of this will get wrapped up a lot faster.

Key Takeaways

- Closing a deal is just as important as making an offer and negotiating. It's not over until it's over.
- Title searches are imperative to make sure the property has no outstanding disputes. Make sure final transactions are made (such as closing costs). Sign the documents (often many of them), transfer the funds, figure out the possession date, and check legal and regulatory compliance.
- Closing entails a ton of paperwork that needs to be signed, including the purchase agreement, insurance proof, loan paperwork, property surveys, deeds, appraisals, title insurance policies, and many others.
- Title companies conduct title search and often provide escrow services.
- Post-closing closing responsibilities include recording the deed to formalize the transfer of the property, updating the property insurance, updating utilities, or changing locks.
- Keep all financial records of the transfer in case you run into issues in the future. If you're going to rent, then you have the responsibility to screen tenants and ensure that their concerns are heard and addressed.

10

STEP SEVEN – EASILY MANAGE YOUR FIRST PROPERTY OR PROJECT & COLLECT YOUR FIRST CHECK

Buy real estate in areas where the path exists...and buy more real estate where there is no path, but you can create your own.

— DAVID WARONKER

Closing a deal is a great milestone that should be celebrated, but you have to start thinking about what your next steps should be, and it's vital that you have a plan. What I like to do after I close a property is review my goals, especially my long-term goals.

To start, ask yourself these questions: Do you want to acquire more properties? If yes, do you plan on diversifying your portfolio, or do you prefer to specialize in a certain niche? Either way, if you choose to continue to buy properties (and I'm not saying right away), you will be looking at ways to grow your portfolio. For that, you need to come up with a strategy to invest in more properties, going back to the various strategies we've talked about.

While you are recovering your money or accumulating more, it's important that you stay in the game. By this, I mean staying informed, checking property values in potential areas that you want to invest in, monitoring trends, and so on. You also have to continue to learn and hone your skills as much as you possibly can, whether it is looking up new strategies or acquiring more knowledge of real estate investing.

Let's take this opportunity to go over some of the things that I didn't talk about but that might be important.

Managing a Fix-and-Flip Project

For any investment you make, you should always start with your due diligence, where you analyze the market, do a property inspection, and so on. You also have to create a budget and look at your financing options.

Now, what's different about fix-and-flip properties is that you need to plan your renovations carefully. You see, the more you budget and understand the things that increase the value of the property for a reduced cost, the more your profit goes up. So, renovation planning starts with devising a well-prepared scope of work where you highlight what renovations you have to do. Start with the essential renovations because these will allow you to pass inspection and sell the property; without them, the property will fail inspection, and you will not be able to sell it. In other words, these are needed. But also, outline all the other improvements and renovations that you think will increase the value of the property.

Then, if you don't have a contractor team, you best get one. Contractors are essential when it comes to fixing and flipping properties, and the more you work with the same company or team, the easier it will get for you—and the cheaper it will get. Then, you have to obtain all the necessary permits and comply with any regulations.

You also have to have project management skills, so creating a timeline for the renovations is important. You don't want to drag these things along because the more time passes, the more money you lose. During this phase, it's also crucial that you keep an eye on your expenses so they don't decrease your profit when you sell them.

When all is done, you have to market your property, which, as you know, comes with a cost, too. An efficient market will bring not just prospective buyers but the right potential buyers, saving you time filtering through buyers who will never buy your home. Then there's the cost of closing the deal and the time it takes to negotiate.

Finding and Screening Tenants

This is a subject that we have yet to develop, but it's quite vital when you become a landlord. This doesn't necessarily mean just finding tenants; it's about finding the *right* tenants. Those who will take good care of your property, pay on time, and do everything a good tenant entails. If you don't find good tenants, chances are that you will find problems down the road, including reduced or delayed profits that might lead to eviction, a very time-consuming and lengthy process.

The first step when screening for great tenants is to market your property properly. There's a lot you can do when it comes to marketing your property, with many different strategies to choose from. Listing your property is important, and choosing the right platforms is, too. Platforms like Realtor.com or Zillow are great places to start. You shouldn't disregard social media platforms either, which are a great way to advertise your properties. You can also advertise them for free on these platforms.

Hiring a professional photographer to take quality pictures of your property can lead to great results and higher chances of your property being viewed. You can certainly do it yourself, but if you lack the expertise, I recommend hiring someone who is equipped. More often than not, the results come out much better. The presentation of the property is also important given this is what tenants will see. If you want to bring in quality tenants, these two things are important.

Then comes the tenant application process. While not necessary, I would have all potential tenants fill out a rental application so you have a better idea of who they are. Here, you should aim to collect personal details, employment information, rental history, and so on. Once that is done, you will analyze all the applications and screen them. This involves doing credit checks to assess for good credit history and a background check to understand if they have any prior convictions, verifying their income, and obtaining any references from previous landlords.

One thing that is quite important to know is the fair housing laws with which you have to comply. These laws are both federal and local, so make sure you understand them. They have to do with any discriminatory practices such as religion, gender, or race. I'm not saying that you'll break these laws on purpose, but if you don't understand them, you might be at risk when screening tenants.

Once you've chosen the right tenants, it's time for the lease agreement. These have to be clear and comprehensive, where you have to add the amount of rent, the date the rent is due, any security deposit, and all the responsibilities you have to fulfill, such as maintenance. Here, it's important that you go to your attorney before sending it out to tenants to sign, just to make sure that everything is done properly.

One last thing on tenants: communication is vital. I've said it many times in the most diverse stages of this whole process, but clear communication is the only way for you to know that everyone is on the same page. Make sure you decide the best way to contact your tenants, and they will contact you from the very beginning. If they have any concerns, make sure you address them promptly so you can build a great landlord-tenant relationship. You should also talk about the ground rules with your new tenants, and it's best that you do so in writing so they have it. These rules can encompass emergency procedures, property rules, and whom they should contact for any urgent repairs. Also, even with tenants on your property, you have to schedule inspections from time to time; it's just the law. So, when that happens, make sure to inform the tenants with a proper notice.

If you like your tenants and their lease is about to expire, you might want to consider offering them a lease renewal where you can discuss any changes to the lease or rent adjustments. However, you also have to be prepared for evictions if tenants violate the lease terms or don't pay rent. There's a whole legal procedure for that, and your attorney can help you with it.

Property Managing Tips

The most common way to get into the real estate business is by buying a property and renting it to tenants, which means you are in it for the long haul. So, I think it's important to highlight some tips when it comes to managing the properties. Keep in mind that some of these I've already mentioned throughout the book, but it's important that you remember them.

Communication is vital, as I've said, so here, you want to respond to tenants as quickly as you can and provide them with emergency contacts if they have an urgent situation at hand. Preventive maintenance is something you want to do regularly, so you don't have to only do it when something happens and it costs you double to fix it. If you do this maintenance in a timely manner, your tenants will also appreciate it. Also, adopt some security measures to protect the property and the tenants, too; this could be anything from proper lighting to secure locks to security cameras.

Always be legally aware so you don't accidentally breach any law, such as fair housing laws or health and safety regulations. The same goes for your lease agreement; it should comply with the law, and you have to pass it on to your attorney before they send it out. Always keep proper records of all the documents having to do with the property, as this paperwork is the only way for you to accurately understand the property's profitability. This goes for the money coming in, but also any receipts or invoices.

To make things easier for you, think about digital solutions when it comes to rent collection so you don't have to waste time physically collecting rent. There are many different platforms that can help you streamline this process.

Scaling Your Real Estate Portfolio

When you start your business, even at the beginning, the aim is to scale your business, acquire more properties, and expand your portfolio. You can also expand your portfolio by simply increasing the value of your investments, which often happens naturally. However, to continue to scale your business, you first need to set some goals. Not only that, but you also have to set a deadline or a timeframe to complete those goals.

Before embarking on a new investment, it's important that you know that you are financially capable of doing so. Look at your finances and evaluate them. You have to create a budget and assess and manage your risk by doing your due diligence. Diversifying your portfolio is a way to reduce the risk of your investments, but for that, you need to look at the different types of property you already have in your portfolio and the investments you have in different locations. These are the two most important factors when it comes to diversifying within the real estate industry.

At this point, you have to start thinking strategically in general, but especially when it comes to acquisitions. There are two important things that you need to take into account: either you improve your existing properties or you purchase new investments. Whatever you choose, you should always pay close attention to your finances and how you can cope with the new investments because they might impact your margins and, ultimately, your profits.

But scaling your business doesn't necessarily mean improving existing properties or purchasing new ones. How you manage them is also relevant. If your idea is to manage all your investments, you will have to come up with an efficient management strategy. This could mean purchasing software management tools or hiring a property management company. The first one is recommended if you want to save money, but still want to manage the properties yourself. Hiring a property management company might cost you more, which can ultimately reduce your profits, but you will save more of your time.

Expanding your network and your connections is also part of scaling your business. Attempting to scale on a daily basis can help you build new relationships in the industry, which might lead to new opportunities. In fact, getting into a partnership is a great way to scale your business because you will have a partner who is willing to make a financial effort and help you expand your business. Usually, this means acquiring more properties or helping you financially increase the value of your existing investments. At this point, becoming more tax efficient can really help you maximize your profits.

Even if you're just starting out in this industry, scaling your business should always be the aim. So, you have to make an effort to constantly network with other professionals.

Exploring Advanced Real Estate Strategies

As you diversify your portfolio and gain more experience, you will inevitably start looking for other strategies that might require a little more knowledge on your part. I'm not going into much detail on any of them, as many require entirely separate books to really know them, but I'll give you the knowledge so that you can dive deeper into them on your own time.

Let's start with commercial real estate. This is not a strategy per se, but when you invest in this type of real estate, it's important that you have acquired some more experience than you had when beginning your real estate investor career. Commercial real estate is a great way to diversify your portfolio, but the approach you have to take is vastly different from, say, residential real estate. Instead of properties where people live, you have to look at office buildings or retail centers, for example. Here, the due diligence you have to do is quite different from that of residential properties, and it's usually more expensive to acquire. On the other hand, it's far more financially stable.

There's also real estate syndication. Here, you pool funds with other like-minded investors, and while this doesn't increase the complexity, there are a few more steps that you have to go through. Also, when doing this, there are usually more properties involved, or at least larger properties, which might contribute to the complexity of the deal. This is especially true when we look at the financial and legal structure of the syndication. Here, it's fairly common to have different types of partners with different powers and functions.

Another more advanced strategy is multifamily real estate. For many real estate investors coming from residential properties, this is the most logical step to follow. Here, you might find apartment complexes that offer multiple income streams. However, the initial investment is often higher than that of single residential properties. There's also more management involved, with more tenant screenings and maintenance.

Tax-related strategies, such as 1031 exchanges that allow you to defer capital gain taxes, are yet another way to dip your toe in more complex real estate strategies. The complexity of these deals often comes from the legal side of things, as, with a 1031 exchange in particular, you have to purchase a property similar to the one you just sold then use the money to purchase the new property, which allows you to defer the capital gained from it. It's important that you work with a tax advisor or an attorney who specializes in these types of deals so you can maximize your profits.

Real estate investment trusts, or REITs, are a simpler but equally successful method. They function similarly to stocks in that they may be bought and sold on the market. However, rather than investing directly in real estate, you are investing in a firm that specializes in real estate property investments. These REIT stocks are structured to provide dividends similar to rental income, giving a consistent income stream, as well as the opportunity for capital development over time. Incorporating REITs into your portfolio is an excellent way to diversify.

Then we have real estate development, which involves buying land and building a property from the ground up. While buying land may be less expensive than buying an existing home, it is important to consider the expenses of hiring workers to complete the building, as well as the time required to finish the project. This approach is more demanding when it comes to due diligence than for already-built properties. It also brings a higher financial commitment.

There are plenty of other advanced strategies, but the ones I've mentioned here are perhaps some of the most common. They are all great ways to get started with these more advanced approaches. They also tend to lead to higher returns, but they carry more risk than the most basic strategies. You often have to have a completely different understanding of that side of the business, so it's important that you really try to get all the necessary knowledge before pursuing any of these advanced strategies.

Scaling your business is something that should be on your mind—if not now, at least in the future. In this case, it means expanding your portfolio, where you need to set a timeline for when you should advance to expand it, assess your finances to understand if you can do it, and improve your existing properties so you can increase your profit. At the same time, you should continue to expand your professional network to allow you to take advantage of other opportunities.

Key Takeaways

- Always be reviewing and checking in with your investment goals.

- Have a team of contractors and repair companies on standby for unexpected problems that arise.
- Make sure you get any necessary permits to renovate your property. This is especially important if you are fixing structural issues.
- It's imperative that you and or your property or project manager stay organized with paperwork, finances, and timelines no matter what strategy you're using.
- Screening tenants is essential to lowering your risk of late rent payment, vacancies, evictions, squatters, or property damage.
- Zillow, Apartments.com, or Realtor.com are great places to find tenants, collect rent, and manage leases.
- Having professional photos and maintaining a seamless application process are key to attracting good tenants.
- Diligently keep records of everything property related for tax and legal reasons.

FREE GIFT #5

The Must-Have Property Rehab Checklist: One mistake can make or break your bank!

Rehabbing a worn-down property is a great way to get a great deal on a property and force its appreciation! Construction also costs time and money which can be a huge money pit if something goes wrong. With this rehab checklist you'll be able to thoroughly understand the process and what things to consider before you start.

To get instant access this free e-book, scan the QR code below or visit this link: https://readstreetpress.com/iwantpermanentpto5

CONCLUSION: YOU CAN DO IT

You are now at the very start of a promising career as a real estate investor, but also at the beginning of achieving your financial freedom, quitting your day job, and especially having the time to do what you love and spend with your loved ones. It won't be easy, especially at the beginning, but you shouldn't be overwhelmed by it.

What you find in this book is everything that you need to know to start. Making changes is the only way we can continue to move forward and achieve things we have never thought of reaching. It's just that first step that we need to make, and from there, we lose the fear of leaving our comfort zone and expand our horizons. There are no more excuses; you know exactly where to start now, and you have the basic knowledge, too. All you have to do now is get out there.

Before I leave you to follow your dreams, I just want to go over the main points we've discussed in this book. However, feel free to peruse those parts you feel you don't fully understand. This is not a one-time read, but a thorough guide to help you navigate the intricacies of real estate investing.

We started by looking at how real estate works, but most importantly, how it can work for you in achieving your goals. We looked at the potential of real estate as a way to build your wealth, how you can maximize your profits through tax, how debt can be leveraged to follow certain opportunities, and how to generate passive income while your investments appreciate. We also looked at the different types of real estate properties you can invest in. The easiest way to get into the industry is to invest in residential properties, but as you gain more experience, commercial properties can be a great way for you to increase your income or even invest in raw land where you have full control of your investment.

Then, we looked at investment strategies and how each presents unique opportunities. Remember, these strategies are not inherently good or bad; it all depends on your situation and how well you can do your due diligence to pick the right one. Then, we moved on to short- and long-term deals, fix-and-flip, and wholesaling. However, everything starts with your very first deal, to which a whole chapter was dedicated. The first deal is often the most important you will make in your career because it will define how you can invest in consequential properties. This is no reason to get overwhelmed by it, though. If you have done your due diligence, understand the market, and have the right people by your side, chances are that everything will go smoothly, and you will be successful.

As we have seen, there are many different steps, such as getting preapproved, creating your budget, and many other things. There will be times when bringing in a partner will make sense. A partner can provide you with enough funds, as well as great insights.

Analyzing deals is perhaps where all the effort lies, but to be very honest, it's my favorite part because I get to understand and be confident about the deals I take on. I went into detail about how you can analyze your deals, but this is something you have to practice, and over time, you will get better at it. Here, you have to go through your due diligence and evaluate the property as well as the market conditions. Once you have all the data, you can make a conscious decision.

The next step is to look for financing, and it's crucial that you know all the different options you can go for. As I've previously said, chances are that traditional financing is the best route when it comes to your first deal. But don't be married to this idea if you are clearly better off with a more creative type of financing, as long as you do your due diligence. Here, finding partners is crucial because they can support you financially, and help when it comes to understanding certain deals.

Once that is all done and decided, it's time to make an offer. At this stage, creating a great offer and knowing how to negotiate can really make your deal successful. But don't forget the closing. Don't think that once the negotiation is done, you are free to do what you want. Your obligations continue, and there's a lot of paperwork involved in closing the deal. This is why you have to work closely with your attorney to make sure everything is in order. After that, you might become a landlord, which often means taking care of maintenance, managing renovations, or screening tenants.

As overwhelming as it might seem, beginnings always feel this way. You have to keep on persevering, and with experience and the confidence you build along the way, things will get easier. And as you continue to move forward in your career, the closer you get to your goal of becoming financially free.

THE ONLY RENTAL PROPERTY INVESTING BOOK YOU'LL EVER NEED:

THE ULTIMATE GUIDE TO FINDING, BUYING, & MANAGING RENTAL PROPERTIES USING LONG & SHORT TERM RENTAL INVESTING STRATEGIES

INTRODUCTION: WHY I LOVE RENTAL PROPERTY INVESTING

"Don't wait to buy real estate. Buy real estate and wait."

— *WILL ROGERS*

What would you do if you had no boss? No set schedule? No clock to punch or to-do list to complete? What if you had nothing but time?

I used to sit at my desk and ponder those exact questions. What would it be like if I wasn't working for the weekend? If the thought of layoffs and downsizing didn't constantly hang over my head?

I like to call that guy Old Andrew because he feels like a completely different person. That guy had a job that didn't challenge him. He made enough money to cover his bills, but not nearly enough to fund the lifestyle of his dreams. He was looking at the typical American life: 9-to-5, climbing the career ladder, retiring at 65 if everything went according to plan, and having a decade or so of freedom to actually enjoy the fruits of his labor.

Old Andrew was surviving, but he certainly wasn't thriving. His frustration mounted every single time he sat down at his desk. And eventually, he got sick of daydreaming about the life he wanted.

So, he took control. He rented out the second story of his duplex and kickstarted a real estate investing journey that changed his life.

How Real Estate Investing Changed My Life

My shift from Old Andrew to New Andrew—aka, the guy writing this book—began when I met my wife. Her passion for real estate sparked my curiosity and pushed me to dip my toe into house hacking (renting out a room or unit of your personal residence with the goal of lowering your expenses). Before I knew it, I had tenants living in the second story of my duplex. When I cashed that first rent check—enough to cover my mortgage—it felt like the sun was peeking through the clouds.

Could real estate investing be my ticket out of my 9-to-5? It sure felt like it. I learned everything I could about the industry, developed my own blueprint for finding great deals, and adapted my strategy as I became more knowledgeable.

Life looks really, really different now. I don't punch a clock anymore. Instead, I spend my time planning and enjoying trips with my wife. I've seen new countries, indulged in some incredible new cuisines, and checked off a few items on my ever-growing bucket list. I have the house of my dreams with plenty of space to tinker with DIY projects and a kitchen that makes me feel like I'm hosting a show on the Food Network.

Real estate investing changed my life. It can change yours, too.

The Book I Wish I Had

At its core, real estate investing is very simple. It's a tried-and-true wealth-building strategy because it's straightforward: buy property. Rent it or flip it. Repeat.

Everyone can do it. Not everyone can be great at it. Being a successful real estate investor is due to tons of tiny decisions that add up to massive results. When I started house hacking, I quickly realized I had a lot to learn. My wife helped a lot, but there are some things only experience can teach you. I went from house hacking to owning multiple properties, including commercial rentals. I went from being a hands-on landlord to employing a team to manage my properties so I could live life to the fullest. Each phase had its own set of challenges, opportunities, and benefits. I learned something new at every single turn.

This is the book I wished I had throughout that journey. It probably caught your attention because you're in the same mindset as Old Andrew. You're feeling broke and frustrated, desperate to provide for your family. You're sick of having your earning potential dictated by your boss or corporate politics. You're a go-getter, and you want to go out there and get it: wealth, assets, and most importantly, control of your time and living life on your terms.

Real estate investing can give you this freedom. This book will give you the blueprint you need to get started and scale, especially if you are:

- Overwhelmed by your real estate options and don't know where to start. There are lots of terms, jargon, and strategies you need to learn to be successful. I'll break them down for you to shorten your learning curve.
- Building your empire. Managing one property is tough. Managing multiple properties is even tougher. And managing more than five is insanely tough, especially if you don't have the systems and team.

I've been there, done that. When you're finished with this book, you'll not only feel confident purchasing and managing your first investment property, but you'll be able to manage a second, third, fourth—as many properties as you want—with ease.

In the next pages, you're going to learn:

- How to find incredible deals
- The ins and outs of creative financing, including how to fund deals with little to no money and a poor credit score
- How to build a system to manage your properties that actually works
- Ways to manage short-term, midterm, and vacation rentals
- How to scale and exit when the time is right

Listen, I'm no mogul. I'm a regular guy who put in the work to learn this business and worked the steps I'm going to lay out for you in the chapters to follow. Jumping into real estate investing was a risk, but most worthwhile things are. If you're ready to take the plunge, read on.

1

HOW RENTAL PROPERTY INVESTING WORKS & HOW IT CAN BUILD YOU WEALTH YOU NEVER IMAGINED

"Ninety percent of all millionaires become so through owning real estate. More money has been made in real estate than in all industrial investments combined. The wise young man or wage earner of today invests his money in real estate."

— *ANDREW CARNEGIE*

"I can't purchase property right now. Interest rates are through the roof."

"I missed the window to invest in property. Best to keep saving and wait until prices come down again."

"I can't risk having a property sit vacant. If I'm not collecting rent, there's no way to make money investing in real estate."

Sound familiar? You're not alone. Lots of people dream of investing in real estate. Many never take the plunge because of thoughts just like the ones above. But most of that fear comes from a lack of knowledge about the industry.

Thankfully, that's easy to fix. In this chapter, you'll get a crash course in real estate investing. We'll go beyond the basics, look at each phase of the real estate cycle, examine four ways investing can make you money, and give you a realistic picture of the pros and cons of starting today instead of in the distant future.

Why Real Estate Investing Is So Powerful

When was the last time you paid rent? Maybe it was a few years ago when you split that four-bedroom house with your buddies from college. Perhaps it was those first few years as a newlywed, renting a tiny house in the city. Maybe it was two weeks ago when you wrote a $1,500 check to your landlord.

Let me tell you what happened to that cash. Your landlord used it to pay the mortgage on the place you live in. While you live in that property and pay their mortgage, the value appreciates, and your landlord racks up tax benefits. They're rolling excess cash flow into new properties.

This is why real estate investing is so powerful. Your hard-earned cash is making your landlord rich. It could be making you rich instead.

The Big Four: How Real Estate Can Make You Wealthy

We all want to make money while we sleep. Real estate investing makes that possible, and there's more than one way to make it happen. Your property can generate value for you in four major ways: appreciation, cash flow, tax benefits, and loan paydowns.

You need just one property to start this process. As value grows, you'll be able to snowball that into more properties and, eventually, more income. Here's how each of The Big Four elements work:

Appreciation

Let's do a little experiment. Head to Zillow and search for the address of your childhood home. Write down the Zestimate at the top of the page. Then, scroll down to the price history and look at the sale price for the last few times the home was bought and sold. You'll likely find a pretty big difference between the current projected value and the recent sale prices. That's appreciation in action.

Appreciation refers to the increase of an asset's value over time. It is split into two categories: natural and forced.

Natural appreciation occurs when market forces outside the investor's control, like inflation, economic growth, or population changes, drive an asset's value up. Forced appreciation occurs when the investor makes decisions that increase the property's value. Investors can create forced appreciation by raising rent or making property improvements.

Natural appreciation is ideal because it doesn't require hands-on work from the owner to increase its value. Instead, the time investment is used on the front end of the purchase when you go through a thorough due diligence process to understand the external factors that can impact the property's value. Forced appreciation requires an investment of time and money after purchasing the property, in addition to the time spent researching the investment before purchasing. In an ideal scenario, an investor can find a property that is not only likely to experience natural appreciation, but also offers an opportunity for improvements that lead to forced appreciation.

Cash Flow

In real estate investing, cash flow is exactly what it sounds like: the movement of money in and out of your property. Every property you own should generate income, typically through rental income. Each property will also come with its share of expenses, like mortgage payments, taxes, and operation expenses.

The easiest way to calculate your cash flow will take you right back to basic mathematics. Add up the expenses on the property, then subtract it from the income. The result is your cash flow.

Income - expenses = cash flow

Accurately tracking your cash flow requires diligence because there are hidden expenses to property ownership and management. Repairs, security, access systems, and property maintenance all need to be accounted for when calculating cash flow. As your real estate empire expands and your team grows, you'll have things like property management fees to account for as well.

If your expenses exceed your income, you are experiencing negative cash flow. If expenses and income are equal, you still have negative cash flow. Your goal is to have positive cash flow, which means your income exceeds your expenses. When that happens, give yourself a pat on the back and celebrate—you're making money!

Tax Benefits

As Benjamin Franklin said, the only certainty in life is death and taxes. Let's talk about taxes.

Taxes are an inevitable part of real estate investing or any income-generating activity. Thankfully, some tax benefits to property ownership and real estate investing can lighten your tax burden. When you invest in real estate, you often qualify for pass-through deductions and tax write-offs, among other advantages. Deductions will lower your taxable income. Some deductions, like taxes and mortgage interest, are fairly obvious. Others, like business equipment or travel expenses, are less obvious but can add up to big savings. Some common tax benefits include:

- Subtracting a decrease in property value from your taxable income
- Using a 1031 exchange to defer taxes after selling an investment property and investing in a new property
- Writing off the value of replacing your investment property's HVAC system

These are just a few examples of the tax benefits of real estate investing. A great accountant or tax strategist can help you make the most of your benefits. They'll prove their value over and over again and quickly become crucial players on your team. We'll talk more about how to find these teammates in the next chapter.

Loan Paydown

You will likely take out a loan to finance property purchases. When you have tenants, their rent payments can go directly toward paying down your loan. As you pay down the principal, you grow the equity on your property. Paying off your loan early can save you money on interest and give you more capital to invest in new properties.

Understanding Rental Property Investing

Real estate investing is a big umbrella. In the broadest sense, it is the act of purchasing a property with the ultimate goal to generate a return. You can do this through residential or commercial properties. We will focus on rental properties throughout this book, but the principles are the same for commercial investing.

There is a big difference between simply buying a house and investing in a rental property. The devil, of course, is in the details.

When you invest in a rental property, you are investing with the ultimate goal of getting a return on your investment, typically through income or appreciation. You might never cook a meal in this residence's kitchen or have a drink on its back porch. Heck, you might not even live in the same city as this residence.

When you purchase a home as your primary residence, you often consider factors unique to your family, like the number of bedrooms or the length of the commute to work. When you invest in rental properties, you become the landlord, and your considerations change. In addition to the property's features like location or size, you also need to consider other factors, like:

- **Maintenance costs:** You are the landlord, which means getting the property move-in ready—and keeping it in that condition—is your responsibility. It's crucial to be honest about whether you can complete the maintenance work yourself or if you have the financial bandwidth to hire someone else to do the work.
- **The desirability for tenants:** It's important to have a clear picture of the potential tenants for the property. Are you offering a long-term rental for families? Mid-term rentals for traveling nurses or other similar professionals? How much work will you have to do to keep the property occupied, and can you handle having the property vacant for a few months between tenants?
- **State and local ordinances:** There are laws and regulations for rental properties, and they often vary by state and location. You'll need to comply with these ordinances and

regulations as well as keep up-to-date on changes after you purchase the property.

- **Your own personal finances:** Can this property generate enough income to make the work worthwhile? What is the average rent for similar properties in the area? How much will it cost to insure the property? Have a clear understanding of your personal financial health before you add another property into the mix.

Remember, your goal is not to build a home for yourself. Your goal is to find the right property, fill it with the right tenants, charge them the right price, and use that income to generate more wealth for yourself. To do this successfully, you need a strategy and a plan. Most of all, you need knowledge of how rental property investing works and how to make decisions based on the phase of the real estate cycle you're in.

Other Pros of Real Estate Investing

For most of us, myself included, real estate investment is an attractive option because it gives us more control over our income and no cap on our earning potential. There are other benefits to jumping in, as I've discovered since taking the plunge.

Unlock the Power of Leverage

You can start investing in real estate without a ton of capital. When you use leverage, you are using borrowed money or debt to set yourself up for a return on your investment. Through mortgages and other purchasing incentives, you can purchase your first property with very little upfront capital and begin your journey. As your cash flow increases, you'll be able to invest in more properties. Leverage makes real estate an accessible way to grow your wealth and scale your business.

Success Is Dependent on the Person

I won't lie to you: making money through real estate investing takes work, especially in the beginning. The great news is that your success is entirely dependent on you. You have the power to improve your skills and expand your real estate knowledge. You have the power to use your personal time to hunt for deals and vet tenants. You have the power to set big dreams for your business and take action to make them happen. Your ability to succeed is entirely in your hands. Yes, it's hard. Is it rewarding? Absolutely.

Everyone Always Needs Somewhere to Live

Though the real estate market moves in cycles, one universal truth remains: everyone needs somewhere to live. People move for jobs, downsize due to retirement, or upgrade their homes to accommodate a growing family. Even when times are tough, a place to live is always a priority, no matter who you are or where you're located.

A Time-Tested Investment and Wealth-Building Strategy

Get-rich-quick schemes come and go. The stock market rises and falls. Real estate is forever. Property has been a wealth builder for generations, and that won't change any time soon. If you want to increase your wealth, investing in real estate is a great way to own a tangible asset that will stand the test of time.

Mostly Stable

Sure, the real estate market fluctuates. But overall, real estate is fairly predictable. If you hold on to a property long enough, its value will most likely appreciate. Rental properties generate consistent revenue. Tax benefits are available year after year. The train will keep moving, even if the journey includes peaks and valleys.

A Variety of Investment Options and Flexibility

Real estate investing is not one-size-fits-all. There are multiple options for investments, from residential to commercial and short-term to long-term. You can buy properties individually or through crowdsourced funding. You get to find the approach that works best for you, your family, and your wallet. When the time comes to change your approach, you also have the flexibility to make changes that suit you.

A Simple Business Model

The business model for real estate investing is pretty straightforward. Buy a property. Find a tenant. Collect payment. Use the cash flow to scale. You do not need to employ a complicated strategy to be successful. You simply start small, learn the business, execute, and scale. It's really that easy.

Buy Low and Negotiate

When you're buying a property, you have the power to negotiate. Your negotiation skills can help you acquire a property below the asking price or place the burden of some of the repairs on the seller. You also don't have to be a superstar negotiator to get started in real estate. It's a skill you can learn and use for life. As you hone your skills, you'll get even more bang for your buck as your business expands.

Many Ways to Profit

Collecting rent is not the only way to profit as a real estate investor. Tax benefits will put money in your pocket. Loan paydowns will, too, as will buying and holding properties to sell down the line. From vacation rentals to purchasing land for future development, real estate investing offers endless opportunities to turn a profit.

Pile Up Passive Income

Trust me, there is nothing better than making money while you sleep. Real estate investing is an incredible way to generate passive income, especially if you have the right systems and team in place to manage your properties. You can collect the cash while someone else deals with the details.

Cons of Real Estate Investing

Real estate investing can be a great way to generate income, grow your wealth, and take back your time, but it's not all fancy vacations and big checks. Like any business, it takes work to build a sustainable real estate company. It's important to know the truth about what you're getting into—cons included.

It Takes Time to Build Real Wealth

Real estate is a long game. It takes patience, persistence, and strategy to be successful. From making property improvements to finding quality tenants, it takes time to get things up and running. Once you do, though, the options are endless.

You Have to Be a Landlord and Manage Properties

Your properties are occupied by actual people, and people can be hard to predict. As a landlord, you'll have to deal with late payments and less-than-ideal tenants. You'll be responsible for handling maintenance and repairs. You will also have to ensure your properties are consistently filled so the money keeps coming in. Although you might be able to hand off these tasks to a property manager down the road, when you're first starting, these tasks will fall squarely on your shoulders.

You Have to Manage Paperwork and Bookkeeping

As a real estate investor, you won't just be touring properties, brokering deals, and doing DIY projects like you're on HGTV. Real estate requires a lot of paperwork, from contracts to logging expenses. Staying organized with your bookkeeping is essential. You won't be chained to your desk, but you will have to spend some time managing your business.

You Can Lose Your Money and Investment

Nothing is guaranteed in life. Real estate is no different. There's always a chance your investment won't produce the returns you anticipated. You can lose money, and it's important to understand that risk exists before diving into real estate.

Takeaways

Hyper-supply. Forced appreciation. Real estate cycles. The Big Four. We packed a lot into this chapter, but every piece of information is absolutely crucial to building your real estate knowledge.

At the end of each chapter in this book, I'll share a few key takeaways. These are things you'll want to remember as we move forward through the book.

Takeaway #1: The Real Estate Market Is Cyclical

After reading media coverage and talking with friends who recently made property purchases, you might be thinking you missed the boat to invest in real estate. You didn't. Every real estate market works through four cycles: recovery, expansion, hyper-supply, and recession. There are indicators to help you determine which phase of the cycle we're currently in and specific strategies to help you thrive during each phase.

Takeaway #2: Look at the Whole Picture When It Comes to Value

Savvy investors consider each element of the Big Four when it comes to real estate investing. Your property can generate value through natural and forced appreciation, cash flow, tax benefits, and loan paydowns. Use each of the Big Four components to your advantage to maximize the value of each investment.

Takeaway #3: Push Past Fear

The more you know about real estate investing, the braver you'll feel. When you understand the real estate cycle, you can adapt your strategy and hold strong when times seem tough. Understanding the Big Four will help you assess a property's potential in its entirety and make investment decisions confidently. And hopefully, knowing the pros and cons of real estate investment will help you dive in without hesitation.

Takeaway #4: Be Patient

Unless you're exceptionally lucky, plan on real estate investing to be a long game. As long as you do it right and know the risks, real estate investing can build significant generational wealth.

What's Next

You've got the basics of real estate down. Now it's time to lay the groundwork for purchasing your first property. In the next chapter, I'll help you pick a strategy, choose a property type and location, build your dream team, and prepare to finance your first deal.

2

EVERYTHING YOU NEED TO KNOW BEFORE BUYING YOUR FIRST PROPERTY

"Buy land, they're not making it anymore."

— *MARK TWAIN*

A t this point, you're probably thinking something like this: *Alright, Andrew. I'm in. In fact, I'm texting my realtor buddy right now to set up some showings.*

Let me stop you right there. Put down the cell phone. Exit out of Zillow. Do not pass go. Do not collect $200. Just like Monopoly, you've got to learn the rules before you play the game. And if you want to dominate the game, you've got to have a plan.

In this chapter, we'll break down everything you need to think about before investing in your first property. From choosing a strategy to organizing the documents for your first loan, by the time you're finished with this chapter, you'll have a clear vision for your first purchase and be ready to hunt for your first deal.

Choose a Strategy

Have you ever tried to lose weight? Before you started, you probably sought some advice from friends who have successfully dropped some pounds. Unsurprisingly, they probably had different suggestions for developing a diet and different preferences for exercising. They all achieved the same result by losing weight, but they all took different paths to get there.

Real estate investing is similar. If you talk to a dozen different investors, you'll find they each had different paths to success. All of the paths, though, can be traced back to one of the five options we're about to discuss.

So, how do you pick the right one for you? Start by asking yourself these three questions:

1. What are your goals? Consider whether you're seeing cash flow, quick returns, or a hands-off investment.
2. Are you willing to handle property management and repairs, or do you want to be more hands-off?
3. Can you handle the ups and downs of the real estate cycle in your local market and nationally?

Keep these answers in mind as you read through these strategies. We'll look at each of them individually.

Long-Term Rentals

A long-term real estate strategy is pretty simple if you have a little patience. When you use a long-term approach, you buy and hold onto properties for the future, possibly even for decades.

You might hold onto your investment for years, but that doesn't mean you have to wait to realize a return. The key to a long-term strategy is to use your rental properties to grow your overall portfolio. To do this, you need to be able to charge enough for rent to cover your mortgage and expenses with a little left over to pay down, build equity, and roll cash into additional properties.

Are long-term rentals right for you? Here's what you should consider:

- **They typically have lease terms of 12 months or more.** Thanks to these lengthy leases, you can anticipate a reliable income. Since this income is funding your mortgage, you can hold on to these properties for longer periods of time, leaving room for the value to appreciate over time.

- **They require less upfront capital.** You can typically find better terms from a lender for a long-term property. These units also aren't expected to be furnished and, due to lower turnover, require less maintenance between tenants.
- **Longer leases can lead to headaches.** A bad tenant might be difficult to remove from your property. There are fewer chances to increase rent, which means you might lose out on some income while you wait out a 12-month lease.
- **Consider the costs.** You might need to perform updates to make the property renter-friendly as well as maintain the property once people move in. If you're comfortable being a landlord, you can save money on property management fees. Long-term rentals have less turnover than short-term or vacation rentals, which means you might not need a full-time property manager if you're comfortable handling property maintenance tasks yourself as they pop up.

Short-Term Rentals

Finding (or creating) a great vacation rental can mean tons of extra cash in your pocket. These properties can often outearn long-term rental properties. The key is to have a place you can keep fully booked while accepting that you'll have to spend more time preparing the house between visitors.

Both of these options are appealing to real estate investors. Before you decide to pursue short-term rentals, though, here are a few things to think about:

- **There's a lot of earning potential.** Since these properties have tons of turnover, there are plenty of opportunities to raise rent prices to keep up with market changes.
- **You can stay hands-off.** You can hire a property manager, cleaning crew, and maintenance crew to keep your day-to-day involvement in the property at a minimum. Hiring a team increases your expenses but makes this approach more passive, especially if you have enough properties and turnover to justify the cost.
- **Location is crucial.** You need to find the right property in the right vacation spot to see the returns needed to make your bank account soar.

- **They can be unpredictable.** You might end up with more vacancies than expected, especially during the offseason. And unlike with a long-term rental, you need to fill your unit with more customers more regularly instead of just finding one good tenant and watching the rent checks roll in for a year.
- **You need to provide some extras to renters.** These rentals need to be fully furnished. You are also on the hook for more costs than a long-term rental because you'll be responsible for listing fees on sites like Airbnb, utility costs, and extras like Wi-Fi.

Mid-Term Rentals

Mid-term rentals are typically booked for short terms, usually in increments of several months. These furnished properties are often located near a hospital, university, or corporate headquarters. Ideal renters include traveling nurses, students, and consultants who need consistent housing for several weeks or months but won't need a long-term lease.

Some real estate investors begin with short-term rentals and shift to mid-term because there tends to be less turnover and, thus, higher profits.

Mid-term rentals can be very appealing, especially if you are in the right location. Here's what to think about before pursuing this strategy:

- **There's demand for this type of rental.** Remote work is here to stay, which makes mid-term rentals very appealing. Since remote workers can work from anywhere, many travel to desirable locations and live and work there for several months at a time.
- **They're a short-term and long-term hybrid.** If you're undecided between a short-term and long-term strategy, a mid-term rental can offer the best of both worlds. They provide the stability of guaranteed rental income for several months at a time. You can also raise rent several times throughout the year since there is turnover every few months.

- **You won't be able to price these at the top of the market.** Typically, short-term rentals can fetch the highest rent, while long-term rentals garner slightly lower prices because tenants are locked in for a longer period of time. Mid-term rentals place you squarely in the middle of the marketplace.
- **You'll need more tenants.** Shorter lease terms mean more turnover. Platforms like Airbnb and VRBO can help you find renters, but be aware that this approach means you will have to prepare the property for new tenants several times per year.
- **Plan accordingly for additional costs.** You have to furnish the property after purchase since tenants won't be moving their furniture in for a short lease. Costs can also mount because you need to get the property move-in ready several times a year.

House Hacking

When you house hack, you rent out part of your home to other tenants. The rent you collect can go toward paying off your mortgage or additional expenses. House hacking is how I started in real estate, and it can be a great way to get your feet wet when it comes to rentals.

The key to house hacking is to have the right type of property. Duplexes and triplexes are popular house hacking options, as are homes with guest houses or garage apartments. Even purchasing land can be a house-hacking opportunity. A large piece of property can house several RVs or trailer homes.

Trust me when I tell you that house hacking has some serious benefits—and some drawbacks. Before you put a listing on Craigslist, consider the following aspects of house hacking:

- **It's favorable for financing.** Since these properties are considered owner-occupied, it might be easier to obtain financing.
- **It will free up a lot of cash.** If you are able to charge enough to cover your mortgage—and then some—you can roll more of your own money into additional properties. It's the start of your empire.

- **Your tenants will literally be your neighbors.** You will be in close proximity to your renters. If they're good tenants, this should be manageable. If they're not good tenants, it could make for a difficult living arrangement.
- **You'll have to be a hands-on landlord.** Your tenants will have more access to you due to your proximity to them. You also need to act as a legal landlord, which means you are subject to local and state laws.
- **You need to have the right property.** Your property needs to be suitable for renters, which might require some renovations. These preparations might include adding or updating a guest house or apartment, or making upgrades to the other side of a duplex.

BRRR (Buy, Rehab, Rent, Refinance, Repeat)

For this strategy, the process is literally in the name. You buy a property, make improvements, rent it out, complete a cash-out refinance, and then purchase your next property.

A cash-out refinance means you convert your equity into cash as your home loan matures. You gain equity as your home value increases or as you pay down your mortgage principal. Once you've built equity, you can refinance and borrow more than you owe on your house.

Confused? Let's look at a real-life example, step by step:

Step 1: You purchase a home for $250,000.

Step 2: You improve the home and rent it out. After 18 months, you've paid off $50,000.You still owe $200,000, so you decide to do a cash-out refinance.

Step 3: You refinance and add a portion of your equity to your new mortgage principal. In this case, you decide to add $30,000. When your new mortgage closes, you'll receive $30,000 that you can use to purchase your next property.

Ready to reno? Think about these things before you don your hard hat:

- **You need to find the right property at the right price.** In order to make this approach work, you'll need to find a distressed property to rejuvenate. You can often find these properties at a discount.

- **There's more effort involved.** You have to handle the rehabilitation, then bring in renters who will contribute to your cash flow. The good news is that their rent will help you pay down your mortgage quicker so you can move to the refinance phase.
- **Financing can be tricky.** Sometimes, purchasing and rehabbing a distressed property can be an uphill battle. It can be difficult to obtain a mortgage for a highly-distressed property.
- **You need a solid plan for renovations.** You also need to do substantial work to make the property livable and attract renters. You should feel confident you can complete these renovations properly on your own or can afford to hire help.
- **Costs can add up quickly.** Property owners often have to sink additional funds into the property to make the necessary—and likely substantial—renovations. The refinancing process also costs money because the property will need to be reappraised.

Which Strategy Is Right for You?

Now that you know the ins and outs of each strategy, it's time to compare them so you can pick the best option for you. We'll talk more about the numbers you need to know to evaluate a property in chapter 3. But until then, let's take a closer look at the difference between long-term, mid-term, and short-term strategies. For this exercise, we're going to pretend we are looking for a property in Nashville, Tennessee.

I picked Nashville because you could effectively run each strategy in the city. It is a popular spot for relocation, and many companies are moving their headquarters there. It is home to a university and several hospitals, so it could be a good fit for a mid-term strategy. It is also a popular tourist location with plenty of events, so it could be a good fit for a short-term strategy.

First, we will use Rentometer to check rent prices in the area. I used Vanderbilt University as the address since it is located downtown. The average rent within a half-mile radius is $2,794.

I'm also going to do my best to estimate my expenses. The median selling price for a home in Nashville is $433,000, according to Realtor.com. But let's assume that I find an incredible diamond in the rough for a little less than that and plan to pay $385,000 for a property with two bedrooms and one bath.

I now need to calculate my mortgage payment, which I can do using a mortgage calculator. For this example, I'm going to use Rocket Mortgage. Nashville is an expensive market, and I'm a new investor, so I'll have to put down less than 20% for a down payment. If I put down $35,000 and choose a 30-year loan term at 6.5% interest, my mortgage will be $2,212.24 just for principal and interest.

Rocket Mortgage also lets me calculate taxes and insurance using their calculator. My estimated taxes will be $112.29, and my estimated insurance will be $131.54. That brings my total estimated mortgage payment to $2,456.07. Over the course of the year, I can expect to pay $29,472.84.

I also need to determine how much I should save for capital expenditures, like maintenance, repairs, and upgrades to the property. There are different ways to calculate this expense. Generally, you should start by saving 1-2% of the purchase price each year for capital expenditures. For this example, that would be $3,850.

Long-Term Rentals by the Numbers

If I purchase a property in Nashville and sign a tenant to a 12-month lease, I can expect to make $33,528 in rental income. To find my expected overall profit, I have to subtract my estimated expenses for the property.

My estimated expenses for this property are:

- Monthly mortgage payments (including insurance and taxes): $2,456.07
- Annual capital expenditures: $3,850

When I subtract these expenses from my rental income, my annual profit is $205.16.

Mid-Term Rentals by the Numbers

Nashville is a healthcare hub. Let's look at the income I can make if I turn my property into a mid-term rental with three-month contracts to accommodate traveling nurses. I will have the chance to reevaluate my rental price every three months.

I decided to price my unit slightly over the average rent at $2,900 per month. With every new tenant, I can raise the rent. Let's assume I raise it by 3% with each new tenant. Here's what my rental income will look like by month:

January: $2,900
February: $2,900
March: $2,900
April: $2,987
May: $2,987
June $2,987
July: $3,076.61
August: $3,076.61
September: $3,076.61
October: $3,168.91
November: $3,168.91
December: $3,168.91

My total rental income for the year would be $36,397.56. Again, you'd have to consider your expenses to turn over the unit, taxes, repairs, as well as mortgage payments. I will have to turn over the apartment four times in this scenario.

Let's assume the turnover cost is $1,000 for each new tenant. That means my expenses will be:

- Monthly mortgage payments (including insurance and taxes): $2,456.07
- Annual capital expenditures: $3,850
- Annual turnover costs: $4,000

In this scenario, you would lose $925.28 after calculating your expenses. With that said, now's a great time to note that you will run into scenarios where you lose money with a strategy. That doesn't mean you should necessarily abandon that strategy. In this example, I could continue to play around with different down payment amounts, property prices, and lease terms to get a clear picture of my likelihood of success with a mid-term rental in the Nashville area.

Short-Term Rentals by the Numbers

Nashville is a popular tourist location, with visitors flocking from all over the country for bachelorette parties, music festivals, and sporting events. According to AirDNA, the average occupancy rate for a short-term rental is 41%, with a nightly rate of $262.10.

If I turn my property into a short-term rental, let's assume I will have renters for 15 days every month. My average monthly rental income would be $3,931.50 per month, which totals $47,178 per year.

I'll mention one last time that expenses will vary for a short-term rental compared to a long or mid-term property. There will be more turnover, which means more fees and possibly more maintenance costs. I'll also have to pay property taxes and my mortgage. I'll also need to cover monthly utilities, like electricity and WiFi.

Let's assume that between fees and utilities, I need to set aside an extra $400 per month. That brings my expenses to:

- Monthly mortgage payments (including insurance and taxes): $2,456.07
- Annual capital expenditures: $3,850
- Annual utilities: $4,800

After subtracting expenses, I will make $9,055.16. Of course, my expenses don't include a property manager or cleaning fees, the latter of which could fluctuate per month based on the length of the stay. I also didn't account for state or local taxes for these short, mid, or long-term strategies. My tax burden will depend on a variety of factors, including how my business is set up.

As you consider these strategies, run your own analysis based on your location and property prices. We'll look more closely at different property types and how to find the right investment location in the next few sections of this chapter.

Choose a Property Type

Once you've picked an investment strategy to pursue, you'll have to choose what type of property you want to work with. Each property type has its own set of pros and cons. There's no right or wrong answer here. You'll need to weigh your options and pick the one that works best for you right now.

Residential Properties

Where do you sleep at night? Whether you're in a city apartment or a farmhouse in the country, if you call it home, it's likely a residential property.

A residential property is a home inhabited by the owner or tenants. In the rental world, this means you'll have tenants on a lease or rental agreement. These properties are specifically zoned for residential use.

We'll get into the specific aspects of each type of residential property soon. But before we do, let's review some overall pros and cons of residential properties.

One of the biggest advantages of residential rentals is income stability. Your tenants will likely be on lease agreements, so you can count on their income each month. You'll also have an advantage if you've purchased property before because you'll be familiar with the process.

However, it's important to know that residential properties have additional tax rules you'll need to follow. When you rent, you become a landlord, which means additional responsibilities and liabilities. You'll want to consider hiring a property manager or educating yourself on your duties as a landlord.

Let's take a closer look at each of your options for residential properties, including the pros and cons of each.

Single-Family Properties

A single-family home is just that: a home that is occupied by one family. From starter homes to mega-mansions, if it's designed to host a single-family unit, it falls in this category. These property types are appealing to renters because they offer privacy and space.

Single-family rentals can be desirable and lucrative because:

- **They often appreciate in value.** Whether you plan to sell quickly or hold on to the property long-term, they tend to go up in resale value.
- **They can be leased for longer periods of time.** People who rent single-family homes tend to sign longer-term leases. With a longer lease term, you can count on income stability and less tenant turnover.

For some people, single-family rentals aren't the right fit because:

- **They don't come with a lot of land.** Single-family homes often sit on smaller plots of land, especially in newer neighborhoods.
- **Desirable properties might not be in renter-friendly neighborhoods.** Some neighborhoods have limitations on rentals or high homeowners association fees that make renting unfeasible.

Multifamily Properties

A multifamily property can house more than one family at a time. In many cases, these properties are not owner-occupied and are rented out to tenants. Apartments, condominiums, mixed-use properties, retirement homes, and duplexes can all fall under this category. (Inspect, 2023)

Real estate investors choose multifamily properties because:

- **There's a tremendous potential for passive income.** Since you collect rent from multiple tenants, it often makes financial sense to hire a property manager. This makes the investment truly passive on your part.
- **There are substantial financial benefits.** Multifamily properties are eligible for financial advantages like tax benefits and are often well-positioned for discounts on insurance policies.

- **It's easier to weather vacancies.** If you have a 20-unit property and one unit is vacant, it's a manageable setback, not a disaster. If you don't have a renter for your single-family property, your income grinds to a halt.

Despite their perks, multifamily properties typically aren't popular choices for first-time investors. This is often because:

- **They require more of an investment.** Due to their size, these types of properties require a hefty down payment, which can be hard for new investors to pull together. You also need to hire a property manager if you want your investment to be truly passive.
- **There is a lot of competition.** These properties are desirable, so when they come on the market, competition tends to be fierce. Experienced investors will have enough cash on hand to make more desirable offers, making it hard for new investors to break in.

Townhome Properties

Townhomes are becoming increasingly popular, especially for people who want a neighborhood feel at a lower price point. Not convinced? In 2021, the construction of townhomes leaped by 28.1%, according to the National Association of Home Builders.

A townhouse typically shares a wall or two with neighboring properties but has its own entrance. Many also have their own backyards. Townhouses are also becoming more widespread and can be found everywhere, from densely populated cities to suburban communities.

Townhomes are an appealing investment option because:

- **Some renters prefer them.** Townhomes offer personal privacy, backyards, and fewer shared walls, making them more appealing to some renters than a condo or apartment.
- **They are a reliable mid-price rental option.** Townhome rental prices typically hover in the middle of the market. They also tend to recover their value after an economic downturn.

Townhomes still have some limitations. If you're considering investing in a townhome, keep in mind that:

- **They are susceptible to market downturns.** Yes, townhouses will eventually recover their value. But that tends to take time, which might be difficult for investors to stomach.
- **There isn't a lot of opportunity for forced appreciation.** Due to homeowners association guidelines, it's typically difficult to make external modifications to a townhome. There are limits to internal upgrades as well. So, while you likely won't be able to adjust the floor plan, you should be able to make cosmetic changes to key areas like the kitchen or bathroom.

REOs/Foreclosures

Foreclosures are unfortunate, but they can also provide an opportunity for new investors. A foreclosure occurs when the homeowner does not make their mortgage payments and the house is repossessed by the lender. The lender then sells the house to recoup costs.

If a foreclosure is not sold at the right price to cover a loan, it becomes REO, or real estate owned. This means that it is owned by the lender and will often be sold at a deep discount.

A foreclosure can be a great opportunity for a deal because:

- **Lenders want to sell quickly.** The longer a lender holds on to a property, the more money they lose. This usually means you can find excellent deals. If you purchase an REO, you will also not have to worry about outstanding debts on the property.
- **You might not need a loan.** Since these properties are cheap, you might be able to purchase one outright.

Purchasing a foreclosure can be tempting, but there are several potential pitfalls. For instance:

- **What you see is what you get when you purchase an REO.** You'll be responsible for any renovations and major repairs. You can also expect to pay a bit more to get the property in rental shape since they are typically not maintained by the lender.
- **You might inherit something you didn't expect.** If you purchase a multifamily home in foreclosure, you might still have tenants to manage. And while an REO will not have any outstanding debts or liens, a foreclosure might. You'll need to be very careful to ensure debts are cleared so you can take ownership.

Fixer-Uppers

These properties are typically purchased at a below-market price and have, to put it kindly, seen better days. Nonetheless, this type of property could end up being a gem in your real estate portfolio if you're willing to put in the work.

Some of the benefits of a fixer-upper include:

- **You can see a serious return on your investment.** Not only can you purchase the down-and-out property at a lower price, but your renovations could add substantial value to the property. This can help you earn a higher price when the time comes to sell.
- **You have options after the renovations.** Some investors will finish their property revamp and immediately put the house on the market to get a return on their investment. Others will hang on to the property and rent it while it appreciates in value.

A fixer-upper isn't all demos and decor, though. You'll also have to understand that:

- **You're not just getting a house—you're getting a project.** Renovations can be expensive, and you could run into unexpected issues that drive the price up even further.
- **You might have to wait to sell.** Depending on the stage you are at in the real estate cycle, the home—even with all of its

upgrades—might sit on the market for a while. If your goal was a fast flip, this delay could lead to financial problems.

Mobile Home Parks

Due to its unique setup, a mobile home park might be your ticket to a thriving real estate business. A mobile home park is a large piece of land divided into smaller lots for mobile homes. The tenant owns a mobile home and rents the land from the property owner.

In addition to the individual lots, many mobile home parks offer the opportunity for multiple streams of income through laundry facilities, vending machines, and storage units.

Mobile home parks tend to be under-the-radar investment opportunities, but they can be real gems because:

- **They are relatively stable investments.** Since they are an affordable housing option, there tends to be consistent demand for them, regardless of the economic landscape. It's also hard to move a mobile home, so tenants tend to stay put.
- **You split responsibility with the tenant.** While you are responsible for the land in a mobile home park, the tenant is responsible for their home. This joint responsibility creates an incentive for both parties to work together to maintain and improve the park.

Mobile home parks can be lucrative, but they certainly aren't perfect. For example:

- **You have less control.** Since your tenants are responsible for their property, upkeep and maintenance fall on them. If they fail to maintain their property, it can impact your park's overall value.
- **There is less opportunity for appreciation.** Appreciation is usually created through upgrades by the owner.

Commercial Properties

From the office building you trek to every morning for your 9-to-5 job to the coffee shop you frequent for your favorite drink, you spend a lot of time in commercial properties. All of those properties are owned by someone—and that someone could be you down the road.

A commercial property generates profit through rental income or capital gain and typically functions as a business. Tenants are typically businesses that lease space on the property for longer lease periods compared to residential properties.

Commercial properties run the gamut from apartment homes to vacant land. Here's a breakdown of each one, along with benefits and drawbacks:

Apartments

Apartments and other multifamily rentals straddle the line between commercial and residential properties. Though they still serve as residences for people, they generate an income for whoever owns them.

Apartments can be a great commercial property investment because:

- **They provide diverse income streams.** Rent is a huge profit driver, but it doesn't stop there. On-site laundry facilities and parking packages can also generate additional income.
- **You can grow your portfolio quickly.** Since these properties create substantial cash flow, you can bankroll more properties to grow your business.

You'll still have your share of headaches, though. Some of the cons include:

- **More tenants, more problems.** Apartments need regular maintenance, and often, the requests for repairs never stop. Even with a property manager, there will be some oversight required on your part, as well as money to finance the repairs.
- **Delayed gratification.** This approach requires patience. Apartment complex purchases take time to close and, depending on your location and other market conditions, can take longer to sell if you determine they aren't the right fit for you.

Condos

Condos are both individually and collectively owned. In other words, people independently own the individual units but share ownership of the common areas. Typically, a homeowners association manages the common areas. The overall building or complex is usually owned by a builder or group.

Purchasing an individual condo can be a great purchase for new investors because:

- **They are fairly easy to manage.** You are responsible for what happens inside the walls of the condo unit, but everything outside of that falls on the homeowners association.
- **There are lower overall costs.** The price to purchase a condo is typically lower than a single-family home.

Still, a condo can come with its own set of challenges. You'll need to consider that:

- **They tend to appreciate slowly.** Don't expect immediate appreciation from a condo. They tend to climb in value more slowly than their counterparts.
- **You can expect additional fees.** Owners typically pay a monthly fee to the homeowners or condo association to maintain other parts of the property. These fees can be pricey, so plan accordingly.

Retail

A retail space houses businesses like shops and restaurants. These properties can feature one business, like a grocery store, or several, like an outdoor shopping center (Tross, 2023).

If you're thinking about investing in a retail property, keep in mind that:

- **You can charge higher rental prices.** If you have an excellent location, retailers will flock to your property. You can charge accordingly, and you'll earn even more if you can host multiple storefronts in one plaza.

- **The renter has substantial responsibility.** Though you're responsible for maintaining the property, the business owner is responsible for taking care of most of the interior upkeep.

You might experience some of these drawbacks:

- **A lot of capital is needed.** These properties are not cheap. Most commercial properties, retail included, require a substantial upfront investment.
- **There are a lot of leases to manage.** If you own a space with multiple tenants, you'll need to manage multiple leases that might start and end at different times. This will impact your cash flow, so you'll need to be on the ball to make sure you don't end up with multiple vacancies.

Office Space

From skyscrapers to office parks, office buildings—and investment opportunities—are everywhere. These properties are classified into three categories depending on their features.

Class A properties are the most prestigious, featuring upgrades that allow owners to charge above-average rental prices. Class B is the middle tier, with standard finishes and average rent prices. Class C properties are typically for groups that need function over fancy finishes.

These properties are worth considering because:

- **They have longer leases.** Rental agreements for office spaces tend to start at 5-7 years.
- **Your tenants will handle upgrades.** As with retail properties, tenants will often invest in aesthetic upgrades to suit their businesses. In most cases, they are also responsible for furnishing the office space.

Investing in office space also means wading into a rapidly changing real estate market. You should know that:

- **Vacancies can be costly.** In this space, you want to hang on to your tenants, which means building strong relationships.

This requires checking in throughout the terms of the lease.
- **The market is changing post-COVID.** As more companies move to permanent remote work, office vacancies might become more prevalent. You need to have a deep understanding of the demand for office space in your market to make wise investment decisions.

Land

That piece of vacant land you drive past every day might just be the real estate investment you've been waiting for. When you have the right property, land can become a valuable asset you can use to rent or develop. The best part? Land tends to appreciate more quickly than other properties.

Renting

When you own a piece of land, you can rent it to others to use for farming or housing. These types of agreements can benefit both the tenant and the property owner.

Here's what to consider before tying yourself to a land investment:

- **The leases are very long.** Some commercial lease terms can be extremely long—we're talking 50 years or more. Therefore, you can count on a guaranteed steady income.
- **The costs are lower.** If you have a tenant, they will often handle improvements. If you rent your land for hunting or fishing, you'll also incur fewer costs.

Renting land isn't necessarily a straightforward process. Some of the potential drawbacks include:

- **You typically need the help of a professional.** Depending on whom you're leasing to and the terms of the agreement, you might need a lawyer to help with the paperwork.
- **There are laws and regulations to consider.** For example, if you plan to lease the land to a company that will be mining natural resources, you might run into red tape. You'll need to do due diligence to ensure the land can be used as you intend.

Developing

Developing a piece of land means you build a structure on a piece of vacant property. You could build on land yourself by adding a house or commercial space, or flip the land to a developer through an outright sale or a contract-to-purchase.

If you're ready to jump into land development, consider that:

- **A high-growth area is key.** Land is limited, so finding the right piece of property in an area that is experiencing a lot of growth can be very lucrative.
- **You will have multiple options for development.** If the property is large enough, you can subdivide it and flip it to multiple people. You could also sell the entire chunk of land to another developer.

Of course, not all land is zoned for development. That perfect piece of land might not be a good option for development if:

- **It's not zoned for the type of development you have in mind.** You have to determine if the land is zoned for commercial or residential development before making your purchase.

Assemble Your Team

Michael Jordan needed Scottie Pippen. Emmett Smith needed Michael Irvin and Troy Aikman. Greg Maddux needed Tom Glavine and John Smoltz.

In other words, every great victory starts with a great team. If you want to rack up wins in real estate, you need a strong team around you. Here's how to build one.

The Core Team

These are your ride-or-dies. They're the people you'll call on time and time again as you launch your business and guide its growth. Consider this group your starting five.

Your Spouse or Significant Other

My girlfriend (now my wife) was the guiding force behind my real estate journey. She knew the industry and helped answer my questions. Whether your spouse is interested in real estate or not, you'll need their support as you pour your time, energy, and money into new investments.

Mentor

This book is meant to be a blueprint for your business. However, your specific needs and circumstances are unique to you. That's where a mentor comes in. They'll supplement what you learn from this book. Find someone in real estate who is a few steps ahead of you and take them to coffee. Build a relationship with them and don't be afraid to ask them questions. You'll soon find they'll be an invaluable part of your growth.

Investor-Friendly Real Estate Agent

The real estate agent you used to purchase your home might not be the best option as you move into investing. An investor-friendly agent will have a deep knowledge of the real estate investing space and possibly be an investor themselves. They will also have a broad network in your desired market, which will help you access off-market properties and find the best tradesmen to help with renovations.

Lender

Your ideal lender shares many of the same qualifications as your ideal real estate agent. They should know the nuances of real estate investing and the specific types of loans you plan to pursue. Ideally, they'll be able to help you navigate creative financing options, which we'll cover later in this book.

Insurance Agent

You'll need to insure your properties, and that's never cheap. As your portfolio grows, so will your insurance needs. An investor-friendly insurance agent can walk you through various coverage methods that will work for your portfolio, like master policies, layered policies, quote share policies, and loss-limited policies.

You'll also need different types of coverage for different types of properties, like tenant legal liability for a residential property.

Bench Players

There's a reason why the NBA has a Sixth Man of the Year Award. The people on your bench can sometimes be the difference between mediocrity and true excellence. Now that you've assembled your core team, it's time to build your bench. As your portfolio grows, you'll rely on this group more and more.

Contractors

When the plumbing breaks or the roof needs to be repaired, who are you going to call? Hopefully, a trusted contractor. The best time to start searching for a contractor is before you need them, so start compiling your list now. Ask for recommendations and keep their numbers handy so you can move quickly when you need assistance.

Bookkeeper

Rent's coming in, money's going out. Your books can become a massive mess if you aren't diligent. You can DIY this part of your business for a while, but as you grow, look for a bookkeeper with real estate experience to help you keep everything in order.

CPA

Your bookkeeper will handle day-to-day tracking. A certified public accountant (CPA) will handle the big-picture stuff, like your taxes. You won't need a CPA the day you open your business, but be prepared to make this hire once your business starts to grow.

Lawyer

When it comes to real estate, there's a lot more to think about besides just selecting a property. A real estate lawyer will help you navigate the buying and selling process and the leasing laws in your area, and draw up the necessary paperwork to protect your assets.

Property Manager

If you truly want your real estate business to generate passive income, you'll need a property manager to handle day-to-day operations like scheduling repairs and dealing with tenants. Ask for referrals and take your time with this hire since they will represent your business in tenant interactions.

Licensed Property Inspector

A licensed property inspector will physically examine the property from foundation to roof to identify a property's shortcomings and potentially expensive repairs. Whether the seller is willing to mitigate some issues or not, you'll want to know about problems with the foundation, roof, home's structure, water damage and mold, not-up-to-code electrical work, a leaky natural gas furnace, and so on.

Assemble Your Personal Finances

We've spent most of this chapter talking about strategy, and you've probably had a lot of fun dreaming about your first property. Now, it's time for the not-so-fun part: going through your personal finances.

Step 1: Take Financial Inventory

Do you have cash saved, or are you in debt? Does your current job feel stable, or are layoffs looming?

Now's the time to pull up your bank statements, investment accounts, tax returns, and credit card statements to determine your financial health. Tally up your assets and liabilities. Your assets are things that have value, like your primary residence and cash savings. Your liabilities are things like your car loan or debt. You need a clear picture of your financial health before you invest in real estate properties.

Step 2: Set Realistic Goals and Expectations

If you have a poor credit score and little cash savings, you might not be able to start your real estate journey just yet. If you are in excellent financial standing with cash on hand, you might be able to acquire a property or two and get the ball rolling quickly.

After you've finished your financial inventory, set some realistic and attainable goals for yourself. Then, make a plan to reach them as soon as possible.

Step 3: Reduce debt and increase your credit score

If you're seeking an investment property loan, you'll need a credit score of at least 640 to qualify—and possibly 700 or higher if you plan on purchasing a multifamily property. You'll also want to start paying down your debt to give yourself more flexibility and limit your financial responsibilities (Ceizyk, 2023).

Step 4: Save for Your Initial Investment

You'll need money for a down payment, closing fees, and appraisal costs, among other things. Pick a target and start saving. Many landlords try to save at least 15% for a down payment on a rental property.

Once you know how much money you plan to save, look into your financing options. You might learn that your lender can only finance up to a certain amount, and you'll need more money to make up the gap. Plan ahead!

Step 5: Emergency Funds and Risk Management

A rental property is a risk. You could have several months or years when a property is unoccupied, or you might experience a downturn in your real estate market. Before you purchase a property, it is crucial to examine your emergency fund and assess if you have enough to cover the unexpected.

Hopefully, you already have an emergency fund for unexpected events like job loss or medical emergencies. You'll need a similar fund for your real estate ventures.

Here are some recommendations to jumpstart your planning:

- You should have an emergency fund for each property you purchase with enough money to go to cash flow expenses like HVAC repair or vacancies.
- If you plan to renovate an investment property, build an emergency fund of 10% for unexpected expenses.
- If you plan to manage rental properties, your emergency fund should total 15% of your annual combined rent.

Just like in Step 4, pick a savings target and put money aside each month to combat any unexpected emergencies. Trust me—you'll be glad you did.

Prepare to Finance Your Deal

Someday, you'll have a team of people available to help you prepare for and finance your deals. Until then, you're going to have to do it yourself. I'm about to show you how.

Know Your Financing Options and How They Work

Unless you have a couple hundred thousand dollars just sitting around, you'll need financing to fund your real estate purchase. The first step is knowing your financing options.

Cash

If you have enough money to pay for your property in full, you'll be able to make a cash-only offer. This type of offer might give you an edge in a competitive market and provide you with immediate cash flow once you finalize the deal.

However, this locks you into one rental. If you have enough money on hand to make a cash-only offer, you have enough to finance multiple properties and supercharge your growth.

Your other option is cash offer financing. In this scenario, your financing company will make the offer on your desired property and pay for it in cash while you make payments to the financing company.

Conventional Loans

When most people talk about home financing, they are talking about conventional loans. These loans are mortgages, typically on a 15-year or 30-year term. You'll need a down payment and, if you put down less than 20%, private mortgage insurance (PMI) to obtain a conventional loan. Your lender will also consider your credit score and debt-to-income ratio to determine if you qualify.

Conventional loans are typically conforming loans, meaning they meet criteria from the Federal Housing Finance Agency.

Portfolio Loans

Portfolio loans are usually non-conforming conventional loans, meaning they don't meet Federal Housing Finance Agency criteria. When you have a portfolio loan, your lender keeps and services the loan in their own portfolio. These loans are not sold on the secondary market. These types of loans are often used by people who are self-employed or have a low credit score.

A portfolio loan can be an attractive option for borrowers because it can be obtained quickly and for a higher loan amount.

Doing a Traditional Loan? Here's How to Get Approved

To get a traditional loan, you'll need to get preapproved. You can apply for a traditional loan through a bank or lender online or by going to one in person. Applying online will be a quicker process, but going in person will help you build a relationship with your lender, which could be beneficial to you as your business grows.

Gather Your Documents

Grab your laptop and park yourself next to your filing cabinet. It's time to do some paperwork. Here's what you'll need to get preapproved:

- Tax returns from the last two years
- W2s from the last two years
- Pay stubs from the last two months
- Personal financial statements that outline your assets and liabilities
- Bank statements from the last two months
- Descriptions of other properties you own
- Purchase and sale documents for the property you want to purchase, if available

Know Where Your Down Payment and Closing Costs Are Coming From

Are you funding your purchase through your cash savings or a gift? Ideally, you'll have enough saved for your down payment and additional closing costs when you apply for your loan. When you are preapproved for a loan, the lender will put a limit on how long the preapproval will last. Most of the time, a preapproval will have a 90-day limit, so you'll want to seek preapproval when you are actually ready to buy.

What to Do If You Have No Money and Bad Credit

Real estate investing is not just for the rich. There are creative ways to finance your first property, even if you have no money and bad credit. We'll cover some of your options in chapter 4. Until then, develop a savings plan and a plan to improve your credit. Both will help you in the long run.

Partnerships and Investors

If you're eyeing more expensive properties, like a retail space or large multifamily property, it might be hard to come up with enough money to finance the deal. If that's the case, you could find an investor or partner to provide some additional capital.

Develop a business plan and start searching for your ideal partner. Your core team might be able to help you connect with potential investors. Meet them in person and vet them thoroughly before entering into a deal with them.

Takeaways

Whew! There's a lot to think about before making your first real estate purchase. From picking a strategy to seeking financing, there's a lot of preparation involved if you want to knock your first investment out of the park.

Here are a few key takeaways from this chapter to keep in mind as we move forward.

Takeaway #1: Don't Rush the Process

You want to have your ducks in a row strategically and financially before you start pursuing a property. I get it—it can be difficult to slow down when you feel like you were ready to start investing yesterday. Taking the time to develop a strong strategy and think through your purchase will help you in the grand scheme of things.

Takeaway #2: Do Your Homework

From picking a strategy to building a team to deciding on a financing option, it is vital to educate yourself. Great real estate investors are constantly learning and always do their due diligence before making a decision.

Takeaway #3: Pick a Path and Commit

If you decide you want to start your real estate journey by house hacking, focus on house hacking. If you decide you want to own mid-term rentals, focus on mid-term rentals. It can be so easy to pick one strategy, like house hacking and then get distracted by a great deal on a retail property. Remember, you can always pivot later. But for now, pick a strategy, pick a property, pick a location, and dial in. Focus is what will make you the big bucks.

What's Next

You've done the dirty work. Now it's time to have a little bit of fun. With your strategy outline, your team in place, and your preapproval letter in hand, you're ready to start hunting for an incredible deal. In the next chapter, we'll go over how to find and analyze your first deal.

FREE GIFT #6

The Must-Have Property Buying Checklist

This checklist can help you avoid common pitfalls when buying a property so you can avoid ugly investing horror stories!

To access this free bonus, head to https://readstreetpress.com/iwantpermanentpto6 in your internet browser or scan the QR code below and I'll send it to you right away!

3

HOW TO FIND AMAZING DEALS NO ONE ELSE CAN

"Every person who invests in well-selected real estate in a growing section of a prosperous community adopts the surest and safest method of becoming independent, for real estate is the basis of wealth."

— *THEODORE ROOSEVELT*

You're driving through a new neighborhood, and suddenly, it happens. Your eyes land on the duplex you thought only existed in your dreams. It needs a little TLC, but it's not in total disrepair. It's fifteen minutes from the nearest hospital and five minutes from a grocery store. And it's for sale. The clouds part. The sun lands on the duplex roof like a spotlight. You swear you hear the angels sing.

Then you wake up.

Chances are, you are not going to stumble upon your ideal investment property by accident. It's going to take some elbow grease, a bit of research, and a well-maintained network to find an amazing deal.

But it's not impossible. In this chapter, I'll show you everything you need to know to not only find an incredible deal, but analyze it so you can be sure you're not wasting your hard-earned money.

Let the hunt begin!

The Four Phases of the Real Estate Cycle

"This too shall pass."

You've heard this saying before, probably more times than you can count. And although it wasn't originally uttered about real estate, it's especially applicable to property investing.

The real estate market is cyclical. A good real estate investor—that will be you!—will understand the nuances of the real estate cycle, know how to identify the different phases, and adjust their strategies accordingly.

The length of a real estate cycle fluctuates, but on average, each one spans about 18 years.

This isn't guesswork, either. Homer Hoyt, who pioneered real estate market analysis and eventually became the chief economist of the Federal Housing Association, first identified the cycle in 1933 after studying land values in Chicago. The cycle is still widely used by investors today to guide their decision-making. The key word here is "average." Hoyt's cycle is a good guideline, but some cycles last much longer than 18 years. Others will be shorter.

In other words, don't pull out your calendar and start marking the arrival and departure of each phase of the cycle just yet. You won't be able to identify which phase we're currently in by looking at your calendar or even browsing Zillow. The real estate cycle is closely connected to other parts of the global and national economy. Global events can cause ripple effects in the real estate industry, which we saw firsthand during the COVID-19 pandemic. Outside factors like inflation, unemployment, and interest rates can impact the real estate cycle, as can shifting demographics. For example, a large business moving its headquarters to a new city could lead to a new phase of the real estate cycle in that housing market. An extreme event like COVID-19 can cause further turmoil.

Regardless of how long each real estate cycle lasts, they will still include four distinct phases: recovery, expansion, hyper-supply, and recession. Let's look at them one by one.

Recovery

In many cases, this phase begins while a region or even the whole country is still in the midst of a recession, and many people are still feeling the pain of tightening their purse strings. Different areas of the country may be experiencing downturns while others are thriving; this dynamic can change constantly. To the average eye, it looks like nothing is happening because new construction is at a standstill. Although it's a difficult time for many people in a region that's struggling economically, it can be an opportunity for investors.

How to identify the recovery phase: You'll start to notice declining vacancies in the market and see an uptick in people looking for new leases. You might also notice a few more foreclosures on the market.

Your strategy: In the recovery stage, vigilance is key. The signs of recovery are often subtle, so good real estate inventors need to be observant and act quickly when opportunities arise. This is the time to pursue below-market value properties and put in some elbow grease into making them rental gems. To make the most of this phase, you'll want to be in a financial position to act quickly on opportunities and wait out the rest of the recovery phase.

Expansion

You know that feeling you get during those first few glorious days of spring when the sun starts to shine a little brighter and the air feels a little warmer? That's the expansion phase of the real estate cycle. In this phase, people are becoming more confident in the economy. They're finding jobs and seeing a little more cash in their pocket. They feel better about making big purchases and might be ready to move.

During this phase, supply has not caught up to housing demand. Instead, there are fewer units available, which drives rent and housing prices up until new inventory comes on the market.

How to identify the expansion phase: You'll start to notice unemployment decreasing. You'll see construction companies break ground on new construction. You might also hear people grumbling about inflation or read a news story about rising interest rates.

Your strategy: Give the market what it wants. Now's the time to update existing properties or pursue new investments that align with people's tastes. With the right upgrades, you can often sell properties above market value to buyers looking for updated homes. In other words, now's the time to invest and upgrade.

The other part of the strategy—and the mark of a great real estate investor—is to stay calm. During this phase, people tend to panic-buy, especially as banks adjust lending requirements and people fear they're about to miss out on a real estate peak. Falling victim to panic leads to mistakes, so you'll need to be vigilant to avoid the panic trap.

Hyper-Supply

The expansion phase leads to heightened demand for housing. Businesses scurry to meet that demand, which leads to a frenzy of investors and developers rushing to increase the housing supply. Inevitably, the market reaches a tipping point, and housing supply begins to exceed demand. Sometimes, this is entirely due to too much inventory. In other instances, an outside factor like a sudden economic shift can lead to a pullback. When that happens, we've entered the hyper-supply phase.

How to identify the hyper-supply phase: You'll notice an uptick in vacancies even as construction continues at a high volume. You'll see properties remain on the market longer, often accompanied by rapid price reductions. Unemployment might rise, and the Federal Reserve might announce lowered interest rates.

Your strategy: It's easy to panic when the hyper-supply phase sets in. Panicked property owners tend to make poor decisions, like liquidating assets if they are vacant. Instead, it's best to hold strong. If you have some extra capital, buying and holding property can also be an effective strategy to survive the hyper-supply phase.

Recession

If you're in the real estate game long enough, you will experience a recession. It's a natural part of the real estate cycle. During a recession, housing supply far exceeds demand. Property owners often have their properties vacant, or they significantly decrease rental rates to accommodate the economic downturn.

How to identify the recession phase: Remember all that ongoing construction in the hyper-supply phase? That comes to an end. Since inventory now far exceeds demand, rental rates begin to drop as housing prices stabilize.

Your strategy: The best time to prepare for a recession is before it happens. You should have a rainy day fund for scenarios like this. Recessions can also be a prime opportunity to expand your portfolio if you can. Keep an eye out for foreclosures that you can purchase and hold on to until the recession passes.

Choose a Location

You've picked an investment strategy and property type. Now the real work begins.

In many cases, the success of your real estate business will come down to location. You could find the best deal on the best property for your chosen strategy, but if the property isn't in the right location, you'll struggle to see the return on your investment that you wanted. Keep in mind the phase that your intended geographical location is in. You may wish to consider a different location to invest in if yours currently doesn't present the ideal conditions.

That's why the best real estate investors spend a lot of time learning how to evaluate a property's location and conduct plenty of due diligence prior to making a purchase.

Local or Long-Distance

Do you want to be within driving distance of your properties, or are you willing to pursue properties in other towns or states to meet your goals? Buying locally is often a good start for first-time investors because you know the area and will be able to manage the property in person. You'll also save money since many lenders consider out-of-state properties to be higher risk.

Of course, this all depends on where you live. Some real estate markets are better than others, so you'll have to run the numbers to see if purchasing out-of-state is worth the effort. Include things like taxes and insurance rates in your calculations.

Neighborhood Demographics

When it comes to real estate, the neighborhood matters. Think carefully about who your ideal renters will be. A young, newly married couple might be willing to pay top dollar for a townhouse if it's in a desirable, walkable downtown neighborhood. A family with young children might be desperate to move into a suburban neighborhood with lush parks and a nearby school.

As you research a property, look at statistics for the neighborhood, like home values and median income levels. This data will help you determine if your purchase will net the rental price you desire.

Job and Unemployment Rates

Can your ideal renter afford to lease your property? Monitoring job and unemployment rates can help you find a property that is in a thriving area. The Bureau of Labor Statistics offers monthly job reports that will help you track changes in median annual wage and overall employment levels.

Population Growth

A growing city means more potential renters for your property, whether your property is a single-family home or a retail space. Population growth will help you understand what type of demand there might be for your property. Before you purchase a property, calculate the population growth of your area.

Let's say you wanted to calculate population growth for your city over the last three years. Start by determining how many people lived in the city three years ago and how many live there now. Subtract the initial population from the current population and divide it by the initial population. Then multiply that number by 100. You'll end up with a percentage for the population growth over the last three years. Divide that number by three to determine the average growth rate per year.

Proximity to Businesses and Amenities

No one likes a long commute. Consider how far your potential property is from local amenities and high-traffic business areas. For example, determine how far your investment will be from the nearest grocery store or the entrance ramp to the freeway. For instance, a mid-term rental near a hospital will be very desirable for traveling nurses. A home 30 minutes away will be less desirable.

School Districts

If you will be renting to families, the quality of the school district your property is zoned for is incredibly important. In 2023, 30% of buyers between the ages of 33 and 42 considered the school district to be the top factor for choosing their home, according to the National Association of Realtors Home Buyers and Sellers Generational Trend Report. In other words, a good school district allows you to charge premium rental prices.

Use resources like Great Schools or Public School Review to research the quality of the schools in your area. If you are purchasing property locally, check with your network to get their feedback on schools in your area, especially if they have children.

Price-to-Rent Ratio

The price-to-rent ratio compares home prices to annualized rent. To calculate it, divide the median home price by the median annual rent. This calculation will help you determine whether the property you are considering is overpriced or not. It will also tell you whether people are more likely to buy or rent.

Trulia offers some recommendations for evaluating the ratio:

Ratio of 1-15: Buying is more favorable
Ratio of 16-20: Renting is typically more favorable
Ratio of 21+: Renting is more favorable

Property Tax and Insurance Rates

Property tax and insurance rates fluctuate based on where your property is located. To calculate property tax, multiply your property's assessed value by the local tax rate. You might also want to seek quotes for insurance. A property in a neighborhood that is prone to vandalism or weather events might mean you'll pay a higher insurance premium.

Vacancy Rates

A city's vacancy rate tells you how many units are currently occupied. If you are purchasing a multifamily property, you will want to determine the vacancy rate for that particular property. You might also want to determine the vacancy rate for neighboring properties and the city where the property is located.

A real estate agency or other landlords can help you determine the vacancy rate for your area. You can also check the U.S. Census.

Find the Deal

Real estate investors don't stumble onto great deals. They seek them out—or, in some cases, create them. You can have the same results, even if you don't have years of real estate experience.

Here's the biggest secret I can give you if you want to find a superb deal: know what you're looking for and know where to look.

Here's how.

Create Your Buy Box

You need to know what you're looking for before you even think about searching for a property. To do this, you need to create your buy box. Your buy box is essentially a list of criteria for your property.

Let's walk through an example together. I want my next property to be a long-term multifamily rental in Wisconsin. Here's a peek at my buy box.

Location	Green Bay, Wisconsin
Property Type	Duplex
Price Range	$200,000 - $250,000
Investment Strategy	Long-term rental
Property Size	Two units

I'll use this buy box to evaluate every property I encounter. A property should meet all this criteria to be considered a serious investment option.

Call Your Investor-Friendly Real Estate Agent

In chapter 2, we covered why it's crucial to have a real estate agent with investing experience. They will understand why you have the criteria you have for your purchase and adhere to your criteria when they present you with properties. Your agent will also have the latest information on houses about to come on the market and be able to offer guidance that will help you find the best deal.

Search for Off-Market Deals

Your ideal property might never make it online. Approximately 11% of home transactions are completed without ever listing the property, according to the 2021 Home Buyer and Seller Generational Trends Report from the National Association of Realtors.

An off-market property is not listed in the Multiple Listing Service (MLS) database. These properties are often off-market because sellers want to list the property privately or it is in foreclosure with tenants. Your realtor and your own network are your best bets for hearing about off-market listings in time to make a bid.

Launch a Direct Mail Campaign

Launching a direct mail campaign is cheap and easy, making it a popular approach for new investors looking for their first real estate deal.

A direct mail campaign is pretty simple: you send letters or postcards directly to homeowners that outline your interest in buying their property. You can target specific neighborhoods or types of properties for your first campaign. Generate printed mailers or write a handwritten note targeting your potential seller's pain points, drop it in the mailbox, and wait.

Check Eviction and Foreclosure Records

You'll have to do some digging to find this information, but it might result in the perfect investment property. You can use a website like foreclosure.com to search for pre-foreclosure properties in your area. When you find one that meets your criteria, you can reach out to the property owner and negotiate a deal.

Reach Out to Wholesalers

A real estate wholesaler is essentially a middleman between a buyer and a seller. They purchase a property from the seller and find a buyer to purchase the home at a higher price.

For example, let's pretend a wholesaler in your area finds a distressed property and purchases it from the owner for a discounted price of $150,000. He sells it to an investor for $165,000 and pockets the difference while the buyer fixes up the property.

Drive for Dollars

The last way to find great real estate deals involves some good, old-fashioned shoe leather. Or, in this day and age, fuel for your car.

This approach is pretty self-explanatory. Using the criteria in your buy box, you pick neighborhoods or areas to explore, hop in your car, and drive around looking for deals. You might find a property for sale or locate the address of a vacant property so you can send a letter directly to the owner.

Analyze the Deal

After weeks of searching, you've finally found it: the property that will help make you rich. It's a great duplex that hits every single criterion in your buy box.

It's perfect. But is it a good deal? A property can look like an excellent investment when you're standing in its front yard. It can look like a disaster once you pull out your calculator and start running some numbers.

It is absolutely critical to analyze every aspect of the property and potential deal before moving forward with a purchase. I cannot stress this enough. You might feel pressure to snap up a property immediately. Don't give in to this impulse. Instead, walk through the process I am about to show you to fully analyze the deal.

Research the Location and Comparables from Other Properties

In chapter 2, we went over some of the factors to consider when you are analyzing a potential real estate market. Now that you have a specific property in mind, we're going to review those factors again. Remember, this analysis includes things like school districts, proximity to businesses and amenities, and specific fees like taxes and homeowners association fees.

In addition, you'll want to consider the neighborhood. Is it growing? Are there plans for expansion or additional amenities?

Furthermore, you'll want to research comparables (or "comps") from other properties. To do this, you need to find several on-the-market or recently sold properties that are similar to the property you are considering.

You'll refine your process for searching for comps over time, but here's the typical workflow:

- **List your home's specifications:** A comp does not have to be a direct replica of your property, but it should be similar to the property in terms of location, condition, property style, property age, square footage, number of bedrooms and bathrooms, and renovations.
- **Conduct an online search for similar properties:** Use the search feature on a site like Zillow or have your real estate agent search the local MLS for similar properties. Do not limit your search to properties that are still on the market. You should look at properties sold within the last six months.
- **Identify your comps:** You might find a bunch of properties that fit your criteria or just a few. Keep your list to four to six properties and make sure they are as close to your potential property as possible.
- **Hit the road:** Drive past the properties to get a feel for their curb appeal and identify anything an online listing might not show, like excessive road noise or nearby construction.
- **Calculate your property's market value:** Use these comps to identify your potential property's market value. You can average the sales price of the homes. You can also calculate the average price per square foot of your comps, multiply that number by the square footage of your property, and use that calculation to understand your property's market value.

Know and Run the Numbers

After you've looked at comps and researched your property's location, it's time to run some numbers.

For this section, we're going to imagine we've found the perfect long-term rental in an up-and-coming Green Bay neighborhood. It's a four-bedroom, two-bath home near breweries, shops, and hiking trails. It's the perfect rental for a young family new to the area and wanting to explore before purchasing a home, or for a group of young professionals willing to live with roommates.

This home is priced at $165,000. You can put down $20,000, and your mortgage will be $972 per month without property taxes and insurance. With the property taxes and insurance, you are paying $1,306 per month. Now that you're armed with this info, it's time to pull out your calculator.

How to Analyze a Deal and What Questions to Ask

The calculations we are about to make require some additional information and numbers. You need to ask yourself things like:

How much can I charge each month for rent?

Look at rental prices in the surrounding area and for similar properties to estimate this number. For our sample property, we'll be able to charge at the higher end of the market because there aren't many houses of that size available. We expect to earn $2,500 per month.

How much will it cost to maintain the property?

In other words, what are your operating costs? These costs can include things like property management fees, repairs, and maintenance. They also include marketing and advertising to generate interest in the property. They do not include your mortgage payment or capital expenditures. Many investors estimate that operating expenses will total half of the annual rental income.

In this case, we are going to manage the property ourselves. We plan to advertise the property in a few Facebook groups, so costs will be low. Let's assume that for this property, our annual operating expenses are 50% of the rental income annually, so around $15,000.

How much will it cost to make the property rentable?

If you need to do a major renovation or upgrade, consider those costs as you analyze your deal.

Numbers to Know

These numbers are not difficult to calculate, but they are vital to understanding whether you are truly getting a good deal.

Here are nine numbers you need to know before purchasing a property:

Net Operating Income (NOI)

NOI = Gross operating income - operating expenses

When you know your net operating income, you can better assess how much money a property will generate, which helps you determine the overall value. This number is also needed to make some of the other calculations in this section.

How to Calculate NOI

Your gross operating income is all of the income you expect your property to generate over the course of the year, including rent, parking fees, and fees from any amenities you might have on the property. In our example, we are just collecting rent from tenants. Your operating expenses are what were outlined in the previous section: property taxes, maintenance, advertising, and so on.

See NOI in Action

In our example, we are just collecting rent from tenants. Here are the numbers:

- Annual operating income: $30,000
- Annual operating expenses: $15,000
- $30,000 - $15,000 = $15,000 NOI

Cash Flow Before Taxes (CFBT)

CFBT = NOI - Debt Service - Capital Expenses + Loan Additions

Before you make a purchase, you need to make sure you will receive the desired return on your investment. This calculation takes your debt into account.

How to Calculate CFBT

We've already calculated your NOI. Your debt service is the amount you will pay on your mortgage over the course of the year. Your capital expenses are potential expenditures like a new air conditioner or other improvements. Loan additions are any money from a nonmortgage loan, like one you take out to improve the property. A loan addition can also be interest from the property, if applicable.

See CFBT in Action

To establish our CFBT, we need to use our NOI and debt service numbers. Here are the numbers:

- NOI: $15,000
- Monthly debt service (just principal and interest): $972/month
- Annual debt service: $11,664
- Capital expenditures: $1,000
- Interest on property: None
- $15,000 - $11,664 - $1,000 + 0 = $2,336 CFBT

Cash Flow After Taxes (CFAT)

CFAT = Cash flow before taxes - income tax

You need to pay taxes on your income, and rental property is no different. Income tax varies by state, so you'll need to know how your state operates in order to calculate this number.

How to Calculate (CFAT)

Research the income tax rate in your state or talk with an accountant. Take into account your tax bracket and other factors your state incorporates. Then, determine how much income tax you will pay on the rental income you will make from the property.

See CFAT in Action

Our example property is in Wisconsin, which has a state income tax rate ranging from 3.5% to 7.65%. Most people in Wisconsin pay 5.3%.

Here are the numbers:

- CFBT: $2,336
- Income tax: $795
- $2,336 - $795 = $1,541

Return on Investment (ROI)

ROI = (Ending value - starting value)/(Starting value)

You don't want to lose money on your purchase. ROI is a percentage that helps determine if your investment generates profit efficiently.

How to Calculate ROI

To calculate ROI, you have to establish two values: the starting value and the ending value. The starting value is your initial costs, like your down payment, closing costs, and any out-of-pocket expenses. The ending value is your annual income from the property, which you determine by subtracting your mortgage payment from your rental income.

See ROI in Action

We have to start by calculating our starting value and ending value. Here are the numbers:

- Down payment: $20,000
- Closing costs: $2,500
- Out-of-pocket expenses: $3,000
- $20,000 + $2,500 + $3,000 = $25,500

Our starting value is $25,500.

Now, we need to calculate the ending value. Here's the breakdown:

- Monthly rent: $2,500
- Monthly mortgage payment, including taxes: $1,306
- Monthly return: $1,194
- Annual return: $14,328

To calculate the ROI, we need to subtract the starting value from the ending value and divide it by the starting value. That brings our ROI to 42%.

Annualized ROI

Annualized ROI = ROI/years held

You probably won't hold on to this property forever. By calculating annualized ROI, you can determine how much to expect on average each year.

How to Calculate Annualized ROI

If you plan to sell the property, it's helpful to know the annualized ROI you can expect. To get this number, divide the ROI you just calculated by the number of years you plan to hold the property. Try this formula a few times with different values for the number of years held.

See Annualized ROI in Action

Let's assume we plan to hang on to this property for five years before selling it. Here's how we'd calculate the annualized ROI:

- ROI: 42%
- Years held: 5
- Annualized ROI: 8%

Capitalization Rate (cap rate = NOI/value)

Capitalization rate is an effective way to compare the potential return for different properties. It helps you assess the risk of purchasing a property. Keep in mind, though, that capitalization rate uses the total value of your property. If you aren't going to pay for the property in cash, it might not be the best comparison tool.

How to Calculate Capitalization Rate

To determine the capitalization rate of a property, divide NOI by the purchase price of the property.

See Capitalization Rate in Action

Even though we're going to use a mortgage to finance our imaginary property purchase, it's still worthwhile to calculate the capitalization rate. Here's the breakdown:

- NOI: $15,000
- Value: $165,000
- Capitalization Rate: 9%

Cash-on-Cash Return (CoC)

CoC = Annual cash flow/cash invested

Cash-on-cash return is a ratio that measures how your cash flow compares to the amount you've invested in a property.

How to Calculate CoC

For this calculation, you need to divide your annual cash flow by the amount you've invested. The amount you've invested includes your down payment, closing costs, and additional fees. Your annual cash flow, as always, is your revenue minus expenses.

See CoC in Action

This number is fairly simple to calculate, especially since we've already established both values.

Here's how it works:

- Annual cash flow: $15,000
- Value: $25,500
- CoC: 58%

Average Annual Return (ARR)

ARR = (ROI1+ROI2+ROI3)/years held

Your average annual return will require a little bit of guesswork. Earlier in this section, we determined our ROI for one year. If we plan to hold this property for five years, the ROI will change annually. If we can increase the rent and lower our expenses, we might have a higher ROI. If we face a downturn in the real estate market and have some costly repairs pop up on the property, we might see a lower ROI.

How to Calculate ARR

To calculate your ARR, estimate how much your ROI will change over the time period you own the property. Try to do a couple of versions of this calculation with varying ROI values and years held.

See ARR in Action

Let's assume our ROI increases by one percentage point every year for five years. Here's how we'd calculate ARR:

- ROI for year 1: 42%
- ROI for year 2: 43%
- ROI for year 3: 44%
- ROI for year 4: 45%
- ROI for year 5: 46%
- Years held: 5
- ARR: 44%

Internal Rate of Return (IRR)

IRR = (future value/present value)^(1/Number of Time Periods) - 1

The internal rate of return is just that: internal. It's a way to estimate how much your property will earn while you own it.

How to Calculate IRR

Most investors do not calculate IRR manually. You can use the IRR function in Excel or a similar program to calculate it.

What to Consider When Analyzing a Short-Term, Mid-Term, or Vacation Rental

We just walked through the numbers for a long-term rental. If you are planning to invest in a short-term, mid-term, or vacation rental, you will need to consider some additional costs.

- Since you aren't locking tenants into a long lease, you'll need to consider seasonality and demand for your property. Will you be able to keep it occupied all year, or will your income severely dip during the off-season?
- You'll also need to invest in more marketing or advertising or use a service like Airbnb to bring renters in. This adds an additional cost, like listing fees.
- Your expenses will be higher because you will have to turn over the unit more often and pay for utilities.

These factors shouldn't deter you from investing in a short-term, mid-term, or vacation rental. You'll just need to add these numbers to your calculations so you can accurately assess the property you are considering to ensure it is actually a good deal.

Paying in Cash vs. Getting a Loan

Some investors swear by paying in cash for properties. Others prefer to use other people's money and build their empires through bank loans. The route you choose will impact your analysis of the property.

Getting a loan is often the route of choice for first-time and seasoned investors alike. It requires less capital to make your first purchase and allows you to grow quickly. As your first property generates cash flow, you can roll that extra money into down payments for additional properties, allowing you to build your portfolio rapidly.

When you use a loan to purchase a property, you have to be ready for the potential downsides. If you choose the wrong property—or worse, properties—you could see its value depreciate sharply. And if you're depending on rental income to cover mortgages, any sustained vacancies can wreak havoc on your finances.

Some investors choose to pay in cash for real estate, which can be a useful strategy if you have enough cash on hand. Paying in cash means you won't have a mortgage, so all that extra rental income can go right into your pocket or be invested elsewhere.

Purchasing a property with cash also means you can move quickly when investment opportunities arise since you won't have to work with a lender to secure a loan. In extremely competitive markets, this type of speed is very helpful.

However, this approach will decrease your tax benefits and limit your buying power. Since you aren't using leverage to acquire more properties, your real estate venture will take longer to grow.

Compare Findings to Your Buy Box

Remember the buy box you created at the beginning of this chapter? It's time to revisit it. By now, you should have several properties you are considering for your investment and a list of all the numbers, like NOI, for each property.

Based on your calculations, which properties meet the criteria in your buy box and provide a return you are comfortable with? Remember, the goal is to build a sustainable real estate empire. You don't want to feel financially crushed by your first investment.

Consider Cash Flow and Appreciation

As you assess your potential investment, it's crucial to consider cash flow and appreciation. There are several ways to determine whether a property will provide good cash flow or not. Many real estate investors aim to have a cash flow that totals 10% of the purchase price each year. If cash flow is higher than that, even better!

You also want to estimate the appreciation. Can you make upgrades over time that lead to forced appreciation? Are there market indicators that lead you to believe the property will experience natural appreciation? Also, consider how long you plan to hold onto the property.

Rule of Thumb and Other Useful Formulas

Experienced investors tend to have some general principles or rules of thumb they follow to analyze a deal. I will give you a quick overview of some now to put you ahead of the game. Use what feels right to you and the property you're considering:

- **The 1% Rule:** With this rule, you aim to have the monthly rent on your property exceed 1% of the purchase price. Investors use this rule of thumb for lower-priced rental properties.
- **Debt Coverage Ratio (DCR):** This ratio is calculated by dividing a property's estimated NOI by the annual debt. You want to aim for a DCR of 1.3 or higher because that means you'll have enough money to cover your mortgage payments each month and still generate cash flow.
- **Loan-to-Value (LTV):** An LTV compares the amount of your mortgage to the appraised value of the property. A high LTV can be risky, so many investors try to build equity in their properties quickly.

Why You Need to Visit a Property Before You Buy

Have you ever sold a house? If you have, this process will seem familiar. Before the photographer arrives, you go on a cleaning frenzy, making sure every speck of dust is swept and every counter crumb is wiped. You pull down all your photos from the wall and pack up your favorite tchotchkes and knickknacks. After all, you want the potential buyers to picture themselves in your house, not you.

You might also do a few surface-level repairs, patch some holes in the wall, and deep-clean the carpets. You break a sweat mowing your lawn, planting a few extra flowers, and giving your mailbox an extra coat of paint.

When the listing is posted, the photos look great. But they don't mention that creaky floorboard on the stairs or the railroad tracks just down the road, or show the neighbor's completely unkempt lawn.

In other words, a picture might be worth a thousand words, but driving to the property and looking at it for yourself is worth a million.

It is vital that you get in your car and physically see the property you are considering purchasing. Look at the condition of the interior and exterior of the home for yourself. Drive through the neighborhood at different times of the day to get a feel for the noise and traffic levels. While you're at it, swing by your comparable properties and be honest about your potential investment comps. Is your property in a better neighborhood? Is it on a noisy street? Does it look like the side gutters are hanging on for dear life?

Your eyes will tell you things that an online listing cannot. Look at properties for yourself and be honest about their actual value. Just because a property is cheap doesn't mean it's a good investment.

How to Identify Common Red Flags

Over time, you will learn how to spot red flags in property listings and on-site more easily. As you learn more about property repair and maintenance, you'll be able to spot costly repairs and shoddy workmanship instantly.

Until then, I'm here to help you spot some common red flags. Here's what I tend to look for:

- **Slow sellers:** This largely depends on your real estate market. If homes in your area are selling within a week and this one has been on the market for six months, be cautious. Ask yourself (and your realtor) why it's taken so long for the property to sell.
- **Quick flips:** If a home was purchased and put back on the market within a few months, it was likely flipped. Some investors are excellent at flipping houses and do solid work. Others take shortcuts, so you'll want to be wary and ask plenty of questions about the renovations done.
- **Water damage:** Water damage often leaves wet spots or yellow spots on walls and ceilings. Keep your eyes peeled for this type of damage when you tour a home. Mold mitigation, whether the seller is responsible for it or you are (in an as-is property—see below), may be necessary to protect the health of your tenants, preserve your property value, and even prevent lawsuits.
- **As-is listings:** If you purchase an as-is listing, you are responsible for every repair that pops up—and they could be major. Sellers are not obligated to tell you about some issues with an as-is property.
- **Roof condition:** You'll be able to see the condition of the roof from the road. Does it look old and neglected? Are shingles missing? Roofs are expensive, so you'll want to know what you're getting yourself into if you purchase that property.

Takeaways

Your first real estate investment is a big deal, and it can be really intimidating to make your first purchase. I had my share of sleepless nights when I purchased my first property, wondering if I was making the right call or setting myself up for a financial loss. I don't want you to feel that way, which is why I'm sharing my best tips in this book.

Here are a few key takeaways from this chapter before we talk more about financing:

Takeaway #1: Have a Vision

Your buy box is your vision for your investment. It is a crucial first step on your investing journey, so don't skip it. Have a clear idea of what you are looking for. It will help you eliminate bad fits quickly so you can spend more time on worthwhile properties.

Takeaway #2: Be Objective

Before you invest in a property, run the numbers. Use the formulas from earlier in this chapter to determine if the property is a good investment. Make a vow to yourself that these numbers—not your desires—will dictate your purchase. It can be so easy to fall in love with the property, realize the numbers don't work, and try everything in your power to manipulate the math so you can purchase it. Numbers do not lie. Use data, not dreams, to make your decision.

Takeaway #3: Do the Legwork

Literally—get in your car and drive around looking for gems. Walk the neighborhoods you love. Get on your hands and knees during a real estate tour and inspect the home. You will not find great deals from your couch. Get out in the world and hunt. This is the best part!

What's Next

You've created your buy box. You've found the property. You've analyzed the deal backward and forward. The answer is clear: this is it. This is the one. This is the property that will jumpstart your real estate portfolio and help you build the life you've always wanted.

It's time to make a deal. In the next chapter, we'll go over how to craft and close a real estate deal. Those house keys will be yours in no time!

4

HOW TO BUY ANY DEAL YOU WANT WITH TOTAL CONFIDENCE EVEN IF YOU HAVE NO MONEY AND BAD CREDIT

"I would give a thousand furlongs of sea for an acre of barren ground."

— *SHAKESPEARE*

You can picture it now. You have that first rental check in your hand. It's going to cover your mortgage and then some. Your first rental property is fully booked, and the money is finally coming in. In a few months, you'll have enough money to buy your second property, then your third, then your fourth.

It's a beautiful vision, isn't it? There's just one small problem.

Minor, really.

Miniscule, when you think about it.

You have no money. And you also have pretty bad credit, thanks to a few years when you were a little too swipe-happy with your credit card.

Alright, so maybe the problem is not so miniscule.

But all is not lost. There are plenty of ways to purchase property without an astronomical credit score and a huge down payment.

In this chapter, I'll show you your financing options, including a few creative ways to get financing without having your finances in tip-top shape. After that, we'll go over every single aspect of closing your first real estate deal, from submitting and negotiating an offer to doing due diligence to closing the deal.

You're going to hear the jingle-jangle of your new house keys in no time.

Financing Options

Many people dream of investing in real estate. Few take the plunge. Often, that's due to finances. They think they don't have enough money for a down payment or the capacity to take on a loan. Or, they think their poor credit score will prevent them from getting any type of loan.

That's not the case. There are plenty of financing options for new investors and people who are trying to obtain their second or third property. These financing options fall into two categories: traditional and creative. Let's look at both of them right now.

Traditional Financing

You do not need a 20% down payment to buy a home. In fact, you can obtain a conventional loan with just a 3% down payment.

But before we jump into the requirements for a traditional loan, let's go over the basics. A traditional or conventional loan is not backed by the government, but most of them conform to guidelines set by Fannie Mae and Freddie Mac.

These types of loans are the ones your parents and grandparents used to purchase their homes. The requirements usually include:

- A minimum credit score of 620
- A down payment of at least 3%
- A debt-to-income ratio below 43%
- Good credit history
- Proof of employment and income

If you meet these requirements, you should be able to obtain a conventional loan.

Creative Financing

If you have a bad credit score and little savings, you won't qualify for a traditional loan. Instead, you'll have to get creative. There are some unique ways to purchase property without obtaining a mortgage or a traditional loan. We're going to talk about five of them now.

Seller Financing

When you purchase a property through seller financing, you pay the seller of the property instead of the bank. The agreement is usually similar to a mortgage, but it eliminates the bank or lender. If your mortgage is issued to you from the seller, it is a purchase-money mortgage. These types of deals generally do not require a down payment or, in some cases, a credit check.

These types of agreements come in many forms, including:

- **Assumable mortgages:** This type of financing lets the buyer take over the seller's existing mortgage, which can sometimes carry lower interest rates.
- **Holding mortgages:** In this agreement, the seller provides the loan and holds onto the property title until the buyer pays for the property.

Seller financing can be a great option for people who want more flexible terms and lower closing costs. It's important, though, to use a professional to help negotiate this type of agreement since there are fewer protections for buyers.

Lease Options and Rent-to-Own Agreements

A rent-to-own agreement is a type of seller financing. This type of agreement lets the renter pay the seller an option fee that allows them to purchase the seller's property later.

A rent-to-own agreement includes a standard lease and an additional portion that specifies the option to buy. In many cases, a portion of the buyer's rent can be applied to the down payment or to the eventual purchase of the home.

You will also pay a nonrefundable option fee even if you decide not to move forward with the purchase.

A lease option is a type of rent-to-own agreement—and it's the preferable one for buyers. Lease options do not require you to purchase the home at the end of the lease, giving you the option to move on to other opportunities if the home isn't the right fit. If you pursue a rent-to-own agreement, take care to ensure that you have a lease-option contract so you can exit if needed.

These types of agreements are excellent options for people who just need more time to get their ducks in a row before purchasing a home. If you live in a high-priced market and would have trouble scraping together enough cash for a down payment, a rent-to-own agreement can help you with your first investment purchase.

Lease Purchase Agreements

Lease purchase and lease option agreements have a lot in common, but they differ in one critical aspect. In a lease purchase, you and the seller are locked into the sale unless something unforeseen happens.

The terms of the agreement are negotiated before a lease is signed. Often, the buyer will pay an above-market rate for rent so that the extra money can be put toward a down payment. Your agreement might also require you to pay insurance, property taxes, or maintenance costs.

The good news is that you can enter into these agreements without a high credit score, and you are contributing to the down payment every time you pay rent. It eliminates the feeling that you are throwing money away while renting because you are building equity.

However, you have to be in the financial position to buy the home at the end of the lease agreement. If you can't qualify for the mortgage, you might lose the ability to purchase the property.

HELOCs and Cash-Out Financing

A home equity line of credit (HELOC) allows you to borrow against the equity in your home. Then, you can use the house as collateral. It typically has a lower interest rate than other loans and is sometimes used to access an additional credit line for other purchases.

We talked about cash-out financing earlier in the book, but here's a refresher. A cash-out refinance enables you to take out a new loan that is worth more than what you currently owe on the house. When you close the deal, you get the difference between your new mortgage and the balance you owned on the previous loan in cash.

A HELOC is essentially a second mortgage since it is separate from your original mortgage. A cash-out refinance covers and eliminates your existing first mortgage. You still have a payment, but it replaces what you owe on your original mortgage.

The interest rates also vary. With a cash-out refinance, you can have a fixed rate or an adjustable rate, while a HELOC offers a variable interest rate.

These can be good options for investors who have already made a home purchase, but wouldn't be able to qualify or can't afford a new down payment. If you already have a property with equity, you can capitalize on that equity to expand your portfolio.

Owner Carrybacks

An owner carryback, also known as owner financing, is an option for people who cannot qualify for a mortgage. When you use an owner carryback mortgage, the loan is provided by the owner and carried by the owner.

When you enter into an agreement like this, the seller hangs on to the title of the property until the loan is fully paid off. In exchange, you make a down payment and take over paying their mortgage. The sale is completed through a deed transfer. At the end of the agreement, the buyer makes a balloon payment for the rest of the mortgage.

This approach is great for people who have poor credit or are strapped for cash. It's also used to seal deals quickly. It can be tricky to find sellers willing to enter into these types of agreements, though. The short loan terms and end-of-term balloon payment can be a burden for many buyers. You might also encounter a higher interest rate.

Why Creative Financing Can Be So Powerful

If you know and understand how to creatively finance a property purchase, you are well-positioned to thrive as a real estate investor.

For your first purchase, you might pursue creative financing out of necessity because of your financial situation. Having access to creative financing is a great thing because it means you don't have to be rich or have made perfect financial decisions in the past to pursue property ownership. Using one of the creative financing options I just described can help you enter the real estate market, and you just need one property to get the ball rolling.

If you don't need to use creative financing to purchase your first investment property, meaning you have a strong credit score and enough money for a substantial down payment, it's still important to understand your creative financing options. As your portfolio grows, you might run into scenarios where creative financing makes sense. For many investors, creative financing is a great alternative to traditional loans during a recession or in times of hyperinflation.

The Risks and Challenges of Creative Financing

Did you ever have to share an art project or writing piece in front of your classmates at school? It can be nerve-wracking to put your work out there. That feeling occurs because doing something creative comes with risks. Heck, writing this book is a risk for me!

Creative financing might not involve personally putting yourself out there, but it does require you to take on some element of risk. These types of financing agreements typically result in higher interest rates and more complicated terms than the traditional mortgage. In many cases, you're dealing directly with the seller, which can be a challenge.

Before you enter into a creative financing agreement, be sure you understand the agreement and are comfortable with the risks. For example, if you are entering using a HELOC, you will have an adjustable-rate mortgage, which means your interest payments could increase substantially. You risk being on the hook for higher payments in the future, so be sure you are comfortable with that.

Submit Your Offer

After you've picked your financing approach, it's time to submit your offer. Before you start drafting your offer, though, make sure you have two things in place: mortgage preapproval, if applicable, and a real estate agent.

Having mortgage preapproval will help make your offer appear more legitimate to the seller because you will have to complete several steps before approval. If you plan to use a traditional mortgage to purchase your property, get preapproved before you submit an offer, and, ideally, before you even start looking for a property.

You should also have a realtor you trust, preferably with experience in rental properties, in your corner before you submit an offer. This real estate agent will help you through the entire purchasing process, which should save you money in the long time. Trust me, if you're purchasing a property for the first time, a good realtor is worth their weight in gold. Pay the commission—it'll pay off down the road.

With all of that out of the way, let's walk through the offer process.

How to Make an Offer

Making an offer on a property is a multi-step process.

First, you'll need to do some research to settle on the price for your offer. This research should include looking at your comps and considering the competition from other buyers. The condition of the house and the time spent on the market might also weigh into your decision-making.

Second, you'll want to consider contingencies. A contingency is a clause that allows you to exit the deal with your earnest money. Contingency clauses are often tied to the home inspection. If you need financing, you might also ask for an appraisal or a financing contingency.

Third, you'll need to look at your budget. How much can you offer in earnest money? What monthly mortgage payment can you afford, and how does it compare to the rent you'll seek from tenants? Decide now what your limits are, and don't go over budget. If this deal doesn't work out, it's OK. There will be other properties. Don't blow your budget out of fear.

Fourth, you'll need to draft your offer letter, preferably with the help of your real estate agent. An offer letter is a detailed document that lays out your proposed terms and conditions for the sale.

What to Include in Your Offer

A real estate transaction is not a back-of-the-napkin deal. These types of transactions take time, and your offer letter is often just the start of negotiations with the seller. Whether you draft your offer letter or seek help from an experienced real estate agent, here's what you'll need to include:

Property Details

As with any important document, you need to outline the stakeholders involved. Include the name and address of yourself and the seller. You should also include the address of the property you want to purchase as well as any other important property specifications, like boundary lines or lot numbers.

Purchasing Information

Now's the time to propose your purchase price. Typically, your offer will be less than the price for which the property is listed. This is OK. Use your comps and your research to decide on a price you think is fair and make the offer. The seller will have a chance to respond.

If you are using financing, you can also include details about how you will pay for the property. You can include your preapproval letter or stipulate that you'll pay in cash.

You'll also want to outline how much you'll put down as an earnest money deposit. We'll talk about that more soon, but basically, it is a deposit that tells the buyer you are making a serious offer.

Contingencies

Your research on the property is not over when you submit your offer letter. You'll need to include details about how much time you'd like to complete your due diligence on the property and the ownership. This process might include inspections and official property searches to ensure you are dealing with the actual owner of the property.

You also need to include a contingency clause. You are not free and clear once your offer is accepted. You could discover a massive issue with the foundation during the inspection or run into an issue with your financing. Lay these contingencies out very clearly and specify that if they occur, you can exit the agreement without penalty.

Closing Dates

The buying process does not—and should not—go on forever. So, include your target date for the closing.

What Is an Earnest Money Deposit?

It can be hard to part with money before a deal is closed, but it's an important part of the buying process. An earnest money deposit is provided in good faith to show the seller you are serious about your offer and intend to buy the home.

If you want to receive your earnest money deposit back if the deal falls through, include that in your offer letter. You can ask to receive your earnest money back if the deal falls through due to something outlined in the contingency clause, or if the seller backs out for other reasons. You can also ask that the earnest money be applied to closing costs or the down payment.

Typically, buyers put down a deposit that totals 1%-3% of the price of the home. Earnest money can also be used as a negotiating tool in a competitive market. If the home is competitive, earnest money deposits can climb up to 10% of the purchase price.

After your offer is accepted, the earnest money is placed in an escrow account with a third party (Chase, 2021).

How to Get Your Offer Accepted

Creativity isn't limited to financing. You can be creative with your offer, too. The best real estate investors have some tricks up their sleeve to make their offers more enticing to sellers. The options are endless, and over time, you'll find a few go-tos. Here are a few of my favorites:

- **Appeal to the seller's motivations:** Your real estate agent might be able to help with this. People sell their homes for a variety of different reasons, and figuring out why your ideal property is on the market can help you beef up your offer. For example, if you learn that the seller is moving soon, you might be able to offer a quicker closing date to help them out.
- **Increase your earnest money deposit:** If you can, offer more earnest money. This gesture indicates just how serious you

are about purchasing the house and can make the seller feel confident that the deal will actually close.

- **Increase your down payment:** The less financing you need, the more confident a seller can be that the deal will close. You can put down a large down payment to ensure the deal goes through or make an all-cash offer if you're able.
- **Offer financial incentives:** From offering to pay moving expenses to paying title insurance fees, you can sweeten your offer with some financial incentives.
- **Be thoughtful about contingencies:** The fewer contingencies in your offer, the better. In a highly competitive market, waiving inspection or financing contingencies can help move your offer to the top of the pile. Just be sure you understand the risks of waiving contingencies.

You don't need to use all of these approaches in your offer. In fact, you should pick and choose which ones to use and when to use them. Consider how competitive your market is and the condition of the home before sweetening your offer. You might find you can close your deal without spending more money.

How to Negotiate

Negotiating a real estate deal is not like you've seen in the movies. There's no yelling or screaming, no staredowns, and often, no fancy boardroom with leather chairs and a long mahogany table.

Instead, most of your negotiating will be done through your agents and include a lot of text messages, number crunching, and paper documents. The process starts as soon as you submit your first offer.

How the Negotiation Process Works

You've finalized your offer and sent it over to the seller. Now, you wait.

When a seller receives your offer, they have three options: accept it, reject it outright, or counter.

If they accept it, congratulations! You're on your way to buying your first rental property and will need to finalize your financing and schedule your home inspection to keep the momentum going.

If they reject it outright, all is not lost. Sellers usually reject an offer because it is too low. If you're still set on purchasing the property, you can work with your agent to craft a new offer. If you don't think you'll be able to reach an agreement that's within your budget, though, move on and hunt for a different property.

If the seller counters, you'll have the chance to review the offer with the realtor and determine if it's worth accepting. If you're not happy with the counter, you can respond with another counteroffer. As you go through this process, you can use some of the strategies outlined in the previous section to sweeten your offer, like waiving contingencies or compromising on the closing date.

Tips for Success

In a perfect world, your first offer will be accepted for 100% of your real estate investment purchases. Unfortunately, we don't live in a perfect world. At some point in your real estate career, you'll have to negotiate.

When that time comes, whether it's on your first purchase or your fourth, I want you to win. These tips will help you do just that.

Play Out Different Scenarios Before Submitting Your Offer

A championship-caliber coach or athlete would never take the field without a solid game plan. You shouldn't submit an offer without one, either.

Before you submit your first offer, game plan how you'll respond in different scenarios. If you plan to offer $100,000 for a home the seller has priced at $150,000, what will you do if they counter at $140,000? Will you walk away? Counter at $110,000? Offer more earnest money?

Walk through every possible outcome and decide how you will react. Know your boundaries, too. Determine the highest price you can afford to pay for the property and stick with it. The last thing you want is buyer's remorse.

Arm Yourself with Data

When possible, back up your offer with data. If your offer is in line with comparable properties on the market, share that in your offer letter and during the negotiation process. Do your research and know your numbers.

If you'll have to put work into the house to make it livable, mention that as well. If the kitchen is out of date or needs new appliances, let the seller know that you've factored that cost into your offer.

Don't Let Your Emotions Take Over

Staying calm is key to winning a negotiation. Think before you respond to a counteroffer. Consider your personal boundaries in terms of price and contingencies.

Our emotions tend to take over when we feel unprepared. Keeping your emotions in check is easier if you've already gamed out different scenarios and done extensive research. Remember, if your offer is rejected or countered, it's not personal. Take a deep breath, put yourself in the seller's shoes, and work your plan.

How to Negotiate through Agents

Your real estate agent is your secret weapon when it comes to negotiating. You want your agent to be a creative problem solver with the backbone to hold firm to your requests when necessary.

A good agent will also be honest with you about what is possible during the negotiation process. They will let you know if your bid is way too low, and they will share ideas for creative incentives to add to your counter.

When you negotiate through an agent, the agent will review counteroffers with you and work with you to determine how you should respond. They'll offer advice and expertise based on their knowledge of the market and your goals. When you decide on a counter, they will negotiate with the listing agent, who will relay your offer to the seller. The process continues until the deal falls through or you reach an agreement and the deal closes.

Negotiation Skills and Creative Financing

You've heard the saying that practice makes perfect, and that's true for real estate negotiation. Your first negotiation won't be your best, but over time, you'll develop the skills you need to make yourself a negotiating powerhouse.

To become a better negotiator, practice:

- **Not taking things personally:** It's just business. Practice separating the seller from the offer. They are trying to act in their own best interests, just like you. Attack the problem instead of holding a grudge.
- **Asking questions:** Ask your realtor questions about the market, the property, and the seller. Be curious. Use what you learn to improve your offers and add incentives that appeal to the seller.
- **Walking away:** It's hard to do, but sometimes necessary. Know your limit and walk away from the process if you don't think you can reach an agreement with the seller.

You can also apply some of the creative financing approaches discussed earlier to your negotiation. For example, if the closing date is a sticking point for the seller, offer to let them lease back the property after closing until they move. Let your real estate agent know if you're open to creative financing approaches and use their expertise to enhance your negotiation.

Due Diligence

When you make an offer, you've usually only seen the house at a basic level. You know the layout and the general condition of the property. Even if you have a background in construction or a keen eye for home repairs, you still need to dig deep to find out if any potential issues are lurking beneath the surface of the home.

The time between when you reach an agreement with the seller and closing on the property is crucial. This is when you do your due diligence on every aspect of the property, from the finances to the overall condition.

Why Due Diligence Is Important

After you enter into an agreement with the seller, it is your responsibility to thoroughly research the property and ensure the property is acceptable. This process is called due diligence.

Due diligence is important because it lets you know if you're actually getting a good deal on the property. You don't want to purchase a property only to find out later that the house has massive flood damage or needs a new roof within the next year.

Effective due diligence examines the property from every angle, typically through careful inspection. As the buyer, you are responsible for hiring inspectors, so it's important to find people that you trust. Your real estate agent, mentor, or colleagues can provide recommendations for trustworthy and skilled inspectors.

Title Inspection

When you take over the title of a home, you don't want any surprises, like liens due to unpaid taxes or outstanding loans. Homes can also become embroiled in legal disputes, like divorces or disagreements over ownership.

A title company will help you discover these issues before your purchase is finalized. They'll verify the property information provided by the seller and conduct a thorough search for unpaid taxes, dues, easements, and other potential financial issues.

The company will also survey the property to determine the boundary lines and usually manages the closing process, including managing the earnest money in escrow.

Document Inspection

Review each and every document provided to you by the seller and your real estate agent. Ask questions about things you do not understand.

Some of these documents will include property disclosures, which can be found on the listing pages. Property disclosures can include things like appliance issues or any work the current owner plans to do before your closing date.

Physical Inspection

You aren't required to complete a physical home inspection—in fact, in highly competitive markets, sometimes people waive inspections altogether—but I highly recommend them. It is worth spending the money before the house closes to avoid a massive, expensive surprise later.

A basic home inspection covers the basic parts of the house and determines its condition. You should always work with a licensed inspector. During their inspection, they'll examine the entire structure as well as the electrical systems, appliances, waterlines, and more. They'll also provide a full report when the inspection is complete.

If you encounter surprises during the inspection, talk with your realtor about how to proceed. You might need to pull out of your deal, particularly if you encounter a problem outlined in the contingency clause.

Other Optional Inspections

A basic physical inspection won't catch every potential issue with a property. Some buyers choose to perform additional inspections, like radon inspections. In some cases, the home's age will impact the inspections you choose to have conducted on the property.

For older homes, you might want to consider having an asbestos inspection or a lead-based paint inspection. We now know that asbestos and lead can be very harmful to our health. So, you might find it is worth it to have an older home inspected for both issues.

Close the Deal

Your new property passed the due diligence process with flying colors. Now, it's time to prepare for your closing date, which is when you'll officially get the keys to your new investment property.

Here's your to-do list as your closing date approaches.

Order Insurance

After your inspections are complete, it's time to start shopping for home insurance. Many lenders want to see proof of insurance in order to finalize your loan, so don't put off this step. You want to be able to shop around to find the best deal for your new property.

Before you shop for insurance, consult your lender to determine their requirements. Some will require you to prepay for a year of insurance and purchase a policy that covers rebuilding your home. Depending on your location, you might also need flood or earthquake insurance.

Start shopping early. Most lenders want to see proof of insurance three business days before closing, and some want to see it even earlier. The more time you have to shop around, the better deal you'll find.

Set Up Your Business Entity

If you haven't already, set up your business entity before your closing. Most investors set up an LLC, S-corp, or a C-corp. Each option has its pros and cons, and all have different tax implications.

What Is an LLC?

A limited liability company (LLC) separates your real estate venture from you as an individual. You can buy, sell, and rent property through your LLC, and it protects you from personal liability for what occurs on the property.

The Pros and Cons of an LLC

An LLC reduces your personal liability for what happens on your property, like an injury. You can also add other people to the LLC, allowing you to build a business with investment partners.

While an LLC reduces your personal liability, it doesn't eliminate it completely. For example, you can still be held responsible for failing in your responsibilities as a landlord.

Tax Implications of an LLC

An LLC offers pass-through taxation, which means you pay personal income taxes. (Snyder, 2022) You can also transfer titles without being taxed on appreciating value, and qualify for additional deductions beyond what you receive when you file your personal tax return.

What Is an S-Corp?

An S-corporation, or S-corp, allows owners to shift their corporate income and associated finances to shareholders.

S-corps are appealing to inventors because they allow you to reduce your self-employment tax. This is because you only have to pay taxes on wages.

Like an LLC, a S-corp is a pass-through entity. However, it operates like a C-corp in that it must have bylaws, minutes for meetings, and a board of directors.

The Pros and Cons of an S-Corp

Reducing your self-employment tax can make an S-corp very appealing to real estate investors, but it isn't always the best option. If you plan to flip the property or be a property manager, saving on self-employment taxes can be a huge benefit. If you aren't going to be as hands-on with your property, an S-corp might hurt more than it helps.

It can be very difficult to remove property from an S-corp without tax implications. You also can't gift property from an S-corp, which can impact your future financial planning.

Tax Implications

If you aren't a passive real estate investor, you might be subject to self-employment tax. For example, if you purchase a property and flip it for profit quickly, that is not a passive investment and thus is subject to self-employment tax. If you have an S-corp, you can place your profit from the sale under the S-corp and pay yourself a portion of it as your wages. Your self-employment tax will be on your wages, not the entirety of the sale (Kaplan, 2024).

What Is a C-Corp?

A C-corporation, or C-corp, means the owners are taxed separately from the rest of the entity. They are essentially double-taxed because their profits are taxed at the corporate and personal level.

The biggest difference between an S-corp and a C-corp, besides taxation, is the amount of shareholders each entity can have. An S-corp cannot have more than 100 shareholders, while a C-corp can have an unlimited amount.

The Pros and Cons of a C-Corp

A C-corp offers liability protection since it is a separate entity from personal property. It's a great option for people who need to offer gains and incentives for capital investors. However, it limits your personal deductions and can be very difficult to maintain since there are a lot of requirements surrounding them.

Tax Implications

When you operate out of a C-corp, you open yourself up to more taxes. You will be taxed twice: at the corporate level and at the individual level. You'll also pay more in capital gains taxes if you sell the property and be subject to taxation if you transfer property out of the C-corp.

Final Walk-Through

Sing it with me—"it's the final countdown." The final walk-through is the last hurdle to clear before you can sign the paperwork and officially take ownership of your new property.

It is important to be thorough in the final walk-through because it is your last chance to check for issues and confirm that the house is in the expected condition.

As you participate in more walk-throughs, you'll learn more about what to look for. Until then, consider this your walk-through checklist:

- Use your inspection summary to check the condition of the house. Ensure every requested repair has been completed to code, if applicable.
- Ask for warranties or receipts for work on the home.
- Make sure the previous owner is completely moved out.
- Test every lock on every door and window.
- Check window screens for holes or tears.
- Run appliances to make sure they are functional.
- Check cabinets, refrigerator, and sinks for mold.
- Test every single outlet in every single room.
- Check for garbage and pests.
- Walk around the yard and perimeter of the property.

Your walk-through will likely happen several days before your closing date and last about an hour, depending on the size of the property. If you find an issue, you can ask the seller to fix it to delay the closing date.

Sign the Documents

Today's the day. Your closing date is the day you officially sign the paperwork for your new property, complete the sale, and receive the keys.

Your closing day will involve multiple people, including the sellers, real estate agents, lenders, title company representatives, and an attorney. You'll spend several hours signing paperwork to complete the sale. The documents might include a loan estimate, closing disclosure, mortgage note, initial escrow statement, mortgage, certificate of occupancy, and a purchase agreement. All of these documents. You will also pay closing costs and other escrow items, typically through a cashier's check or wire transfer.

Takeaways

If you have poor credit and no money, home ownership is not out of reach—you'll just need to get a little creative. In this chapter, we covered the entire home-buying process, from finding creative financing solutions to officially receiving the keys to your new investment.

Here are a few key takeaways from this chapter:

Takeaway #1: Think Positively

Traditional financing is not your only option when it comes to purchasing a property. Consider the creative options I've outlined in this chapter and pursue the one that works for you. Purchasing a home is a complicated process, no matter which financing option you choose. There will be times of frustration and delay. Be positive. Take a deep breath. It will all work out.

Takeaway #2: Have a Strategy

You need a strategy for financing your home. You also need a strategy when the time comes to make an offer. Always game-plan for different scenarios. Know your target price for the property and the highest amount you can afford before you submit your offer.

Takeaway #3: Don't Take Shortcuts

When it comes to purchasing property, you need to do your due diligence. Take your time on the title, document, and physical inspection process. Be thorough during the final walk-through. And when your closing date finally comes, read every document carefully

5

HOW TO CREATE AN EASY PROPERTY MANAGEMENT SYSTEM & AVOID ALL THE HEADACHES

"As a real estate professional, if you're trying to build a big business, you need to invest in that business."

— *GLENN SANFORD*

You've invested your time in researching an investment strategy. You've invested your money in your dream property. Now, it's time to invest in your processes.

As a real estate investor, your ability to effectively manage your properties will make or break your business. After all, to be a successful real estate mogul, you need to have multiple properties. And in order to have multiple properties that actually turn a profit, you need to be able to manage them.

To do this, you need to invest in your processes and your team. You need to be able to find good tenants and streamline the turnover process. You need a network of efficient and economical contractors you can trust.

In this chapter, I'm going to tell you exactly how to build the processes and team you need to keep your business running smoothly.

What Does a Landlord Do?

If you own a property and lease it out to tenants for payment, you are a landlord. Being a landlord means you are responsible for filling your property with tenants, appropriately maintaining the property, and following city, state, and federal regulations.

You can make big decisions about your property, like raising rent based on your agreement with tenants or evicting tenants if they fail to pay. You also have to make sure the property is in the proper condition for rentals and prepare it for new tenants.

It's a big job. But if you want that sweet passive income, you'll need to do a bit of heavy lifting.

Should You Hire a Property Manager?

If you or your business entity owns a property that is rented to others, you are a landlord. But you can outsource the day-to-day operations of maintaining the property to a property manager.

A property manager you can count on is worth their weight in gold. They can take plenty of time-consuming tasks off of your plate, like:

- **Coordinating maintenance:** A good property manager will have a list of reliable contractors who can help with maintenance and repairs.
- **Finding new tenants:** When you have a vacancy, a property manager can take the lead on finding a new tenant and researching the market value for a new lease agreement.
- **Vetting tenants:** A property manager can handle the background and credit check process to help you find the best possible tenant.
- **Collecting payment:** Your property manager can follow up with tenants if they miss a rental payment and help with the eviction process if needed.

In other words, you get to sit back and collect your rental checks while someone else does all the work. Sounds great, right?

Hold that thought. Property managers are like any other type of employee. Some are really good at their jobs; others aren't. Good ones aren't cheap, and for new investors, it's sometimes easier to handle these tasks yourself until you can afford an excellent property manager.

A property manager typically charges a percentage of the rental price. The cost can range from 6% to 12%, depending on your location and the property manager's experience. Their pay will reduce the cash flow for your rental, so you'll need to analyze your options carefully before making a hire.

Having a property manager also reduces the amount of control you have over your property. You're still the landlord, of course, but different property managers (or their companies) have different processes for screening tenants and handling repairs. They might also take a different approach to filling a vacancy than you would. If you're OK with having less control over the day-to-day operations of your rental, this won't be a problem.

Some real estate investors choose to manage their properties on their own. This is an excellent way to learn the nitty-gritty details of property and tenant management. If you decide to manage your first property on your own, don't be afraid to change course if the process becomes overwhelming. If you feel stressed about dealing with tenants and chasing down rent payments, consider outsourcing property management. Your peace of mind will offset the hit to your cash flow.

How to Prepare Your Property for Long-Term Tenants

Whether you hire a property manager or handle it yourself, the real work begins when it's time to prepare for tenants.

When you purchased your property, you had a target rental price in mind. Now, it's time to finalize your asking price and lease terms and draft the lease. You'll want to have the lease on hand and ready to go when you find the perfect tenant.

You will also need to review the legal requirements for rental properties in your area. Every city and state has different requirements. Make sure you know the rules and regulations before you list your property.

You'll also need to put in a bit of elbow grease—or hire someone else to put their elbow grease into the property instead. Start by inspecting the house from top to bottom for safety hazards and possible upgrades. You can handle the repairs yourself or hire a professional to make sure every repair is done correctly.

You'll also need to clean the property thoroughly to make it move-in ready. For most landlords, this process includes deep-cleaning the entire home, from the baseboards to the ceiling fans. You might also want to spruce up the property with a new coat of paint or updated flooring.

Long-term properties are not usually furnished. They do come with appliances, though, so you'll want to make sure every appliance is in proper working order. If an appliance seems to be on its last legs, start preparing to replace it.

Once your property is in tip-top rental condition and you have a property management plan in place, it's time to find your first tenant.

Finding Tenants

Ask your fellow landlords for their best tenant stories, and you're sure to hear some doozies. One will tell you about the tenant who left the home in shambles after an eviction. Another will tell you about the mystery stains they found throughout the house after tenants moved out, or the weird smell that took weeks to dissipate.

Your tenants are people. People come with issues. Eventually, you'll have a tenant you'd rather forget. If you screen tenants properly, though, great tenants will far outweigh the bad.

Here's how to find tenants who pay on time and treat your property as if it's their own.

How to List the Unit

When you list the unit, your goal is not only to find a good tenant but also to fetch the highest possible rental rate for the property. Your ability to do this hinges on your ability to market your property and all its features effectively.

How Much to Charge for Rent

When you purchased your property, you had an estimated monthly rental price in your head based on comparable properties in your area. This estimate is a great place to start as you nail down your official asking price. Remember that market values change over time, so conduct this analysis again before you officially list the property and anytime you bring in a new tenant.

You want your rental rate to be in line with the rest of the market. You also want it to align with the actual value of your property. When you purchased your property, you received an appraisal value for the home. If you made substantial improvements to the property, seek a reappraisal to determine the home's current value.

Many real estate investors aim to charge a monthly rent that is between 0.8% and 1.1% of the appraised value. For example, a home appraised at $300,000 might fetch between $2,400 and $3,300 in rent each month.

At the very least, you want to charge enough in rent to cover your monthly mortgage payment and, preferably, the rest of your expenses, like maintenance, insurance, and repairs.

Before you settle on a monthly rate, review the laws for your state and city. Some states, like California and New York, have rent control laws that will limit how much you can increase rates. Consult an attorney to make sure you understand the laws and restrictions.

How to Take Listing Photos

When you stand in line at the grocery store checkout, your eyes probably wander to the candy and magazines that separate the registers. What catches your eye? If you're anything like me, you're probably drawn to magazines with a striking headline or an eye-catching photo. Even if I don't care about the subject matter, the right cover is often enough to capture my attention while I wait to ring up my groceries. And if the cover is really good, I might even pick up the magazine and flip through the pages.

The right listing photos will have the same effect on your potential tenants. Eye-catching photos will encourage them to click on your listing. If they like what they see, you're one step closer to bringing them on as tenants.

After all, your potential tenants will be scrolling through dozens of different listings as they search for their new residence. If you want to stand out from the crowd, you need photos that show off your property's incredible features and allow your potential tenants to envision themselves living there.

Some real estate investors prefer to hire a professional photographer for their listing photos. Others do it themselves. Choose the right approach for your needs and budget. A high-quality camera is helpful if you want top-of-the-line photos, but many people can also get great results with a camera phone with a little practice and patience.

If you decide to take the photos yourself, here's how to make sure they capture your dream tenant's attention:

- **Consider staging the home:** Yes, you can take listing photos of an empty home. But vacant rooms tend to look smaller and less inviting, which is the exact opposite of what you're aiming for. Stage your photos with simple furniture and décor, or work with a staging company to set up your property for the photos.
- **Make it seem like home:** Add some fresh flowers and decorative features to each room to make it seem lived in. The decor doesn't need to be flashy but should make the unit feel like a home.
- **Use natural light:** Pick a sunny day and open the windows to feature the home in its best light. Artificial and flash photography can make the photos look dull instead of bright and inviting.
- **Make it seem spacious:** Use a tripod and set it up in the doorway of the room to give viewers a clear picture of the entire room. Set up your camera at various heights and take several photos to give yourself options for the listing.
- **Don't forget the details:** If the home has beautiful details, like a cozy fireplace or hidden storage nooks, snap some photos to highlight them. These elements can help increase the home's value in the eyes of your potential tenant.
- **Make editing easy:** Take tons of photos so you have plenty of options to choose from when you compile your listing. When you take photos, make sure the camera is straight and that you leave room to crop photos as needed.

As your real estate portfolio grows, you'll become an expert at taking amazing listing photos. Keep practicing, and don't be afraid to reshoot photos when tenants move out or you relist the unit.

Where to List

You have your rental price. You have your photos. Now it's time to actually list the property. After all, your dream tenants aren't going to find you by chance!

There are a lot of rental platforms out there, and each one has its pros and cons. I will break down three of the most popular ones to help you find the best option for you.

Apartments.com

When tenants look for a new place to live, Apartments.com is often one of their first stops, making it an excellent place to list your property. They've invested a lot of money into marketing the platform so tenants know and trust them.

They can also help you manage the property once you find a tenant. You can conduct tenant screenings, collect rent, and manage maintenance requests through Apartments.com.

There are fees associated with some of the features on Apartments.com. For instance, you can upgrade to a premium listing for a fee. This website also charges for tenant screenings and includes a transaction fee for rent payments.

Facebook

If you want to find renters without opening your wallet, Facebook is a great option. With over two billion daily users, it is the best way to get your rental property in front of as many people as possible.

You'll need a Facebook account to set up your listing, and you'll want to include all relevant details and photos in your description.

Facebook is an excellent way to generate leads for your property, but you'll need to be prepared to field messages and have a system in place to vet potential renters. It's also not a one-stop shop, so you'll need a process for setting up showings, preparing leases, and collecting rental payments.

Zillow Rental Manager

Like Apartments.com, Zillow offers a one-stop shop for landlords. You can list your property for free on the platform, which has over 30 million visitors each month between Zillow, Trulia, and HotPads. It also offers tenant screenings, a lease builder, and a rent collection tool.

Zillow Rental Manager allows you to list your rental for free, but you'll need to upgrade to premium to truly stand out from the crowd. You also need to be careful using Zillow's data since it can be inaccurate.

Research, as always, is your friend when it comes to finding places to list your rental. Try some traditional listing methods like the ones listed above, and experiment with other up-and-comers until you find the approach that works best for you. Try posting your listing on local Reddit forums, Craigslist, and other social media platforms. Build an email list or social media account and update your audience about vacancies. Connect with other local businesses that can recommend your property to new employees. Remember, your goal is to make it easy for your prospective tenants to find you.

How to Screen Tenants

You've posted your listing and received your first inquiry from a potential tenant. Hooray! It's exciting to learn someone is interested in renting your property. But that doesn't mean you should hand over the keys to them just yet.

You want to make sure the tenant will be able to pay the rent each month and treat your property with respect. The tenant screening portion of the rental process is incredibly important because it's your chance to vet the potential renter thoroughly. Just like you performed your due diligence before buying your property, you need to perform due diligence on anyone who wants to rent from you.

What Questions to Ask Potential Tenants

You'll have the chance to ask tenants questions multiple times throughout the application process. Many landlords have screening questionnaires that potential renters complete at the start of the inquiry process. These questionnaires help the landlord determine whether the potential tenant is a genuine lead or not.

You will also have the opportunity to talk with potential renters when you show them the property or during a phone call.

Before you develop a screening questionnaire or talk with a potential tenant, sit down and write down all the questions you'd like to have answered. Some of these questions might include:

- When do you plan to move?
- How do you generate an income?
- Do you have any pets?
- Do you or any other potential tenants smoke?
- Have you ever been convinced of a crime?

Some of these questions might be uncomfortable to ask, but they are necessary. After all, your property is a big investment. You want to make sure that your tenants can meet their financial obligations and treat your property with respect.

When you prepare your questions, avoid any that could be considered discriminatory. Federal law protects people from discrimination. Do not ask questions or make comments pertaining to:

- Race
- National origin
- Color
- Gender
- Religion
- Marital Status
- Disabilities

If you ask any experienced landlord, their list of tenant screening questions is probably very different than when they started. You'll find that your list of screening questions also evolves as you become more experienced as a landlord.

How to Conduct a Background Check and Credit Check

Running a background and credit check on a potential tenant is non-negotiable for landlords. You want a trustworthy, reliable tenant. Taking the time to vet them thoroughly will reduce the risk of tenant-related headaches later.

To run a background check, you need written consent from the tenant. You can add this to your rental application or send it separately.

Then, you need to collect the information needed to run the check. You should ask for the date of birth and social security number of anyone who will be living in the house. You'll also need two previous addresses and the name of their employer.

Finally, use a background check service to complete the check. There are various options available, so check with other investors to find the ones they recommend. You can run background checks through services like RentPrep and E-Renter, among others.

To pull your potential tenant's credit report, use a service like Experian, TransUnion, or Equifax. You can also hire a tenant-specific agency. RentPrep also offers a credit check service.

Helpful Hints for Screening Tenants

Conducting background checks and asking plenty of screening questions will help you find reliable tenants, but you shouldn't stop there. I've learned over the years that there are other steps you can take to improve your screening process. Learn from my experience and take these steps to optimize your screening process:

- **Know your own personal screening requirements:** Decide what your ideal tenant's income, credit score, and required references are. Also, decide whether you will allow tenants with pets or children (some landlords won't rent to pet owners and some prefer the 55+ age group). Finalize these requirements before you list your property.
- **Use screening applications to your advantage:** Collect basic information like names, addresses, smoking, and pet information in your first communication with a potential renter, preferably through a form. This will reduce the amount of time you spend talking with unqualified applicants
- **Learn and adjust:** Don't be afraid to adjust your process as you learn more about the market and the real estate business. You might learn you need to ask for more

references or lower your criteria for income. Follow the data, and don't be afraid to pivot as you grow.

What to Know About Tenant Applications

You've pored over tenant applications, run your background and credit checks, and intensely vetted every potential tenant. Now, it's decision time.

Perhaps you've narrowed the pool to two or three prospective tenants, or maybe you have just one finalist. Either way, you're in the final stretch of the selection process.

Showing the Property

Your tenants will likely want to see the property in person before signing a lease. Showing a property is a multi-step process that begins before the tenant ever pulls into the driveway. Before you have an in-person showing, you'll want to:

- **Schedule an appointment with the prospective tenant:** Set up a date and time to meet with the potential renter at the property. Make sure you leave yourself enough time to get to the property beforehand and make sure it's up to par. If you're doing multiple showings in one day, leave a buffer zone so tenants aren't running into each other between appointments.
- **Clean the property:** Inspect the property before the potential tenants arrive to make sure it is clean and looks well-maintained. Empty the trash, spray air freshener, tidy the yard, and verify that the property looks pristine.
- **Have a safety plan:** Even if your potential tenant seems great, you still don't know them. Make sure you meet in broad daylight and let someone you trust know where you are going and how long you expect the tour to last.

When it's time to meet the tenant and show the property, make sure you put your best foot—and the property's best foot—forward. Make a great first impression by:

- **Dressing professionally:** You don't have to wear a full suit, but be sure to look presentable.

- **Being prepared:** Your potential tenants will have questions about the history of the property, the neighborhood, and the surrounding area. Do some research and game plan how you will answer potential questions.
- **Treating it like a business meeting:** Whether this is your first property or your fifth, real estate investing is your business. Treat it like you would any other business meeting. Shake your prospective tenant's hand, be on time, and act like you would in the workplace.

After you've talked with the tenant, showed them the property, highlighted its features, and answered their questions, you'll probably have a hunch about whether they'll be interested in signing a lease—and whether they're the right tenant for your property. Set a time and date to follow up and make sure you reach out.

How to Approve or Deny a Potential Tenant

When you follow up with a potential applicant, you'll learn whether they are still interested in the property. The final decision to offer a lease agreement, though, falls solely on you. You have the power to approve or deny a tenant.

If they have pets, you can charge a pet deposit and a monthly pet fee to cover wear and tear. Make sure these additional fees are aligned with local practices.

If the tenant meets your desired requirements for a renter and wants to move forward, let them know they've been approved and send them the lease agreement. This lease agreement should be thorough and include addendums and clauses to protect you, the tenant, and the property for the duration of the lease agreement. A lawyer can review your lease before you send it over to confirm you didn't miss anything.

Unfortunately, sometimes a potential tenant just isn't the right fit. If this happens, politely let them know that you've denied the application. Hold firm to your criteria and make sure you apply the same criteria to every potential tenant.

How to Collect a Security Deposit

When you and your tenant agree to the lease, you can collect a security deposit. If you've ever rented a house or apartment, you are likely familiar with this process.

A security deposit is a predetermined amount of money you hold on to for the duration of the lease. If the tenant damages the property, you can use the security deposit to pay for the damages. If there are no damages when the tenant moves out, you must return the security deposit to them. In most states, a security deposit should not exceed one month's rent.

You can adjust the security deposit based on factors like the tenant's credit score or expected income. For example, you might ask for a higher security deposit from a tenant with pets or unreliable income, or a reduced security deposit to entice a tenant with an excellent credit score to sign the lease.

Outline the terms and conditions for the security deposit in the lease. Always collect it before handing over the keys to the property.

How to Write a Lease That Protects You

A lease is a contract between you and the tenant. It specifies what you will give them (access to a property) and what they will give you (the rental payment). It also details stipulations that you will be required to follow as the landlord and that the tenant will be required to follow as the renter.

Before you draw up a lease for your property, there are a few things you must consider, starting with the lease terms.

Month-to-Month vs. Long-Term Leases

When you create a lease, you have the power to determine how long the lease will last. A month-to-month lease renews every 30 days unless it is terminated by you or the tenant. A long-term lease has a set duration for the terms. Some popular options include three months, six months, or 12 months. In a long-term lease, you and the tenant lock in the rent price for a specific amount of time. If a tenant breaks the lease early, you can collect a penalty outlined in the lease.

A month-to-month lease is helpful for tenants who need flexible housing. You can charge a premium price for a month-to-month lease, but you'll have to accept that the tenant might leave the agreement at any time, leaving you with a vacancy.

A long-term lease provides stability for you and the tenant. The tradeoff is that you'll likely have to charge a little less for rent than for a month-to-month lease, and you won't be able to raise rates to meet market value for the duration of the lease.

How to Get a Lease Contract

I strongly, strongly recommend you seek help from a professional to prepare your leasing agreement. This document is crucial to your business, and it's worth investing in. The lease is your opportunity to lay out your expectations for tenants for payment and cancellation. It also lets you set guidelines for the tenant's responsibilities for maintaining the property and lays out what will happen if your property is damaged. Trust me, this is not a document you want to throw together at the last minute.

You have several options for creating the lease, including:

- **Hiring an attorney:** A licensed attorney with real estate experience can draw up a lease that covers all your bases. Ask for recommendations from other real estate investors and do your own research before selecting an attorney.
- **Generating the document online:** Sites like Zillow Rental Manager offer free lease templates you can update for your property. If you use this option, make sure your lease meets all the necessary state requirements.
- **Check with local associations:** If your area has a professional association for realtors, landlords, and attorneys, check to see if they offer free lease templates. These documents will align with your state requirements and can be a great starting point for creating a lease.

What to Include in a Lease

You can—and should—adapt your lease to each of your properties. But regardless of how you adapt your lease, every version should include:

- **Contact information:** Your lease should include contact information for you, the tenant(s), and, if applicable, the property manager. Each party should provide their full name, mailing address, phone number, and email address.
- **Property details:** Property details include the address and a list of anything provided with the property, like appliances or furniture.
- **Utility payment details:** Will you pay the utilities or the tenant? Outline expectations in the lease, including if there are required utility providers for the property.
- **Duration and payment terms:** Include how long the lease will last, the amount due for rent each month, how rent should be paid, and the due date. Be specific about when rent is considered late and what happens if you don't receive payment.
- **Termination and eviction terms:** Outline the procedure and expectations for terminating the lease and the process for eviction.
- **Insurance requirements:** Research the insurance requirements in your state and include the details in the lease. If your tenants are required to have renter's insurance, describe the type and amount of coverage they need in this section of the lease.
- **Property policies:** Lay out the policies for smoking, pets, parking, and guests. If there is a pet fee or an additional charge for more parking spaces, specify that in the lease.
- **Rules and expectations:** Does the tenant dispose of trash, or do you handle it? Will they plow the driveway and maintain the yard, or is landscape maintenance provided? Be clear about what the tenant needs to do to maintain the property and describe what you will handle as the landlord.

As you can see, your lease should be a very specific document. This is the time to decide what you expect from a tenant and lay it out clearly. Take the time to write a lease that is clear, thorough, and all-encompassing. It will save you time down the road.

Signing the Lease

Your lease is complete. Now it's time to sign the paperwork and hand the keys over to your new tenant.

After you've approved the tenant and they're ready to move forward, send over an unsigned lease and set a deadline for its return. Give them enough time—usually several days—to review the agreement before they sign it.

Once the tenant has reviewed the lease and signed it, they'll send it back to you. Once you sign the lease, it is binding. Print out a copy to save for your records and provide a copy to the tenant for their records. If issues arise, refer back to the lease agreement to determine how to proceed.

Tenant Management

The day has finally arrived. Your tenant is officially moving into your rental property and their new home. It's exciting, but your work as a landlord is not done, especially if you decide not to hire a property manager.

Tenant management is an ongoing process. In this section, we'll go over various aspects of keeping your tenants happy, your property protected, and the rent checks rolling in.

Move In

When a tenant moves into your rental, excitement is at an all-time high for both of you. The tenant is filled with expectations about their life in your rental unit, from cozy dinners in the breakfast nook to watching TV in the living room. You might also have some visions of your own, like a quiet tenant and perfectly maintained property.

As a landlord, move-in day is a chance to welcome the tenant to your property and set expectations for how the tenant-landlord relationship will unfold. Your move-in process should include two key components: an inspection and a welcome packet.

Move-In Inspection

Before your tenant arrives, complete a walkthrough of the property. Check every room in the house for damage. Make sure the appliances, plumbing, and electrical systems are working properly. Check the garage and yard for signs of damage or wear and tear. Take videos or photos to record the state of the property before the tenant moves in.

When the tenant arrives, walk through the property again with them or provide them with a checklist to walk through it themselves. Note any damage, big or small, on the property. When you are finished with the inspection, you and the tenant should sign the checklist.

This process allows you and the tenant to get on the same page about the condition of the property. If the tenant notices an issue, you can develop a plan to address it. It also prepares you for the move-out process, whenever that may be. If there is damage to the property when the tenant moves out, you can hold them accountable according to the terms of the lease.

Welcome Packet

The welcome packet is your chance to provide necessary information about the property to your tenants as well as welcome them to the area. This packet should be robust and include everything they need to know about their new residence.

Make sure you include basic paperwork in the welcome packet, including a copy of the lease, contact information for you or the property manager, and the move-in inspection checklist. Outline the procedures for paying rent and requesting repairs or maintenance, as well as the rules for the property.

You'll also want to provide everything your tenant needs to access the home, including several copies of the keys, remote door openers, and information about access codes if there is a security system.

If you want to go above and beyond, welcome the tenant to the area with a map of the city and a list of local establishments. Some landlords choose to provide a small gift, like a gift card to a local pizza shop or a bottle of wine, to welcome tenants to the rental. It's a small touch, but it can help start your relationship with the tenants on the right foot.

Rent Collection

Let's be real: you're not investing in real estate out of the goodness of your heart. You're running a business, and you need to get paid. There are a few ways to collect rent, including by cash or check. If you want to make the process incredibly easy, though, you need to set up an online rent collection process.

Most of your tenants will expect to pay their rent online. It's a win-win for you and the tenant. You'll receive your payments quickly and on time, and your tenants won't have to worry about waiting for a check to clear or missing a payment.

To collect rent online, you can use a bank transfer or a collection software system. Zillow Rental Manager and Apartments.com offer rent collection services. You can also be paid via Venmo, PayPal, or Apple Pay. You can also set up a process for collecting rent via credit card.

What If Your Tenants Don't Pay?

It's the second of the month, and your tenant still hasn't paid rent. It's officially late. Now what?

When a tenant doesn't pay rent on time, they are violating their lease and breaching the contract both of you signed. When this happens, it's best to start with the basics.

Before you contact your tenant, check your records and bank account one more time. Make sure the payment hasn't been processed. After all, everyone makes mistakes—it's possible you missed the payment when you were reviewing your accounts.

If the tenant is indeed late, it's time to create a paper trail. Send them a notice about the missed payment and let them know about next steps. If the missed payment was an oversight, the tenant will pay it and the late fee, and you'll both be able to move forward. If you still don't receive payment, you can try to call the tenant. Do not call more than once, though. The phone call is a courtesy. Multiple calls will feel like harassment, which you want to avoid.

If you still don't receive payment, it's time to start the eviction process. Begin by sending an official document called a pay or quit notice, which should clearly state the next steps. Tell the tenant that you plan to evict if you are not paid in full, including late fees. Set a deadline for receiving payment.

After you've posted the pay or quit notice, find a lawyer with experience in evictions. Depending on your state, you can start the eviction process after several days of nonpayment following the pay or quit notice. Your lawyer can guide you through the specific steps of the eviction process in your state.

Listen, I know that waiting on rent payments can be frustrating. The longer you wait to receive the money that is owed to you, the angrier you become. If you find yourself in this situation, the best advice I can give you is to be patient, stay calm, get as much as you can in writing, and seek the help of an experienced eviction lawyer. The eviction process can take time, but trust that it will work out in your favor. Don't let it keep you from moving forward with real estate investing.

Grace Periods and Extensions

We've all fallen on tough financial times, and your tenants might experience hardships while renting from you. There are a few ways to handle these situations so that your tenant can meet their obligations to you. The most popular options are grace periods and extensions.

Grace Periods

Grace periods are extremely common in the rental world. Some states require them, and others leave it up to the landlord's discretion. A grace period is just what it sounds like—an extra cushion that gives tenants a few extra days to pay rent. For example, though rent is due on the first of the month, it isn't considered late until the fifth. Those extra few days are the grace period.

If you provide a grace period, you need to include the details of it in the lease agreement. When does the grace period end? What is the late fee? These details ensure that you and the tenant are clear about the expectations for payment.

A grace period protects you and the tenant. Things happen, and sometimes bank transfers are delayed due to errors or holidays. A grace period gives your tenant time to pay their rent without being assessed a fee and helps you maintain your relationship with the tenant.

Rent Extension

If your tenant falls on particularly hard times, like a job loss or other financial hardship, they may ask for a rent extension. Granting an extension can help you maintain the relationship and retain the tenant. If they are a reliable tenant, you might decide it is worth it to give them some extra time to come up with their payment.

If you decide to grant a tenant an extension, detail the conversation in writing and lay out the terms for payment. Consider asking for a partial rent payment along with additional installments until the rent is paid in full.

If you don't feel comfortable granting an extension, don't. Use your judgment.

Communicating with Tenants

Ideally, you won't need to communicate much with your tenants. Hopefully, they pay their rent on time, rarely request repairs, and adhere to the terms of your lease.

But we don't live in a perfect world. Chances are, you'll have to chat with your tenants in some capacity, whether it's to set up a maintenance appointment or discuss lease renewals. You can vary your method of communication based on the topic.

Email

Email is an excellent option for tenant communication because it provides a paper trail for your interactions with the client. It's an easy way to share paperwork or general announcements about the property without interrupting the tenant's daily life.

If you plan to use email to communicate with tenants, have a system in place to remind you to follow up when needed. It's easy for an important email to get lost in someone's inbox. Be sure you're ready to follow up via another email or escalate the conversation to a phone call or text message if necessary.

Texting

Texting is a great way to communicate with tenants, but you'll need some boundaries in place to keep your phone from buzzing at all hours of the day and night. If you decide to use texting to connect with tenants, ask for their consent when they move in. Let them know what you will share with them via text, and try not to text them beyond business hours.

Texting should be used for specific circumstances. Text messages are great for reminding tenants about upcoming maintenance or rent payments. They are not ideal for in-depth conversations with tenants.

Phone Call

Phone calls should be used for urgent matters that are best discussed face-to-face (or voice-to-voice). Let tenants know that they can call you if there is an emergency on the property, but specify what you consider an emergency. Let them know how quickly they should expect a response from you if you miss their call.

Keep in mind that phone calls are not ideal for legal conversations because you can't document them. If you think you'll need to revisit details about the conversation later, try to conduct it through email, mail, or text message so you have documentation of the interaction.

Written Notice

Sometimes, you need to communicate with a tenant the old-fashioned way: on paper. For example, if you offer the tenant a lease renewal, you might send them details via email and follow up with a letter through the mail outlining the details for their personal records.

How to Handle Maintenance and Repairs

As a landlord, you have a responsibility to provide a livable environment for your tenants. It's up to you to respond to maintenance requests and complete repairs in a timely manner. It's good for business and your reputation.

Some maintenance tasks, like changing batteries in the smoke alarm, are the tenant's responsibility. The rest falls on your shoulders, and tenants won't hesitate to reach out when something needs to be fixed.

And here's the thing—as annoying as an unexpected maintenance request can be, it's a good thing when a tenant lets you know something is wrong with your property. It gives you a chance to fix it, keep your tenant happy, and maintain the value of your property. That's a win-win for everyone involved.

It will be easier to handle maintenance requests efficiently if you have a process in place. Here's what to consider as you design your process:

- **How should tenants submit requests?** You need one streamlined way for tenants to let you know when the property needs maintenance or repairs. Decide if you want them to communicate with you via text, email, or an online application.

- **How will you organize repairs and maintenance?** You need to track every request received, document how you addressed each one, and monitor the cost of repairs. Try setting up a spreadsheet to get you started.
- **How will you confirm the issue has been resolved?** You'll want to follow up with the tenant via email, text, or an online application to confirm the issue has been addressed and officially close the request.
- **What is considered an emergency?** In the case of a true emergency, like a busted AC unit in the summer or a major plumbing issue, you'll want your tenants to reach out to you immediately. Decide what constitutes an emergency and let the tenant know to call you if an emergency occurs. Detail these expectations in the welcome packet when they move in.

I hate to break it to you, but chances are these maintenance issues will arise at really inconvenient times. It can be easy to delay addressing them if you are busy with something else. I encourage you to avoid procrastinating when it comes to handling maintenance requests from tenants. Addressing these issues quickly strengthens the tenant-landlord relationship and makes it more likely that the tenant will renew when their lease expires.

Always acknowledge maintenance requests and try to provide a timeline for repairs. Try to address urgent issues, like a broken washing machine, within 24-48 hours. Non-urgent issues, like a squeaky stair, can be addressed within a week or two.

How to Reduce Expenses and Increase Your Income

Your goal for every single property you own should be to maximize your profits. There are plenty of ways to do this without cutting corners or inconveniencing your tenants.

As you generate cash flow, you might want to reinvest those funds into the property. This helps you in two ways: it increases the value of your property, and it provides a better experience for tenants. Some investments you can make to cut costs and maximize your income include:

- **Making the property energy-efficient:** Consider upgrading your heating or cooling system to a more energy-efficient model or swapping out appliances for updated versions.
- **Learn maintenance skills:** The more repairs you can do yourself, the more money you'll save on maintenance costs. Take some time to learn basic maintenance tasks and enjoy the extra cash in your pocket.
- **Reevaluate the landscaping:** Could you swap grass for turf and eliminate the need for a lawn care service? Consider making some adjustments to the landscape to cut costs.
- **Examine your plumbing:** If you are paying the water bill, try switching out shower heads and calibrating toilets so they use water more efficiently.

If you want to reduce your expenses and maximize your income, you should also focus on keeping your tenants happy, especially if they are your ideal renters. When a tenant leaves, you have to invest money into finding and screening a new tenant and making the property move-in ready. Build a good relationship with your tenant, address their maintenance needs quickly, and communicate as needed. If you do these things, they'll be more likely to renew their lease when the time comes.

How to Handle Common Tenant Issues

It's impossible to plan for every tenant issue you'll encounter as a real estate investor. There are some issues, however, that tend to pop up no matter what. Here are three common problems and guidance on how to handle each one:

Tenant Issue #1: "There are bugs in this house!"

Pests want the pleasures of home, too. If ants and other pests have taken up residence in your rental, your tenants will let you know about it. When this happens, head out to the property as soon as possible to evaluate the extent of the issue. Develop a plan for exterminating the critters and share it with your tenants. Hire an exterminator and make sure the problem is taken care of thoroughly.

Tenant Issue #2: "The neighbors are making too much noise!"

If you are renting out both sides of a duplex, you might encounter this complaint and be able to do something about it. In most cases, a short conversation with the person complaining about the noise will help you address the root of the issue. Then, you can have a short conversation with the noisy neighbor and ask them to be more considerate. If it's a continuous problem, address it based on the terms laid out in the lease. If you don't have a noise complaint clause in the lease, consider adding one.

Tenant Issue #3: "I want my security deposit back!"

When a tenant moves out, you'll have the opportunity to review the property for damages. If there is damage, you can keep the security deposit. Some tenants are not happy about this. If they ask for their deposit back, refer back to the photos and checklist from move-in and highlight where the damage has occurred. In some cases, this can evolve into a legal issue, so consult an attorney if things escalate.

What to Know About the Fair Housing Act

The Fair Housing Act protects renters from discrimination. As a landlord, it is your responsibility to understand the Fair Housing Act and other protections granted to renters in your state.

The Fair Housing Act protects people from discrimination based on race, color, religion, national origin, familial status, sex, and disability. Some states have additional protections, like age or sexual orientation.

In order to stay compliant, you need to be very careful about how you communicate in all aspects of your rental business. For example, if you state a preference for female renters in your rental listing, that can be a violation of the Fair Housing Act.

This principle also applies to questions you ask potential tenants during the screening process. For instance, asking a potential tenant where they go to church could be considered a violation of the Fair Housing Act.

How to Streamline Your Property

As you add more rental properties to your portfolio, you'll be desperate to start streamlining your operations as much as possible.

Why wait? Whether you have one property or several, it's never too early to start incorporating the newest technology into your rentals. Here are three ways to upgrade your rental and make your life a little bit easier.

Smart Locks

A smart lock makes physical keys a thing of the past—or at least keeps them buried in your pocket or purse. Adding a keyless entry system is a great way to upgrade your locks and make life easier for you and your tenants.

Smart locks provide easy access for tenants, regardless of whether they have their physical keys with them or not. For landlords, smart locks are a game-changer for security and tenant transitions. If you have smart locks on your property, you can provide different codes for service providers, maintenance companies, and tenants. When someone enters the code, you'll be notified.

Smart locks are more expensive to install, but they will help you save money in the long run. One of the biggest benefits comes when tenants move out. Instead of changing the locks on every door in the property, you can simply switch out the code for the new tenants.

Smart Thermostat

If you (or your tenants) dread opening the electric bill every month, it might be time to install a smart thermostat. Smart thermostats automatically adjust the temperature in the house based on your schedule. It's connected to the Wi-Fi in the home and allows the user to control the thermostat remotely.

Smart thermostats are popular in short and mid-term rentals because the landlord often foots the electric bill. A smart thermostat gives the landlord some control over the temperature in the house, allowing them to reduce costs.

For long-term rentals, tenants are typically covering the electric bill. As a result, a smart thermostat is a money-saving perk for tenants. Having one in your rental might be an extra incentive that keeps tenants happy and makes them more likely to renew.

Smart Safety Devices

One of your biggest responsibilities as a landlord is to keep your property and tenants safe. Thanks to technology, there are now more devices than ever to monitor your rental.

You might want to consider investing in a Ring camera or another security device to protect your property. Ring cameras can be a deterrent to crime. After all, no thief wants to be caught on camera!

It can also provide a sense of security to your tenants. Having the extra layer of security a Ring camera provides can make your tenants feel more comfortable at home. It might even be the feature that sets your rental property apart from others.

How to Remove Tenants

We talked a bit about evictions earlier in this chapter. Now, we'll explore how and when to remove tenants in more detail.

There are several reasons you might need to evict or remove a tenant, including:

- **Failing to pay rent:** As discussed earlier, if a tenant habitually pays rent late or doesn't pay at all, you can remove them.
- **Damaging the property:** If a tenant intentionally destroys your property or allows gross negligence to occur, you can pursue removing them from the rental.
- **Using the property for illegal activities:** If you can prove that your tenant is participating in illegal activity on your property, you can remove them.
- **Violating the lease:** If a tenant has an unauthorized pet or participates in an activity that violates the terms of the lease, you can pursue removing them from the property.

There are two common ways to remove tenants: cash for keys and eviction. Let's take a closer look at both of them.

Eviction

Evicting a tenant is a lengthy process. No landlord wants to do it, but sometimes it is necessary. Hopefully, this is a rare occurrence throughout your real estate career.

If you do end up deciding to evict a tenant, here's how to do it:

- **Review the law:** Check the laws for your state or consult an attorney before moving forward with an eviction. Different states and municipalities have different landlord-tenant laws. You want to be sure you can win.
- **Consider alternatives:** Evictions are expensive and stressful, even for landlords. Ask the tenant if they want to leave the property on their own or offer them a cash-for-keys exchange, which will be discussed in the next section.
- **Serve the eviction notice:** The type of notice depends on the violation. A pay or quit notice is used when a tenant owes unpaid rent. A cure or quit notice is used if a tenant is in violation of the lease, but can fix the problem by removing an unauthorized pet or roommate. An unconditional quit notice is used when the tenant needs to vacate immediately due to illegal activity or gross negligence. If the tenant doesn't take the necessary action to address the notice, it's time to move on to the next step.
- **File a lawsuit:** Hire an attorney to file your eviction suit and walk you through the process. An eviction lawyer will know exactly what you need to file in your state.
- **Gather your documents:** Your attorney can advise you on what paperwork you will need to bring to court for your hearing. In most cases, you will need the original lease agreement, documents related to the eviction, and copies of any communication you had with the tenant.
- **Complete the eviction:** If you win in court, local law enforcement will receive a Writ of Restitution. Then, they will go to the property and remove the tenant. You will also receive a financial judgment. The judgment typically requires the evictee to pay the rent you are owed and additional damages.

See? It's a lengthy, tedious process. Thankfully, it's not the only way to remove a tenant.

Cash for Keys

Cash for keys is an alternative to an eviction. In a cash-for-keys exchange, the landlord pays the tenant an agreed-upon fee to vacate the property.

I know what you're thinking—why on earth would any landlord pay a bad tenant? I get it, but there's a method to the madness.

Landlords tend to use this option because it is more time and cost-efficient. As you saw earlier, evictions can be costly and time-consuming. A cash-for-keys exchange allows landlords to avoid this process and remove the tenant faster than going through the legal eviction process. It also typically saves them money.

If you decide to pursue a cash-for-keys exchange, you will need to:

- **Serve an eviction notice:** Research the eviction process in your state and serve the appropriate notice. You aren't legally required to serve an eviction notice, but it can help you in the negotiation process.
- **Make a verbal offer:** Talk with your tenant to see if they'd be open to a cash-for-keys exchange. Discuss the dollar amount and the move-out date.
- **Put it in writing:** If the tenant agrees, send them a written contract. Hire an attorney to help with this if possible.
- **Finalize the exchange:** Sign the documents and exchange the keys and cash. Conduct a move-out inspection, wave goodbye to your tenant, and move on.

Whether you choose to evict or use cash for keys, removing a tenant is never fun. If you find yourself in this situation, use it as a learning opportunity for your business. Review your application and background check process. Consider adjusting your income and credit score criteria for your next tenant. Don't dwell on this chapter of your real estate career—use it to make the next chapter even better.

Moving Out

All good things must come to an end. Eventually, your tenant will move on to a new city or a new property. When that time comes, you want to have a clearly defined move-out process to ensure your tenant can exit the property quickly and smoothly. Also, you'll want to ensure you can recoup any potential costs for damages or repairs and can quickly prep the property for your next tenant. This process isn't lengthy, but does require several key components.

Move-Out Packet

The move-out packet provides all the information your tenant needs to leave the property, from cleaning guidelines to instructions for inspections. Most move-out checklists include:

- **Confirmation of the move-out date:** Reiterate when the tenant is supposed to exit the property. Include the date and time (for example, by midnight on April 1).
- **Forwarding information:** The tenant should provide a way to reach them via phone, email, and mail.
- **Inspection details:** Let the tenant know how to schedule their move-out inspection and any details about what to expect during the process.
- **Cleaning instructions:** Outline how the tenant should leave the property. For example, you might ask them to sweep, dispose of trash, wipe down the walls, clean out the fridge, clean the carpets, remove pet waste from the yard, etc.
- **Utility guidelines:** Let the tenant know how long they must keep utilities on. In many instances, utilities should remain on until after the move-out date.
- **Key return details:** Outline when and how the tenant will hand over the keys to the property.

Move-Out Inspection

The move-out inspection is your opportunity to walk through the property with the tenant and check for damage. Now's the time to pull out the move-in inspection checklist you created when the tenant arrived at the property, including photos. You can use the move-in checklist to compare the condition of the property at move-out to the condition at move-in.

During the inspection, you should look for damage that exceeds normal wear and tear. Normal wear and tear include things like reasonable scratches on the walls, worn carpet, and nail holes. This type of damage is reasonable for any space that has been lived in. Remember, your property was the tenant's home, so it is reasonable for them to have hung photographs on the walls or walked on the carpet.

However, damage can sometimes exceed what is reasonable. In these circumstances, you can use the security deposit to cover the repairs. This damage is called tenant property damage and can include large holes in the walls, broken windows, torn window screens, or missing fixtures. If you spot tenant property damage, notify the tenant during the inspection. In many cases, the security deposit will cover the repairs. If not, estimate the total cost of repairs or, if appropriate, give them the opportunity to fix the damage.

Returning the Deposit

If you complete the move-out inspection, it's time to return the security deposit. If there has been some level of tenant property damage, you might need to use some of the security deposit to repair the damage. In this scenario, you will need to create documentation about how much of the deposit you are keeping and why. This document should include tenant information, a description of the damage, the amount needed to repair the damage, and the amount of the security deposit the tenant will receive after deductions.

If there is no property damage, you need to return the security deposit in full to the tenant. Check your state and local laws for guidance on how to approach this process. Many states have specific time frames for when you must return the deposit.

If property damage exceeds the amount of the security deposit, you may need to take legal action if the tenant is unwilling to cover the costs.

Preparing the Unit for the Next Tenant

After the tenant moves out, it's time to prepare the property for your next move-in. Before your next tenant moves in, be sure to:

- Repaint the walls
- Change all locks and make new sets of keys
- Clean the property thoroughly
- Complete any necessary repairs
- Take updated photos of the property

Contractors

Real estate investing might seem like a solo endeavor, but it is not. You need a network of reliable contractors to help you repair and maintain your property. These extremely skilled workers will help keep your properties in tip-top shape.

How to Find Good Contractors

The process of finding good contractors is similar to building any other type of network. You need to ask for recommendations, check references, and understand the exact type of skills you need for each project. When asking for recommendations, make sure contractors are skilled in the area you need help in. For example, not all landscaping companies do masonry repairs on walkways because their skills may apply only to lawn care.

Ask other real estate inventors and realtors for recommendations. Take note of any work trucks you see in your neighborhood and ask other homeowners for recommendations. As you start to hire contractors, ask them for recommendations as well. Your favorite plumber might know an excellent carpenter and vice versa.

Once you have a list of potential contractors, check their references. Call previous clients to see what they think of their work and search for the company name online to see if there are any reviews. You should also check that contracts have appropriate licenses and insurance policies, if applicable. Check online reviews. What's most important with reviews is how they handle negative reviews. Did they ignore them? Respond with a half-hearted apology? Or, did they respond professionally and demonstrate genuine concern for the customer's satisfaction? Everyone makes mistakes, and some people like to leave bad reviews just because they're angry people. So, focus more on the contractor's response than the review itself—unless there are consistently bad reviews, in which case, don't hire this individual or company.

Eventually, you'll have a list of several contractors to speak with. Determine exactly what you need to be done for your project and pick up the phone. Ask them for a price estimate, and be sure to shop around to compare costs and timelines.

How to Manage Contractors

Your role does not end when you hire a contractor. Just like you, contractors are running a business, which means they have their own project requirements, timelines, and costs to think about.

There should be a contract in place before work begins. Make sure you read and thoroughly understand the contract before you sign it. The contract should include specifics about the project timeline, expected costs, and details on other aspects of the project, like using subcontractors. This part of the process is your opportunity to outline your expectations for the project and get on the same page with the contractor.

When work begins, your contractor might have questions about the project or other tasks you need to complete, like acquiring permits. Have an established process for communication in place, and do your best to respond promptly. Communication is key to completing projects on time. Prioritize it!

Tip: always hire contractors or handymen who hold professional liability insurance. You are running a business, so hire professionals who carry the necessary insurance for your protection (in the case of injury) or property damage.

Why You Need a Handyman on Speed Dial

Sometimes, you don't need a specialist to complete a home repair project. While a plumber, carpenter, or electrician can help you with high-level home projects, a handyman can handle some other projects.

A highly skilled handyman can complete a lot of detailed home improvement tasks, like repairing a deck or installing cabinetry. In some cases, these projects might be things you could learn to do yourself, but hiring a handyman saves you valuable time. From fixing a faucet to replacing a window, a great handyman can tackle your to-do list quickly. They also tend to charge a daily or hourly rate, while a contractor typically charges by the project.

Licensed vs. Unlicensed

A handyman is a great option for many home projects because the tasks they complete don't require specific licenses. An unlicensed handyman can still complete basic repairs.

On the other hand, you will most likely want to hire a licensed contractor for in-depth projects. Most states require licenses for contractors, electricians, plumbers, and HVAC installers. Confirming a contractor is licensed helps protect you from scams. As you meet other real estate investors, you will likely hear horror stories about contractors who performed shoddy work or took a customer's money and never completed the project. In many cases, you'll learn that these contractors were not licensed.

Using an unlicensed contractor can lead to issues with permits, safety issues, and damages to your property. Before you hire a contractor, ask for their licensing information and confirm that it's up to date on your state's licensing website.

As previously mentioned, make sure anyone working on your property is well-insured so you're not left holding the tab for property damage they caused while on the job.

How to Screen a Contractor

You should always speak with your potential contractor before hiring them for your project. In addition to personally checking their references and talking with former clients, you should also ask them:

- Will you handle permits, or will I?
- Do you use subcontractors? If so, how do you hire them?
- Can you supply information on your license and insurance?
- How will you protect my property?
- What is the timeline for the project?

You should also discuss the payment structure. Different contractors take different approaches to project pricing. Some common structures include:

- **Guaranteed maximum prices:** This sets a maximum price for the project so you don't encounter any surprises. Before the project begins, the contractor shares a cost breakdown for it that you approve. If the project comes in under budget, you and the contractor will split the difference.

- **Lump sum:** With this approach, the contractor provides a lump-sum total price for the project without breaking down individual costs. You pay the lump sum, and if there is any excess, the contractor keeps the extra money.
- **Cost:** If a project is completed at cost, you pay for the cost of the project and the contractor's rate. If a project encounters delays or unexpected costs, you foot the bill.

What Types of Contractors Will You Need?

You'll need many different types of contractors during your lifetime as a landlord, from roofers to flooring contractors. Most commonly, though, you'll call on these four different types of contractors:

- **Lawn/snow:** This contractor will help maintain your property's lawn and landscaping as well as remove snow and help with winter prep. Choose landscape maintenance companies that can handle everything your property needs, including tree and shrub care, masonry repair, and outdoor lighting. That is, unless you just want a "mow and blow" service that does the bare minimum to keep the property attractive.
- **Electrician:** This contractor will complete tasks like running wiring and installing light switches.
- **Plumber:** This contractor will install pipes and connect drains to established piping systems.
- **Carpenter:** A carpenter will make your property stand out by installing molding, creating built-ins, and handling other woodworking tasks.

Bookkeeping

You entered the real estate business to make money. Staying on top of your bookkeeping is crucial to understanding exactly how much you are making and spending in your business.

How Bookkeeping Works

Bookkeeping is essentially the recording of monetary transactions within a business. Typically, a bookkeeper will sit down weekly or monthly and record the business's transactions, including rent payments and property expenses. They'll also handle financial paperwork, like payroll, invoicing, or preparing financial statements for further analysis.

Why Bookkeeping Is Necessary

If you want a viable real estate business, you have to be able to make good financial decisions. Having up-to-date and balanced books helps you do that. The financial records a bookkeeper maintains can inform your decisions on your business's budget and help with tax preparation.

Do You Need to Hire a Bookkeeper?

Bookkeeping requires someone who is diligent, precise, and organized. You can handle bookkeeping duties yourself, delegate them to another employee, or hire a professional bookkeeper.

Whether you handle bookkeeping internally or outsource, decide on software to use or set up a spreadsheet to update regularly. Designate time to look over receipts and bank statements and update your books. Ideally, this should be completed weekly.

The key to keeping your books up to date is being organized and disciplined about recording transactions regularly. Be honest about whether you have the time to stay on top of this. If you don't, consider hiring someone to manage your bookkeeping for you. You won't regret outsourcing this task—having your books in order will help your business thrive and give you peace of mind that you're financially on the right track.

Build Your Document Library

As a landlord, you'll find that there are some forms and paperwork you will use over and over again. Building a library of necessary forms and documents will help streamline property management and make it easier to grow your team in the future.

Some key forms you will need include:

- **Rental forms:** Have your rental application, welcome letters, and background check authorizations templated and ready to send.

- **Leases:** In addition to a basic lease agreement, you'll also want to have a month-to-month agreement, renewal agreement, addendums, and subleasing agreements ready to go.
- **Tenant notifications:** These forms can include disclosures, notices to enter, rental increase notices, maintenance updates, and eviction notices.
- **Violation notices:** Be prepared to inform tenants about past-due payments, smoking violations, pet violations, noise violations, damage, and other issues.

Takeaways

You didn't enter real estate investing to sit behind a desk managing tenants or handling repairs. By implementing the process I've outlined in this chapter and carefully growing your team, you'll be able to grow your business over time so you can be more hands-off. Trust me, there's nothing better than enjoying a drink with your partner or friends while your property manager handles the day-to-day operations of your business!

Takeaway #1: You're Only as Good as Your Tenant Screening Process

Tenants are the lifeblood of your business, and having good tenants who pay on time and respect the property as if it were their own is worth its weight in gold. Invest in designing a tenant screening process that thoroughly vets applicants. Track your procedures and processes so you can outsource these screening tasks when the time comes.

Takeaway #2: Don't Hesitate to Grow Your Team

You might not be in a position to grow your team right this moment. But one day, you will be ready. Have a plan for how you want to grow. Will you hire a property manager first, or outsource your bookkeeping? Develop a growth plan and create your processes with outsourcing in mind. It will be easier to seek help if you have a plan in place.

Takeaway #3: Always Be on the Lookout for Talent

The best time to search for a contractor or a property manager is when you don't need one. Keep a list of highly recommended tradesmen on hand and work to build relationships with them before you need assistance. After working together, don't hesitate to send them referrals or offer positive feedback. Relationships matter in this business.

What's Next

Your property management process is in place, and you have a plan to grow your team over time. Now, it's time to figure out exactly how to manage a short-term and mid-term rental so that your guests will return again and again.

In the next chapter, we'll cover how to set up each type of rental and what to expect from your guests. You'll be fully booked in no time at all!

FREE GIFT #7

The Complete Guide & Checklist to Tenant Screening:

This comprehensive guide will take you through the step-by-step process to find and keep good tenants. Avoid common mistakes and safeguard your investment with this essential tenant screening guide.

To access this free bonus, head to https://readstreetpress.com/iwantpermanentpto7 in your internet browser or scan the QR code below and I'll send it to you right away!

6

HOW TO MANAGE SHORT-TERM, MID-TERM, & VACATION RENTALS BETTER THAN THE RITZ CARLTON

"If you don't own a home, buy one. If you own a home, buy another one. If you own two homes, buy a third."

— *JOHN PAULSON*

Long-term rentals can provide a stable rental income. If you're in the right location, though, short-term, mid-term, and vacation rentals can be incredibly lucrative.

The key to making these types of rentals work is managing them effectively. A well-managed short-term, mid-term, or vacation rental can provide more upside for tenants than a hotel stay. For investors, these types of rentals can generate a lot of income in a short time frame because you can consistently bring in new tenants while increasing your prices.

In this chapter, I'm going to break down how you can turn a short-term, mid-term, or vacation rental into a cash cow.

Short-Term/Vacation Rentals

Demand for vacation rentals has outpaced hotels since 2022, according to an article from NerdWallet.

This shift makes sense. Short-term rentals offer perks like a kitchen, individual bedrooms, and backyards, making them a home away from home for travelers. They're the perfect option for digital nomads trying to work while they travel or large families who want to spend time together without splurging on multiple hotel rooms. While hotels offer some perks, they can't quite match the benefits of a vacation rental in the minds of many consumers. And it's not just budget-minded consumers. For example, a wealthy family planning a family reunion might be more amenable to renting a luxury home where everyone can be together and have privacy, rather than a busy hotel with shared common areas.

That's where you come in. With the right house in the right location, you can offer a vacation solution for travelers that far exceeds their hotel options.

Pros of Short-Term Rentals

There's a reason why short-term rentals are popping up in both established vacation destinations, like Nashville, and under-the-radar destinations, like Milwaukee. The benefits of owning a short-term rental are numerous, and real estate investors are trying to take advantage of this window of opportunity.

Here are some of the pros of owning a short-term rental:

More Cash

Short-term rentals can generate more cash per month than long-term rentals due to one simple factor: more tenants. For example, let's say you have a property within walking distance of the beach in a prominent vacation spot. You could charge $3,000 per month for a long-term rental. That's great money! But with a short-term rental, you can charge $2,500 per week. If you rent the property for four weeks a month, you collect $10,000. That's even better money!

Tax Benefits

Short-term rentals have a lot of expenses that can count as deductions, like cleaning fees, utilities, and insurance. These deductions can help you save money on your taxes. As always, work with a tax professional to fully understand the potential tax benefits of a short-term rental in your area.

More Control

Want to take a vacation at your rental? You can block out several weeks or months to live in your unit. Want to increase your income? You can raise prices for your next vacancy instead of waiting for a lease to expire. Want to perform some quick maintenance? When the current guests leave next weekend, you can knock out your tasks without anyone underfoot.

Cons of Short-Term Rentals

Do short-term rentals sound too good to be true? They can be a great investment, but they certainly aren't perfect.

Here are some cons to consider for short-term rentals:

Inconsistent Income

Yes, you can make more money on a short-term rental. However, you always have to be willing to accept that the income might be inconsistent based on seasonality and other factors. Have a plan for the months your unit sits vacant. That ski-in condo that's booked solid from November to April will sit vacant during "mud season" until the summer alpine activities draw more visitors. It will be vacant again in the fall after the foliage lovers have departed.

Increased Risk

Having an unpredictable income is a risk. If the economy tanks and people cut back on vacations, you could struggle. Your guests are also a risk. When you have more guests each month, the amount of time you have to vet them decreases. As a result, short-term rentals are more prone to theft or damage than long-term rentals. You can mitigate these risks to some extent by asking for a security deposit.

Area Limitations

Some areas are cracking down on short-term rentals. These restrictions might limit your ability to find a great property you can rent to vacationers. And, if you purchase a property and the restrictions change, you might have to sell the property much earlier than you intended. Check the local laws about short-term rentals in your area before you buy a property for that purpose.

How to Furnish a Short-Term Rental

Your guests can't bring their own furniture for a one-week stay in your beach house. You need to completely furnish a short-term rental so your guests can have a relaxing stay. These costs can add up quickly if you're not careful. Thankfully, there's a way to furnish your property without taking out a second mortgage.

What to Include

It might feel like you can furnish your short-term rental with leftover furniture from your college apartment, but I urge you not to take the easy way out. The way you furnish your rental impacts the amount you can charge and the overall satisfaction of your guests, which, in turn, influences your future earnings.

Before you create your shopping list, ask yourself the following questions:

- **Who is my ideal guest?** Will most of your guests be young women in town for a bachelorette party? Extended families enjoying a family reunion? Couples indulging in a romantic getaway? Each category requires different types of furnishing and amenities.
- **How big is the property?** The number of bedrooms and bathrooms will influence what you purchase. If you want to sleep more people than the bedrooms allow, you might want to add bunk beds, trundle beds, or a convertible sofa to your shopping list.
- **What is the property's vibe or aesthetic?** If your rental is a cabin in the woods, you might want to skip modern furnishings. Decide which look you are going for so you can pick furniture and décor that creates an experience for your guests.
- **How much do I want to charge?** If you want to charge luxury prices, you need to spend a bit more on luxury furniture. If not, you might be able to save some money by finding durable pieces for a lower price.
- **What is my budget?** Do not go into debt furnishing your short-term rental. Examine your expenses and determine how much you can spend. Give yourself time to shop sales,

and don't be afraid to reuse and recycle furniture as long as the pieces fit the vibe you are going for.

Once you know the profile of your ideal guest and the aesthetics you want to create, it's time to create your shopping list. Here are some recommendations to get you started:

- **Bedrooms:** At bare minimum, you'll need beds, nightstands, and a dresser. Think about how many people you want to sleep in each room. You might want a mix of king, queen, twin, and bunk beds to maximize your space.
- **Living areas:** You'll have couches, chairs, end tables, and, most likely, an entertainment system for the main living area of the house. Extras like a coffee table, dining table, and space for games and activities can also make the living area more inviting. A sleeper sofa can be an option if you cater to large families or groups.
- **Bathrooms:** Add a blow dryer, toiletries, and, if needed, extra storage to the bathroom to make it suitable for guests.
- **Kitchen:** Your guests will want dishes, cooking utensils, and a seating area so they can cook at home. Don't forget a coffee maker!
- **Backyard:** If you have an outdoor space, you might want to add some deck chairs, an outdoor dining table, or a grill so your guests can enjoy the space.

How to Estimate Costs

The cost to furnish your furniture can vary depending on your location and your shopping approach. To estimate costs, consider things like:

- **Your shopping style:** Are you a thrifting machine or do you prefer to buy new? Searching estate sales, thrift stores, and garage sales can help you save money and find some hidden gems.
- **Your location:** If you're in a remote area, you might need to ship items to your property, which can cost more. You might also need to rent a moving truck to transport furniture to the location.

- **Your timetable:** If you have several months to set up the property before guests arrive, you have more time to wait for sales or search for the perfect item. If you need to get the property ready quickly, you might need to snag items as soon as you find them.

After considering these factors, you can start to estimate your costs. If you ask ten short-term rental owners how much it cost to furnish their property, you'll get ten different answers. Let's do a sample estimate together.

For this estimate, let's pretend we're furnishing a four-bedroom, two-bathroom beach rental. The property is two blocks from the beach in a walkable beach town that's perfect for a family vacation. We want the property to be able to sleep ten people comfortably.

Here's the budget breakdown:

- **Bedrooms:** Two bedrooms will have queen beds, one will have a pair of twin beds, and the other will have two sets of bunk beds. We need to budget about $1,000-$2,000 for each bedroom.
- **Living room:** We want enough seating for ten people, a solid TV system, a coffee table for games, and plenty of lighting. This should cost about $2,000.
- **Kitchen/dining area:** We want a table that can seat ten people and a few bar stools for the island. This should cost $750 - $1,000.
- **Backyard:** The backyard is a huge selling point for this property. We want an outdoor dining area, nice chairs for the lawn, and a seating area for the porch. This adds $750-$1,000 to our budget.
- **Linens, toiletries, and utensils:** You'll need sheets for each bed, towels for each guest, and supplies for the kitchen. Plan to spend $2,000 - $2,500 on these items.
- **Appliances:** You want to offer a nice coffee maker in the kitchen, appliances like a toaster and blender, and hair dryers in the bathrooms. Set aside $750 for this category.

In this scenario, we live near the rental, so we'll transport most of the items ourselves. As you can see, all these expenses can add up really quickly. When you build your shopping list, do some research to determine the price range for each item and budget accordingly. If you find ways to save, take advantage of them!

Amenities

If you want to truly wow your guests—and earn great reviews that can help you charge premium prices—you'll want to have some amenities. The types of amenities you offer varies greatly based on your ideal guest's profile, location, and budget.

Some items to think about include:

- **Wi-Fi:** This is an amenity, but in reality, it's a necessity. Most guests expect super-quick Wi-Fi, so make sure you provide it. Multiple USB ports in the common areas and bedrooms are a nice perk, too.
- **Security:** Smart locks and Ring cameras can help you protect your property and make your guests feel safe.
- **Kitchen appliances:** A fully-stocked kitchen complete with a coffee bar and popular appliances will make it easier for guests to eat at the rental.
- **Extra toiletries:** Mini shampoo bottles, extra toothbrushes, and other easy-to-forget items can save your guests a late-night run to the pharmacy.
- **Entertainment:** A deck of cards, board games, and paperback books can help your guests stay entertained during their downtime. You can also include items related to the location, like a boogie board or beach chairs for a beach rental or a sled and cozy blankets for a mountain rental.

Guest Books

Have you ever flipped through the guest book at a short-term rental? Whether you look through it at the beginning or the end of your stay, it probably left an impression on you about guests' overall experience at the rental.

A guest book can be a great opportunity for your guests to leave their best tips for future visitors and feedback for you. They can also help you collect more information on your guests so you can follow up with them later to see if they'd like to book another visit or build an email list for marketing.

Your guest book does not have to be complicated, either. A beautiful journal from a local shop and plenty of pens are more than enough to encourage your guests to leave a note.

Welcome Packets

Your visitors are in town for the vacation of a lifetime, but they're also guests in your home. A welcome packet helps you set expectations for their stay and gives instructions for check-out.

Feel free to get creative with your welcome packet, but always include these essential components:

- **Property information:** This is the place to let your guests know important info, like parking guidelines, Wi-Fi passwords, and how to contact you in case of an emergency.
- **Rules:** Let guests know any rules for the property, like noise guidelines and quiet hours.
- **Appliance guidelines:** Let them know which appliances are available and include instructions on how to use them.
- **Check-out instructions:** What do you need guests to do before you leave? Provide a checklist so they can prepare for their exit. Some popular tasks include stripping the beds, collecting towels for the laundry, or running a dishwasher cycle.

Your welcome packet is a living, breathing document. Don't be afraid to add pages and information to it as you receive feedback from your guests.

Guest Promotions and Local Suggestions

Your guests will be looking for fun things to do in the area, and this is your opportunity to be an excellent host. Consider what your guests might want to do locally and put together some recommendations to help them find local gems.

For instance, share your recommendations for:

- A local pizza place that will satisfy their hunger after a long day
- A vibey coffee shop that locals love
- A cute shop for gifts and souvenirs
- A nearby restaurant with photo-worthy views
- Kid-friendly activities the entire family can enjoy
- Breweries, wineries, or cocktail bars worth adding to a bar crawl

You can also partner with some of these businesses to offer guest promotions or discounts. Your guests will love saving a few dollars, the businesses will be grateful for the extra customers, and you'll build relationships with local venues that can pay off down the road.

Check-Out Instructions

You should include check-out instructions in your welcome packet so guests know what to expect. When putting together this document, it's important to be thorough and clear about your expectations.

Make sure these instructions include:

- **Check-out time:** Let guests know when they need to exit the property and any potential repercussions if they stay later than expected.
- **Lock-up information:** Tell guests where to leave their keys and remind them to lock every door when they leave.
- **Cleaning instructions:** Let guests know where to place dirty towels and linens, how to dispose of trash, and any other expectations for cleaning the home before they depart.
- **Lights and utilities:** Remind guests to turn off all lights and let them know the desired temperature for the thermostat.

How to Price Your Short-Term Rental

Ready to make some money? If you want to maximize your profit, you need to price your short-term rental appropriately for your goals and location. You need to ask yourself several questions before setting your rental price. I'm going to break them down one by one.

How Much Will It Take to Operate?

Just like a long-term rental, it takes money to operate a short-term rental. Write down the cost of your monthly mortgage, expected utility payments, insurance, listing fees, and additional fees for cleaning services and a property manager, if you have one.

What Extras Do I Want to Provide?

If you want to provide extras like cable or satellite TV, a welcome basket filled with local goods, or amenities like bicycles or kayaks, add them to your operating expenses. You don't want these items to come out of your pocket, so calculate how much you spend on these items per visit and roll them into your price.

What Should My Nightly Rate Be?

After you calculate your operating expenses, it's time to calculate your nightly rate. The average month is 30 days, so divide your expenses by 30. This will give you the bare minimum you should charge per night.

Of course, your goal is to make a profit, not just cover your expenses. Think about how much you might need over the course of the year for repairs and maintenance, as well as your desired profit, and add that to the bare minimum nightly rate.

What Are the Service Fees?

You will need to clean the property after every visit. You might also want to allow pets, in which case you will likely charge a pet fee. If you list through a platform like Airbnb or Vrbo, you might also have to consider listing fees. Decide what you will charge for each of these services and outline them for your guests.

What Is My Expected Vacancy Rate?

Chances are, your property will not be booked for every night it's available. For example, if your property is located in an area that is great for weekend visits, you might not have the property booked during the week. If your property is a cabin in a popular ski area, you might not be booked during "mud season." Think about how often you expect your property to book, and be realistic about the location and potential seasonal ebbs and flows.

If you expect your property to be vacant for days or months at a time, you need to consider how you will cover expenses like your mortgage, HOA fees, landscape maintenance, and utilities. In some cases, you may want to increase your rental price during busy times to offset the losses later on.

After you've answered these questions, it's time to experiment with your prices. Set aside some time with your calculator and play around with potential rates. Look at other rentals in your area to determine what other property owners charge for comparable properties. Be prepared to adjust your prices as the market changes and as you rack up positive reviews about the property.

How to Set Up an Airbnb Listing

Airbnb changed the game for short-term rentals, and you'll have to list your rental on the platform if you want to find renters, especially in the beginning. Consider this section your crash course on the platform.

How to List on Airbnb

Depending on your location and property type, you will likely face a lot of competition with other rentals for bookings. Your listing can help set you apart and shoot you to the top of the search results—if you have the right approach.

- **Conduct SEO research:** Think of Airbnb as the Google for short-term rentals. You need to know what your ideal renter is looking for so you can include those terms in your description. Enter various keywords into Airbnb and see what pops up. How do popular properties describe their rental?
- **Write a good description:** The more information you can include in your description, the better. Include the information you gathered from your research and be as descriptive as possible. What amenities do you offer? How close is your property to desirable entertainment? Great photos will get your property rented fast, even more so than a description. We've included some photo tips below.
- **Set competitive prices:** Know the average price for rentals in your area and set your prices accordingly. Understand how

your rental compares to listings at the highest price point in your area and the lowest.

- **Consider outsourcing:** Yes, there are people who write rental listings for a living. These professionals are experts in optimizing your listing for each platform, so consider investing in their services to get a leg up on the competition.

What to Know About Fees

Airbnb is a business, not a charity. As a host, Airbnb helps you by marketing your property to guests through their advertising and name recognition. It also offers protections, customer support, and resources to help you run a profitable business. As a result, it charges fees.

The fees Airbnb charges fluctuate based on the property location and cancellation policies. You have two options when it comes to paying these fees: you can cover all the costs as the host, or you can split the fee with your guests.

In some cases, you will be required to use the host-only option, also called the Simplified Pricing option. Simplified Pricing applies if you are a software-connected host, which means you use some sort of software to manage your property. As of 2024, hosts paid 15% to Airbnb using the Simplified Pricing structure. However, guests see that the service fee is $0. This lack of service fee can often lead to a higher booking rate because it benefits guests compared to splitting the fee.

With split-fee pricing, the host pays about 3% of the Airbnb fees, and the guest pays anywhere from 13%-20%. This structure helps offset your costs, but can be a deterrent for guests wanting to book your property.

If you have the option to use split-fee or Simplified Pricing, play around with different rates to determine how much you will profit from either option. Pick the option that is right for you.

What to Include in Your Listing Photos

You can include up to 100 photos in your Airbnb listing, but don't let that overwhelm you. A handful of incredible photos will have a bigger impact on your booking rate than 100 subpar photos.

You can hire someone to take photos of your listing. If you prefer doing it yourself, implement these tips to make them stand out:

- **Keep the unit clutter-free:** Make sure surfaces are clear and there are no papers on the countertops or other areas.
- **Make sure it's clean:** Take photos after thoroughly cleaning the property.
- **Spotlight amenities:** Add a photo of the stocked coffee bar or the board game collection to let guests know about the perks your property offers.
- **Work your angles:** Shoot from the corner to capture the entire space, or take a photo looking down at the open living space from the second floor.
- **Make sure it's well-lit:** Use natural lighting to depict the brightness of the rooms or turn on lamps in the bedroom to give it a cozy vibe.
- **Add photos of local attractions and amenities:** These photos may include a quaint downtown street, a sandy beach, a boat dock, ski slopes, hiking trails, lakes, etc.

What to Know About Reviews

Reviews will make or break your success as a short-term rental owner. You want your guests to leave great reviews after every stay because reviews increase your visibility in Airbnb's search results and encourage future guests to book your property.

Ultimately, you can't control if guests leave a review or not, but you can do a few things to encourage them. My favorite ways to encourage reviews include:

- **Making the request at check-out:** Add it to your check-out checklist to remind guests to leave feedback.
- **Posting signage around the property:** Type up a one-sheet asking guests to leave a review. Frame it and display it near your guestbook or welcome packet.
- **Reviewing the guests:** Airbnb offers double-blind reviews, which allow you to review your guests after every stay. When you review a guest, they receive a notification reminding them to review you as well.

How to Become a Superhost

Airbnb is a crowded platform, so you need to stand out to secure listings. The Superhost badge is one way to do this, but it takes some time to achieve.

When you become a Superhost, Airbnb adds a badge to your profile indicating your status. The badge helps potential guests identify hosts who offer great properties. Approximately 20% of hosts earn Superhost status, according to AirDNA.

To become a Superhost, you need to:

- Maintain a 4.8 overall rating.
- Maintain a cancellation rate of under 1%, with the exception of cancellations that meet requirements for extenuating circumstances.
- Have a 90% response rate or above.
- Complete ten trips or three reservations that total 100 nights of occupancy.

See? It's not easy to reach this status. Airbnb evaluates hosts quarterly and hands out Superhost badges automatically based on the above criteria. If you land the coveted badge, there are some benefits, including:

- **Additional promotion:** Airbnb includes Superhost properties on promotional materials and offers a search filter for travelers so they can separate Superhosts from other listings
- **Referral bonus:** You can receive 20% more than the standard bonus for hosts you refer to the platform.
- **Extra coupons:** If you maintain Superhost status for a year, you receive a $100 coupon.
- **Priority service:** Customer support will prioritize your needs if issues arise.
- **Early access:** You'll have access to new features before anyone else.

In addition, you might see an increase in bookings. The Superhost badge can build trust with potential guests, which can set you apart from other properties in your area.

How to Manage a Short-Term Rental

Just like long-term rentals, short-term rentals require hands-on management. From maintaining listings to handling repairs, there are plenty of day-to-day responsibilities that need to be handled to own a successful short-term rental.

Most real estate investors use one of four options to manage their property rentals. The right option for you will depend on your budget and goals for your real estate venture.

Self

Yes, you can manage your short-term rental yourself. This approach saves you money but costs you time. To manage your short-term rental effectively, you will need to:

- **Price your rental:** You will need to set prices for your property, keep up to date with the rental market in your area, and adjust prices accordingly.
- **Manage the money:** You will have to keep your books balanced and manage income and expenses to make sure your property is actually generating a profit.
- **Market the property:** From coordinating listing photos to updating property descriptions, you will need to market your property properly.
- **Protect your property:** You want your property to stay safe, which means enforcing house rules and screening guests.
- **Maintain the property:** This entails managing the cleaning service and scheduling or performing maintenance.
- **Handle customer service:** If the barbeque grill doesn't have gas or the air conditioning breaks, guests will call you for help.

Property Manager

You can outsource all the aforementioned tasks to a property manager. A property manager allows you to be hands-off. They handle the listings, bookings, and inquiries (and can list the property on multiple platforms). Once the guests arrive, the property manager will provide customer service, handle logistics such as linens and toiletries, and take care of cleaning the property after guests check out.

Some managers charge a commission, meaning they charge 25%-40% of the rental income. Others work on a fixed-price basis, meaning you pay them a set fee every month. Shop around for a property manager who performs the services you need for your rental at a price you can afford. Some states require that a property manager be licensed. Property managers are full-service and charge accordingly. For a cheaper option, consider a co-host.

Co-Hosting

You can also hire someone to co-host your property on Airbnb. Co-hosting means you hire someone to help you manage the property, especially the guest experience. Co-hosting benefits owners who don't have the time to manage a listing once guests arrive. You can find co-hosts in your area or through marketplaces like CohostClub. Typically, a co-host charges 20%-25% of the rental fee or a fixed price rate. Unlike property managers, co-hosts do not handle the bookings; their role is simply to ensure an outstanding guest experience.

Virtual Assistance

You also don't have to delegate every aspect of property management. You can hire a virtual assistant to take certain tasks off your plate. There are virtual assistants who have extensive experience assisting real estate investors. They can perform tasks like responding to guest inquiries, managing your listing, and coordinating cleaning and maintenance.

Other Short-Term Rental Platforms

Airbnb is a great way to market your short-term rental, but it's not your only option. Explore other platforms like:

- Vrbo
- PlumGuide
- FlipKey

Every short-term rental platform has its own unique criteria and client base. Research the right ones for you based on your location, property type, and cost. You might find a platform that generates more bookings than Airbnb!

Mid-Term Rentals

A mid-term rental is a happy medium between vacation rentals and long-term leases. With the right location and target tenant, it can be incredibly lucrative.

Pros of Mid-Term Rentals

Mid-term rentals provide housing to a typically under-served portion of the rental marketplace: people in a time of transition. Some of the pros of mid-term rentals include:

Longer Lease Terms

Mid-term leases typically last 3 to 9 months, making them the middle ground for people who aren't looking for a short stay, but can't commit to a long-term lease. As a landlord, you receive the benefits of a steady income while still being able to bring in new tenants and periodically raise prices.

Good Tenants

Most people seek mid-term rentals because they want the comforts of home for a short time frame. Your tenants will typically be traveling nurses, digital nomads, professionals working a consulting or other limited gig, students, or families who are relocating.

More Stable

The short-term rental market can change with the seasons—and the weather. Vacationers might cancel their trip due to impending weather, financial issues, or family emergencies. Tenants in mid-term leases are using your property as their residence, so they're less likely to change a booking at the last minute.

Cons of Mid-Term Rentals

There are some challenges associated with mid-term rentals. Some of the cons include:

Less Potential Income

Mid-term rentals will typically generate less income than short-term rentals because you are housing one tenant at a time for a locked-in price. You'll also need to consider the price your tenant can afford to pay in rent. A student might be able to afford less than, say, a traveling nurse.

Higher Turnover

We've talked about the cost of preparing a property for new tenants several times throughout this book. Mid-term rentals face more turnover than long-term rentals, albeit less than short-term rentals.

Increased Upfront Costs

Unlike long-term rentals, mid-term rentals need to be furnished. You'll have to fund furnishing the home, just like a short-term rental, without the benefit of premium rental prices.

How Mid-Term Rentals Compare to Short-Term Rentals

There is a lot of overlap between mid-term and short-term rentals. Both types of rentals need to be furnished, although you can likely reduce the amenities offered for a mid-term rental.

When it comes to pricing, both mid-term and short-term rentals will likely generate more income than a long-term rental. On paper, a short-term rental could generate the highest return—but you would need to keep it fully booked, which is hard to guarantee. A mid-term rental might generate less income per month, but you might see fewer vacancies, depending on the location and your target tenant.

A Hidden Moneymaker: Traveling Nurses

If your property is near a hospital, you might be sitting on a gold mine. Hospitals regularly employ traveling nurses who take on new assignments in new cities every few months. They need stable housing, but don't want to lock themselves into a year-long lease.

This group needs a fully furnished rental, but they aren't looking for extras like toiletries. They also tend to prefer 3 to 9-month leases.

If you want to reach these renters, list your property on Airbnb, Vrbo, or FurnishedFinder. You can also let your local hospital's recruiting department know that you have housing available for their new hires.

Corporate and Business Rentals

If you have several local corporations or large businesses in your area, you might be able to fill your mid-term rental with people relocating for a job or consultants on months-long projects.

Searching for permanent housing can be stressful. If you have a property in a good school district and desirable location, it can be a good option for families who are relocating due to new employment or a transfer. A mid-term rental is ideal because it provides permanent housing for a short time while they look for their dream home and explore the area.

Takeaways

The real estate space is filled with gurus promising quick returns on short-term and mid-term rentals. They can be lucrative, but they can also be challenging. Consider everything I've laid out in this chapter before deciding what type of rental you want to offer. Once you've made your decision, do everything you can to make your rental the most desirable on the market!

Takeaway #1: Consider Your Location and Target Renter

Your location and target renter will influence a lot of your decision-making as a real estate investor. A short-term rental might not work in a college town, while a mid-term rental might not be the best choice for a beach haven. Let the market drive your decision, not your emotions.

Takeaway #2: Understand the Costs

There are more costs associated with a short or mid-term rental, especially upfront. You'll need to furnish the property and provide amenities. There's also a time cost, too. If you plan to manage the property yourself, be prepared to spend more time marketing and maintaining the rental.

Takeaway #3: Set the Right Price

Do plenty of market research before setting your price and experiment with potential rates to find the sweet spot for your property. Understand that seasonality can impact the price you can charge at different parts of the year, and make sure you charge enough during busy times to offset vacancies.

What's Next

You've learned everything you need to know about purchasing and renting your first property. In the next chapter, we'll dream big. I'll teach you how to grow your portfolio so you can become a real estate mogul.

FREE GIFT #8

The Only Maintenance Checklist for Rental Properties You'll Ever Need: don't let anything fall through the cracks!

Repairs and maintenance on your investment is unavoidable but does not have to be overbearing. With this maintenance checklist you will learn how to upkeep your property, prevent small issues from becoming major problems, keep your tenants happy and maintain your property value.

To access this free bonus, head to https://readstreetpress.com/iwantpermanentpto8 in your internet browser or scan the QR code below and I'll send it to you right away!

7

HOW TO BECOME A REAL ESTATE MOGUL BIGGER THAN ROBERT KIYOSAKI

"Often in the real world, it's not the smart who get ahead, but the bold."

— *ROBERT KIYOSAKI*

That Robert Kiyosaki quote above? It fires me up, especially as I grow as a real estate investor.

There will always be someone who is technically smarter than you. But bolder than you? That's entirely in your control.

You took a bold step when you picked up this book. The rest of your real estate journey will also be built on bold steps as you scale your portfolio, learn to manage multiple properties, and grow your network with other people who can help with your journey.

In this chapter, I'm going to break down each of those bold steps individually. By the end of it, you'll be well on your way to becoming a true real estate mogul.

How to Scale a Bulletproof Portfolio

Earlier in this book, you learned how to find excellent properties and finance their purchase. Any real estate investor can find a solid property once and turn a profit. But to do it over and over again takes a combination of skill, creativity, and capital.

Create a Growth Plan

Yes, you want to be bold as you scale. That doesn't mean you need to be foolish. You wouldn't take a road trip without bringing a map. On the same principle, you don't build a profitable real estate business flying by the seat of your pants.

Review the strategy you developed in chapter 2. What did you target for your first property? Consider finding a similar property for your second purchase. This approach allows you to build on what you already know, and, hopefully, find, purchase, and list your next property quickly.

However, you will eventually want to diversify. Include this timeline in your growth plan. For example, if your first property was a long-term residential rental, you might want to move into the commercial space.

Revisit this plan regularly to make sure you are on track and adjust as needed.

Find and Leverage More Capital

Once your first rental property starts generating income, it can be tempting to sock the cash into your personal bank account. Don't do it. To build a real estate business that can truly free you from your 9-to-5, you need more properties.

Instead, use that money and, if needed, some of the financing options we discussed in chapter 4 to purchase the types of properties you identified in your growth plan. Once you've purchased your second property, use that income to fund your third. Rinse, repeat, get rich.

Search for More Value

When you purchased your first property, you might've had very little to put down for a down payment or had a poor credit score that limited your financing options. Hopefully, you will be in a better position for your next purchase.

Review your financial standing again. Can you contribute more for a down payment this time around, thus lowering your mortgage payment and increasing your rental profit? Can you look forward to better loan terms due to better credit?

You might also be able to search for more value within the property you buy. For example, you might be able to use the rental income from your first property to make more improvements in the second property that can increase its rental value. Be creative as you search for more value in the properties you plan to purchase and the properties you already have in your portfolio.

Expand and Adapt

As you look toward the future, consider expanding into new markets. For example, if you've already purchased a rental property in your current city, consider adding a short-term rental in your favorite vacation destination to give you access to a whole new market.

Above all, keep learning. Be a constant student of real estate. Read more books like this, sign up for email newsletters to receive the latest updates about the industry, and pursue every opportunity to learn from real estate moguls a few steps ahead of you.

Managing Multiple Properties

We talked a lot about how to manage a property in chapter 5. As your portfolio grows, you'll need those tips more than ever. Here's what you can do as you scale to manage multiple properties without losing your mind.

Get Organized

Simple? Yes. The difference between success and failure as a real estate professional? Absolutely. Think about everything you need to keep track of for your first rental: receipts, contracts, rental agreements, forms, and more. In addition to the paperwork, you also need to pay taxes, balance your books, and field inquiries from potential new tenants.

It's a lot of work. Now multiply that by 3, 5, or 10 properties. It would be unmanageable. That's why you need to be organized. Develop a system to remind you about important deadlines and other dates. Create a filing system for digital and paper files so you always have them on hand. Whatever you create, make sure it is something you can teach to a new hire.

Build a Team

It is possible to manage your first few properties by yourself. But you only have so much time and energy, so you'll eventually need to hire team members as you scale. For example, you might decide to hire a bookkeeper after purchasing your second property, or a property manager after purchasing your third.

Trust me, you will expand your team eventually. This is why it's helpful to be organized and build scalable systems for rental applications, bookkeeping, and other tasks from the beginning. When you hand the reins over to your new employee, they'll be ready to jump right in and pick up where you left off.

Utilize Software

It's pretty great living in the future. We can ask Alexa to turn on the lights, set the thermostat from our phone, and talk into our Apple watches to respond to text messages. Technology certainly makes everyday life easier—and it can make managing your rentals easier, too.

Consider implementing software programs to streamline key portfolio management tasks. Some popular options include:

- AppFolio Investment Manager
- SyndicationPro
- DoorLoop

Research your options and ask your network for recommendations.

Growing Your Network and Doing Bigger Deals

You can hardly believe it. The chance to purchase a 15-unit apartment building in a prime location in your growing city just came across your desk. The only problem? You have nowhere near the capital to invest in a property like that on your own, no matter how much money you make.

To complete a big deal like that, you'll need a partner. The best time to start looking for a real estate partner is before you need one.

How to Network

Real estate investing is all about relationships. Yes, you might compete with other investors on a deal or two. But having friends in the industry, from new investors like yourself to established veterans with a phone-book-sized portfolio, can help your business grow in ways you can never imagine.

Start networking as early as possible by:

- Attending local real estate events
- Traveling to national real estate conferences
- Joining professional associations like the National Real Estate Investors Association
- Cultivating relationships with everyone you meet

Networking can be intimidating, especially when you are first starting out. Keep pushing! You'll find some friends and mentors who provide encouragement and knowledge.

How to Complete Bigger Deals

If you want to participate in bigger deals like the apartment scenario I outlined above, you might need a partner. There are typically two types of partnerships: active partnerships and passive income partnerships. In an active partnership, you and your partners share operations tasks equally. In a passive partnership, you raise money from investors who won't be as involved in the operations.

Partnerships are a great way to combine your resources and lean on the expertise of more experienced investors. However, you'll be splitting the earnings and will have to compromise as you purchase and manage the property.

Your network will be a great resource for potential partners. You could also search for investing partners online or through crowdfunding platforms.

Takeaways

You picked up this book because you had big dreams about investing in real estate. You're well on your way to making them happen. Scaling your portfolio, managing multiple properties, and taking on bigger deals will take some bold steps. You can make them happen by implementing the steps I outlined above.

Takeaway #1: Start Right Now

If you have just one rental property right now, you have the gift of time. You have time to develop a plan to diversify your portfolio. You have time to get organized and create systems to use in your business as you purchase new properties. You have time to grow your network and prepare for partnerships. Take advantage of this additional time and use it to set your business up for success.

Takeaway #2: Keep Learning

It can be intimidating to learn real estate management software. It can be scary to walk into a networking event when you don't know anyone. It can be downright terrifying to purchase another property when you're still learning how to manage one. Remember that every scary step is a chance to grow your knowledge. But as they say, "Fortune favors the bold." Every expert was once a beginner. Ask the questions, do the research, and pursue relationships. Above all, keep learning.

Takeaway #3: Don't Stay Stuck

Making bold moves means you might make some missteps. That's okay! The worst thing you can do as a real estate investor is stay stagnant. Pursue diverse types of properties, explore new markets, and pursue bigger deals.

What's Next

In this chapter, you prepared to acquire new properties and scale your business. Daydreaming about your business's growth is a lot of fun, but it's also important to think about the end game for every property you purchase. In the next chapter, we'll talk about potential exit strategies.

The Ultimate Tax Planning E-Book for Real Estate Investors: don't miss out on any deductions!

Learn about the various deductions and tax benefits available in this e-book. From depreciation and mortgage interest, this book will help you catch potential tax savings. Keep more of your hard-earned money! Ask your CPA for more information about the potential deductions your real estate portfolio can create for you.

To access this free e-book, head to https://readstreetpress.com/iwantpermanentpto9 in your internet browser or scan the QR code below and I'll send it to you right away!

8

THE MUST-KNOW EXIT STRATEGIES TO PROTECT YOUR EMPIRE

"Every exit is an entry somewhere else."

— *TOM STOPPARD*

When you're handed the keys to your first rental property, the last thing you're thinking about is your exit strategy. This oversight is a mistake.

Whenever you invest in something, whether a real estate property or a stock, you should have an exit strategy in place when you make your purchase. An exit strategy is essentially a contingency plan. It is your plan for how you will liquidate an asset once you've met or exceeded a specific set of criteria.

In real estate investing, there are several exit strategies you can use. In this chapter, I'll review each one so you can make the best decision for your business with each investment you make.

Hold Forever

This exit strategy is exactly as it sounds. When you purchase a property with a "hold forever" exit strategy, it means you plan to hang on to it for the rest of your life. In many cases, you might pass it on to your heirs when you die. This strategy allows you to build equity in the property, collect rent, and upgrade the rental to increase its overall value.

Investors tend to choose this strategy to generate recurring income and hedge against inflation. It also offers some tax benefits, like owner expense deductions.

The downfall of this strategy centers on the real estate cycle. As we discussed in chapter 1, the real estate market ebbs and flows. Changes in the local, state, and national real estate market can impact the home's monthly rental prices. If you plan to hold on to the property long-term to generate recurring income, be prepared for those prices to fluctuate.

Sell and Cash Out

This exit strategy is the most popular for real estate investors. In this scenario, you plan to eventually sell the property for a profit. This sale could take place immediately after a little rehabbing or a decade from now after collecting rent.

This exit strategy has similar benefits and drawbacks to a hold forever strategy. The only difference is that you envision selling at some point, usually when the market reaches its peak.

Seller Financing

In chapter 4, we discussed seller financing options. Remember, seller financing is a way to purchase a home without using a traditional lender. When you use this as an exit strategy for your property, you are in the seller's position instead of the buyer's. This approach allows you to collect monthly payments, spread out your tax burden, and sell the property at the end of the deal.

However, this approach can be risky. Since your buyer is responsible for the monthly payments, but you still hold the title, any default will impact you. If the buyer can't pay, you could enter foreclosure.

1031 Exchange

Capital gains taxes can be pricey. A 1031 Exchange is a popular strategy investors use to minimize their tax burden. With a 1031

Exchange, you essentially swap one property for another and defer taxes in the process. For example, if you profit $15,000 from the sale of your first rental property, you can use the proceeds on your next property. When you do this, you don't defer paying capital gains taxes, which is typically 15%-20% of the sale.

This approach is a great way to consolidate your properties as your business grows or increase your ROI for your money by upgrading your portfolio.

As you can imagine, this type of exchange is complicated. Make sure you work with a tax professional to execute it properly and avoid additional scrutiny from the IRS.

Takeaways

Many new real estate investors purchase properties without an exit strategy in mind, and it gets them into trouble down the road. Consider each of the strategies outlined in this chapter carefully and enter into each purchase with your exit in mind. It will make it much easier to decide whether to exit the property when the time comes.

Takeaway #1: Consider the Market

Revisit the real estate cycle as you decide your exit strategy, especially if you plan to sell and cash out. Consider how long it will take to get the desired ROI on your investment based on the phase the local, state, and national real estate market is in. Make sure you can financially handle keeping the property longer than planned.

Takeaway #2: Seek Assistance

Exit strategies like 1031 Exchanges or seller financing can be difficult to execute on your own. Seek help from an attorney to help you create contracts to use with your buyer for a seller financing agreement. Use a tax professional to assist with a 1031 Exchange.

Takeaway #3: It's Okay to Change Your Mind

Yes, you might've bought a property intending to hold it forever and pass it down to whoever inherits or buys your business in the future. But things change. Don't be afraid to pivot your exit strategy if your circumstances—or the market—dictate it. Your exit strategy should be written in pencil, not permanent ink.

What's Next

Whew! This chapter might've been short and sweet, but we've covered a lot of ground throughout this book. We'll wrap everything up in the pages to come.

FREE GIFT #10

Free Chapter From Our Upcoming Book: *The Complete LLC Beginners Guide: The Easy Way to Create & Manage Your Limited Liability Company, Save on Taxes & Avoid Costly Mistakes*

Creating an LLC is an essential part of running your real estate portfolio and protecting yourself. Get a sneak peek into our upcoming book with this free chapter on creating and managing your LLC. Learn the easy steps needed to establish your LLC and take advantage of tax benefits. Whether you're just beginning or looking to optimize your existing business, this chapter will give you the place to start your path to success.

To access this free chapter, head to https://readstreetpress.com/iwantpermanentpto10 in your internet browser or scan the QR code below and I'll send it to you right away!

CONCLUSION

"When one door closes, buy another one and open it yourself."

— *ANONYMOUS*

Sometimes, I think about who I was before starting my real estate journey. That version of myself feels like a completely different person, so much so that I still call him Old Andrew in my mind.

Old Andrew was miserable. He was bored. He had so many dreams and so little time to actually chase them.

I like New Andrew—the version writing this to you right now—so much better. Now, I don't think about commuting to the office; I think about the next plane I'm hopping on with my wife. I don't think about packing a soggy sandwich to eat at my desk; I think about the next gourmet meal I'm going to whip up for friends and family. I don't sit up at night, worrying about my next annual review with the boss; instead, I dream about the DIY projects I'm going to tackle around the house.

Real estate investing made that type of financial and time freedom happen for me. Now that you've read this book, it can happen for you, too.

What to Remember

We covered a lot in this book. If you're feeling a little overwhelmed right now, don't worry. You're not alone—I felt overwhelmed a lot when I started my real estate investing journey. It's why I wrote this book!

I hope you refer back to this book often as you pursue your first deal, welcome your first tenants, and grow your business. In the meantime, remember these key takeaways:

- **Don't skip the strategy:** You need a strategy for purchasing a property, financing a property, and growing your business.
- **Real estate investing is not one-size-fits-all:** Think creatively about searching for properties and financing your deals, and think about how much risk you're willing and able to take on.
- **Know your market:** Do your research and make decisions based on data, not feelings. Study your market and keep learning.
- **Just start:** This book is your blueprint for launching and growing your business. It's useless if it just sits on your shelf or on your Kindle.

This book exists because I know anyone can find success in real estate investing. You just need the right strategy and the knowledge to make it happen. There's room for all of us in this industry. Use this book to build the business of your dreams.

Your New Life Is Just Around the Corner

Before we end our time together, I want you to grab a piece of paper. On one side, describe the current version of yourself. How do you feel? How do you spend your time? What are your dreams?

Then, I want you to turn the paper over and picture the new version of yourself. How does that version of you spend time? What are your hobbies and dreams? What are your relationships like?

It is possible to be that new version of yourself. I'm living proof of it. And I want that for you—it's why I wrote this book. Now, it's time to snag your first real estate deal and start your journey. I'm rooting for you!

To your success,

Andrew

FREE GIFT #11

The Ultimate House Hacking E-Book for Real Estate Investors: The start of your multi-million-dollar portfolio starts as a seed.

All investors start small, and the first step is the hardest part. Why not break into the real estate game by house hacking? From this book you'll learn what house hacking is and why it helps investors start at zero and end up a real estate hero.

To access this free e-book, head to https://readstreetpress.com/iwantpermanentpto11 in your internet browser or scan the QR code.

FREE GIFT #12

The Complete Guide to Building Your Elite Real Estate Investment Team: It's about who you know!

Learn the essential skills needed to build your elite real estate investment team. Assemble the dream team of professionals to support your rental property investment journey, including real estate agents, accountants, lawyers, and property managers with the tools in this guide.

To access this free e-book, head to https://readstreetpress.com/iwantpermanentpto12 in your internet browser or scan the QR code and I'll send it to you right away!

THANK YOU

THANK YOU so much for buy and reading my book! You could have picked from many others, but you chose this one.

Before you go, I want to ask you for one small favor.

 **Can you please leave this book a review on Amazon?**

Leaving a review is the best way to support the work of independent authors like me. You can scan the QR code or visit the link below:

https://www.amazon.com/review/create-review/?asin=B0D6Q93SN3

Your feedback will help me to keep writing the kind of books that will help you build the real estate empire of your dreams. It would mean a lot to me to hear from you.

 Our mission is to inspire and empower others to break free from the constraints of traditional employment and achieve Permanent PTO through entrepreneurship. We believe everyone can transform their financial future and live the life they've always dreamed of and spend life living.

If you would like more resources, please visit our website: www.permanentpto.com

WOULD YOU LIKE MORE OF OUR BOOKS FOR FREE?

Join Our Exclusive ARC Team—Limited Spots Available!

Do you love being the first to discover groundbreaking books? If so, you're invited to apply for our Advanced Review Copy (ARC) Team!

As a member of this elite group, you'll receive early copies of our upcoming books—completely free. All we ask in return is your honest feedback so we can improve the quality of our content. This is your chance to get exclusive access, influence the book market, and connect with authors and fellow readers.

Why Apply?

- **Early Access:** Be among the first to read and review new titles before they hit the shelves.

- **Influence Others:** Your insights help guide other readers and shape future publications.

- **Exclusive Content:** Get free access to new articles, tools, and more!

Spots are limited to ensure a quality experience for all members. Don't miss this opportunity to make a real impact in the world of real estate and entrepreneurship literature.

Apply online with the QR code or visit https://readstreetpress.com/freebooks to join our ARC Reviewers Team. We look forward to having you!

REFERENCES

To see the references for each book, please visit:
https://permanentpto.com/book-references/